Peter 〵 ⟍

1979.

SARTRE
ON THEATER

Jean-Paul Sartre

SARTRE ON THEATER

Documents assembled, edited,
introduced, and annotated
by Michel Contat and Michel Rybalka

*Translated from the French
by Frank Jellinek*

QUARTET BOOKS

LONDON

First published in Great Britain
by Quartet Books Limited 1976
27 Goodge Street, London WIP 1FD

ISBN 0 704 32120 3
English Translation Copyright © 1976 by Random House, Inc.

CONTENTS

INTRODUCTION

Nearly everything that Sartre has said or written about the theater and his own plays is assembled in this book. It is the only one of his books that he did not compose as such. Unlike *Situations*, volumes made up of essays, lectures, and interviews which were not originally intended as a collection either, this book was not Sartre's own idea. We suggested it to him because we found, even before our combined annotated biography and bibliography, *The Writings of Jean-Paul Sartre*, was published (in French by Gallimard in 1970), that a book of this kind would fill a need and would be useful as a working tool both from the historical and documentary standpoint and from the standpoint of present-day relevance.

The importance of Sartre's work in the theater and its leading part in the history of the contemporary drama are now fully recognized. In the postwar period in France his plays dominated the stage at least until 1951 (the year of the first performance of *The Devil and the Good Lord* [*Le Diable et le Bon Dieu*], which more or less coincided with the emergence of what came to be known as "the theater of the absurd"). Sartre's international reputation since the end of the war is undoubtedly due far more to his plays than to his novels, essays, or works on philosophy. Many of those who consider him one of the three or four great contemporary writers have read nothing of Sartre's but one or two of his plays. Their lasting success with wide sections of the general public is attested by their large printings in pocket books. His plays are part of the literary history of our time; he already ranks as a classic. His name appears on the reading lists of the French secondary schools and universities. It was felt, therefore, that both the general reader and the student were in need of a handy book containing the documentary material essential for an understanding of Sartre's work on and in the theater.

In the late sixties it was contended, with some show of reason, that Sartre's plays were better for reading than for hearing or performing; but that judgment seems to require correction, or at least qualification, today. It is true that Sartre's plays call for a careful reading which gives ample time for reflection, because of the complexity, depth, and breadth of their themes. It is equally true that Sartre himself took the view that they were not so much stage experiments designed to remodel the drama as elements in a philosophical and political enterprise whose shape certainly shows up more plainly in reading than in performance. The misconceptions to which Sartre laid himself open by paying too little heed to the conditions in which his plays were produced are notorious. It may well be that he has always thought of them as *writing* rather than stage material. Serge Reggiani once told us of an incident which is rather significant in this respect. One evening after *The Condemned of Altona* (*Les Séquestrés d'Altona*) had been playing to full houses for several weeks, Sartre turned up, as he often did, for a drink with his players after the show. He was carrying the book of the play, which had been published that day. Displaying the copy hot from the press, he exclaimed with a smile, "This is what really counts—the *book!*"

There can be no doubt that Sartre himself has some share in the responsibility for the loss of interest in his plays among the playwrights and producers who were looking for new methods of production during the period—roughly 1955 to 1965—when they were experimenting with the lessons they had learned from Brecht. And in any case, the themes of his plays seemed to belong to an era that had ended; the anguished or playful metaphysical questionings of the avant-garde seemed to have put the imperatives of commitment wholly out of date. But here too, it may be suggested, many things had changed by May 1968. One of the two performances that strikingly marked the rebirth of political drama in France from the ruins of the theater of the absurd was the revival of *The Devil and the Good Lord* by the Théâtre National Populaire (TNP) in September 1968, the other most undoubtedly being the excellent *1789* at Ariane Mnouchkine's Théâtre du Soleil. The movement is now growing (chiefly at Villeurbanne), enriched with all the experiments of the sixties. We are not asserting that Sartre has taken, is taking, or will take any decisive part in this movement through his plays. The reason why he has given up writing new plays nowadays is that he is convinced that the time for individual creation is over and that the dramatist's new role is to share in a theatrical company's collective work. The urgency of the political tasks he has set himself and his decision to complete his study of Flaubert made it out of the question for him to devote himself to such absorbing work in the theater, which would also require a radical alteration in his creative habits. On the other hand, several of his plays—as was found with *The Devil and the Good Lord*, but also with *Nekrassov* at the Théâtre national at Strasbourg in 1968—would be extremely well suited to a drama designed to be both political theater and people's theater. And lastly, inasmuch as he is the only French playwright who has tackled the question of political drama, and as early as 1943 at that, any consideration of the prerequisites for this form of theater must necessarily, we think, proceed by way of Sartre. For this reason the documents assembled in this volume have more than a purely historical interest; their relevance is contemporary.

Sartre's theatrical bent dates back to his childhood. It is bound up with his calling as a writer, the origins of which he has elucidated in *The Words (Les Mots)*. In his childhood Sartre thought of the writer as primarily a novelist, but as equally bound to make a career in the theater. He recalls writing his earliest plays at La Rochelle in 1917–1920, while still at the *lycée*, and he had a great taste for the operettas at the Municipal Theater, which his mother took him to see regularly. Somewhat later, when he was about seventeen, he wrote, according to testimony from his fellow pupils at the Lycée Henri IV, a play called *Prophesy Without Power* (*Vaticiner sans pouvoir*), inspired by Jarry, a description of Rodin's *Thinker* on the lines of *Ubu Roi*. At the École normale supérieure in the rue d'Ulm he distinguished himself in the end-of-year revues by his talents as a satirist as much as by his gifts as singer and actor. He wrote two short plays while he was doing his military service after graduating. One of them, *Epimetheus*, was allegorical, an adaptation of a Platonic myth for the stage, in which he contrasted Prometheus, the artist and solitary, with Epimetheus, the engineer and average man, thereby developing a theme which is also to be found in a contemporary philosophical and literary essay, *The Legend of Truth* (*La Légende de la vérité*). The other play was entitled *I Will Have a Fine Burial* (*J'aurai un bel enterrement*) and was derived, Sartre tells us, from Pirandello; it dealt with someone meticulously preparing his own funeral. None of these early plays seems to have survived.

In 1932 Sartre met Charles Dullin, who was to play such a decisive part in bringing his theatrical bent to fruition, through Simone Jollivet (whom Simone de Beauvoir calls "Camille" in her memoirs). This enabled Sartre and Simone de Beauvoir frequently to go backstage at the Atelier and watch the most imaginative, rigorous, and demanding of the Cartel producers at work. They became close friends of Dullin's and saw a great deal of him in the thirties and during the Occupation, and Sartre shaped most of his ideas about theatrical techniques from contact with Dullin. He testifies to this repeatedly in several of the documents collected in this volume.

There can, therefore, be no doubt whatever that as a dramatist Sartre owes a great deal to the most important French theatrical venture of the period between the wars. He did not try to renovate its forms, but sought to chasten its content by a return to the tragic. It was Dullin again who gave him an opportunity to broaden his knowledge of the theater by entrusting him with the series of lectures on the history of the theater at his School of Dramatic Art in 1942–1943. The course was concerned mainly with the Greek drama, and it was then that Sartre read Hegel's *Aesthetics* and built up his own concept of drama as the representation of a conflict of rights. We have been unable to find any lecture notes from this period, but Sartre as a teacher of drama appears in several of his later lectures which are reproduced in this volume.

Sartre's attitude to the theater is perhaps more pragmatic than theoretical. He has never cared to elaborate and systematize his ideas about dramatic techniques, as he has the techniques of the novel. We have from him as regards the theater no equivalent of *Situations I* or *What Is Literature? (Qu'est-ce que la littérature?)*. Most of the documents presented in this volume are oral (such as lectures or conversations) and in their assemblage here contain a number of repetitions. But their interest resides precisely in the spontaneity deriving from a long practice of the stage. We must acknowledge, however, that they do not have the weight of Sartre's specifically literary writings.

Though the nature of Sartre's contribution to the theater still has to be studied in greater depth and specificity, the reader of this volume will certainly be persuaded that Sartre has a great deal to say about the theater and that he excels in commenting on his own works. These two considerations have led us to divide this volume into two sections.

The first comprises the full text of a number of general pieces on the theater, many of them little known and hard to come by, and some of them hitherto unpublished, such as the long lecture entitled "Epic Theater and Dramatic Theater" delivered at the Sorbonne in 1960. We have also included two fairly long extracts from *The Idiot of the Family* (*L'Idiot de la famille*), in which Sartre expounds his ideas about the actor.

The second section is an attempt to throw light on Sartre's own dramatic works by means of selections from various documents and interviews given at the time of performance, grouped together play by play. The whole is an attempt to bring out the plays' essential significance and presents Sartre's most illuminating statements about them. Originally we had hoped to compile a detailed file of the criticisms of each play, but we have had to defer this project owing to lack of space.

As it stands, this volume should serve as a useful supplement to Francis Jeanson's excellent *Sartre par lui-même* [Sartre on Sartre] (Paris: Éditions du Seuil, 1955 and 1967) and Pierre Verstraeten's essay, *Violence et éthique* [Violence and ethics] (Paris: Gallimard, 1972), a philosophical study couched in such abstract terms as, unfortunately, to be accessible only to academic specialists. These are at present the only two critical works in French devoted to Sartre's dramatic work. For criticism in English we should single out Dorothy McCall's *The Theatre of Jean-Paul Sartre* (New York: Columbia University Press, 1969), interesting but in many respects inadequate.

A list of Sartre's pieces on the theater and cinema not reproduced here will be found at the back of this volume. For more detailed information we refer the reader to *Les Écrits de Sartre* and its supplement published in the *Magazine littéraire* (no. 55) for September 1971, and to the American revised and augmented translation, *The Writings of Jean-Paul Sartre*, published in two volumes in 1974 by the Northwestern University Press.

Lastly, it should be explained that the introductory notes for each piece and the notes at the back of the book were included mainly with an eye to contributing to the history of the contemporary French theater.

MICHEL CONTAT
MICHEL RYBALKA

We wish to express our gratitude to Arlette Elkaïm, Lena Zonina, Philip Berk, Gilbert Guisan, Sylvère Lotringer, and Jean-Luc Seylaz for their assistance and contributions.

I

DOCUMENTS, LECTURES,
AND CONVERSATIONS
ON THE THEATER

For a Theater of Situations

This article was published as "Pour un théâtre de situations" in *La Rue*, November 1947. The following translation is by Richard McLeary, and is reprinted from *Selected Prose*, volume 2 of *The Writings of Jean-Paul Sartre*, edited by Michel Contat and Michel Rybalka (Evanston, Ill.: Northwestern University Press, 1974, pp. 185–86).

The chief source of great tragedy—the tragedy of Aeschylus and Sophocles, of Corneille— is human freedom. Oedipus is free; Antigone and Prometheus are free. The fate we think we find in ancient drama is only the other side of freedom. Passions themselves are freedoms caught in their own trap.

Psychological theater—the theater of Euripides, Voltaire, and Crébillon *fils*—announces the decline of tragic forms. A conflict of characters, whatever turns you may give it, is never anything but a composition of forces whose results are predictable. Everything is settled in advance. The man who is led inevitably to his downfall by a combination of circumstances is not likely to move us. There is greatness in his fall only if he falls through his own fault. The reason why we are embarrassed by psychology at the theater is not by any means that there is too much greatness in it but too little, and it's too bad that modern authors have discovered this bastard form of knowledge and extended it beyond its proper range. They have missed the will, the oath, and the folly of pride which constitute the virtues and the vices of tragedy.

But if we focus on these latter, our plays will no longer be sustained primarily by character—depicted by calculated "theatrical expressions" and consisting in nothing other than the total structure of our oaths (the oath we take to show ourselves irritable, intransigent, faithful, and so on)—but by situation. Not that superficial imbroglio that Scribe and Sardou were so good at staging and that had no human value. But if it's true that man is free in a given situation and that in and through that situation he chooses what he will be, then what we have to show in the theater are simple and human situations and free individuals in these situations choosing what they will be. The character comes later, after the curtain has fallen. It is only the hardening of choice, its arterio-sclerosis; it is what Kierkegaard called *repetition*. The most moving thing the theater can show is a character creating himself, the moment of choice, of the free decision which commits him to a moral code and a whole way of life. The situation is an appeal: it surrounds us, offering us solutions which it's up to us to choose. And in order for the decision to be deeply human, in order for it to bring the whole man into play, we have to stage limit situations, that is, situations which present alternatives one of which leads to death. Thus freedom is revealed in its highest degree, since it agrees to lose itself in order to be able to affirm itself. And since there is theater only if all the spectators are united, situations must be found which are so general that they are common to all. Immerse men in these universal and extreme situations which leave them only a couple of ways out, arrange things so that in choosing the way out they choose themselves, and you've won—the play is good. It is through particular situations that each age grasps the human situation and the enigmas human freedom must confront. Antigone, in Sophocles' tragedy, has to choose between civic morality and family morality. This dilemma scarcely makes sense today. But we have our own problems: the problem of means and ends, of the legitimacy of violence, the problem of the consequences of action, the problem of the relationships between the person and the collectivity, between the individual undertaking and historical constants, and a hundred more. It seems to me that the dramatist's task is to choose from among these limit situations the one that best expresses his concerns, and to present it to the public as the question certain free individuals are confronted with. It is only in this way that the theater will recover its lost resonance, only in this way that it will succeed in *unifying* the diversified audiences who are going to it in our time.

On Dramatic Style

This unpublished piece is a lecture given by Sartre on June 10, 1944, at the request of Jean Vilar, who had organized a series of lectures on the theater, followed by discussion. The next lecture was to be given by Camus, as Jean Vilar announced when introducing Sartre, but we do not know whether the series was continued or was interrupted by the circumstances of the time. We reproduce the stenographic record of Sartre's lecture in full, but not revised by him, followed by the rather superficial discussion that ensued, given here for its documentary interest. Simone de Beauvoir has been kind enough to supply the text. She notes in *The Prime of Life* (New York: World Publishing Co., 1962, p. 462) that the lecture was delivered a few days after the dress rehearsal of *No Exit*, adding: "The meeting took place in a hall overlooking the Seine, and was well attended. Barrault and Camus both raised points with Sartre afterward, and so did Cocteau—this was the first time I had seen him at close quarters." Armand Salacrou, whom Sartre was seeing quite frequently at the time, also took part in the discussion. The names of the other speakers, except for Vilar, are not known.

Before I deal with dramatic style, I must tell you how I see the theater and why it brings up the problem of style.

In a very good book on "the essence of theater," Monsieur Gouhier[1] observes that an actor is present in the flesh on the stage in a way in which he is not on the screen. And as a matter of fact, we often do speak of an actor as having "presence"; it is practically a term of theatrical jargon, even; and the audience rather tends to look at actors from that point of view. For instance, when "Rigadin in the flesh" was advertised at La Rochelle just before the 1914 war, people thronged to the performance precisely to view someone they had seen on the screen in his absence, so to speak.

I may not be putting this quite accurately, for basically we are concerned in both cases with imaginary persons, with the absent. Obviously, if you are watching Hamlet, you are not seeing Hamlet, and if you do see Hamlet, it is not Hamlet who is there, that is to say he's not on the stage, he's in Denmark, a long way from the Comédie-Française, and so you cannot truly speak of his presence in the flesh.

So, to approach the matter from the other end, I shall draw a distinction between the cinema and the novel, on the one hand, and the theater, on the other, by what I may call a distancing between characters and audience in the theater, a distance of manner which exists in neither the film nor the novel. In the traditional novel I usually choose a hero—or rather am made to choose one, it's really a matter of forcing a card—and I identify with him to a certain degree, I see through his eyes, and his perception is my perception. You can get rather interesting effects from this joint responsibility—I might even call it complicity—especially if the reader (whether he likes it or not) and the author are made jointly responsible for perceiving something rather ugly, rather unpleasant. So that while you are reading, you don't know to what extent you are and to what extent you are not yourself. In any event, since the hero's

eyes are my eyes, a tree in a novel is not a tree, it is always
a tree as seen by Julien Sorel, for instance, and consquently,
if I identify with him, it is a tree as seen by me. And since
I see it with whatever of the hero's past has stayed with me
since I read about it, and something of his future as well,
the tree is individualized.

In the film something rather ambiguous happens, because we do not see things directly, but through the camera
eye, that is, through an impersonal witness which has come
between the spectator and the object seen. I see things as
someone who is not me sees them; I am, for instance, a long
way from the character, yet I see him close up. There is a
sort of detachment here, but—and this is what is ambiguous
about it—this eye also often becomes the eye of all of the
characters, for instance the hero's eye. If the hero hears a
sound, we first see the character turn his head and then, as
the camera moves, the object which has made the sound, just
as the hero can see it.

So there is a shift here, and for an instant I identify
myself with the person seeing the thing.

This identification can be taken further; experimentally,
it could and should be taken to the point where the camera
eye was completely identified with the hero's eye. We—that
is, the director and I—once tried to produce a scenario with
a character who was never seen and was identified solely
with the camera eye: anything that was happening would
happen only as the character saw it.[2]

This proved extraordinarily difficult, and the idea was
dropped during the shooting, but not because it was im-
practicable.[3] If we examine the state of mind of someone
watching a film, we find that he very often identifies with the
character he prefers, the strongest or the most attractive,
the character who gives him the finest idea of himself. In the
theater, however, all this is replaced by an absolute distance.
To begin with, I see with my own eyes and I am always at
the same level and in the same place, and so there is neither

the complicity we have in the novel nor the ambiguous complicity of the film; hence to me a character is always definitely someone else, someone who is not me and into whose skin I cannot slide.

Consequently, the emotion in a play to some degree does not have the same quality and very often not the same intensity as it has in a film. It is an emotion that is always a little farther away from me, since all the characters in a play are external to me; but it is also true that the person I see is not, to me, specifically someone else; for in real life someone else is not only the person I am looking at but also the person looking at me. For instance, when I observe a couple quarreling in some public place, if they suddenly pay attention to me when I turn my head their way, I abruptly feel myself observed, and I jump back into my skin, immediately shrink away, and suddenly have the sensation of being looked at.

In the theater the "someone else" never looks at me; or should he happen to look at me, then the actor, the imaginary character, vanishes. Hamlet or Volpone vanishes and it is Barrault or Dullin[4] looking at me. What is wrong with addressing an audience is that it causes the imaginary character to vanish and to be replaced by the presence of the real person. This can be amusing in a music hall, where there is a sort of flicker between the moment when the actor is simply someone else and the moment when he addresses the audience, to ask it to take up a chorus, for instance; but this sort of flicker is impossible in a play, and consequently the spectator is precluded from participating in it. He may look, but he will never be looked at. The three knocks following the species of initial ceremony of taking one's seat might be thought of as representing a magical ceremony of annihilation. The spectator loses his awareness of self, and he remembers it during the performance only when tedious stretches occur. Indeed, actors may suggest cuts because the seats in the theater in which they are performing have creaked at some particular moment, showing that some of the audience have remembered that they have legs and are uncomfortable.

Normally at the beginning of a performance the spectator should simply be a pair of eyes and should be fully aware that he is helpless. During popular melodramas you often hear spectators shout "Don't drink it!" when there's a poison or "For God's sake, hurry!" when the heroine has to be rescued. But even as he shouts, the spectator feels that he is helpless, for he knows quite well that nothing will happen; in essence, indeed, this is the origin of the need for distancing. Though this need is absolutely essential, it does not in any way rule out the hero's freedom nor does it mean, as some have supposed, that he is the victim of some fatality or subject to some sort of determinism, but simply that the event, no matter what happens and even if I can to some extent foresee it, cannot in any way be stopped by me; if I shout, I would be stopping the actor, but not Hamlet. And it is this sense of necessity—the projection of the spectator's impotence—that is in fact the origin of the tragic and the comic and should be regarded as something like the impotence of someone who is dreaming and knows there is nothing he can do.

The running commentary and objurgations of the chorus in the classical Greek drama are rather a good demonstration of this impotence: no one takes the slightest notice of them. The result of this initial distancing is that the settings remain conceptual. What individualized the setting in the novel was the relation between the character I had assumed, in whom I had embodied myself, and the tree or table he was looking at. What individualizes an object in life is that I, with my memories, in my situation, face it, touch it, and act on it. Similarly in the film, if I am made to look at the branches of a linden tree at the precise moment when I ought to look at them and in the precise way I am supposed to look at them, here again I am driven to individuation.

But in the theater I do not see the object, because to see it would be to connect it with my universe, in which it would be a cardboard tree, since actually seeing it would be seeing it as something painted on a flat or a designated object. My only connection with the set is the characters' gestures; the only way I can be connected with the tree is to see a character sit down in its shade. It is not the sight of the character, therefore, that makes the settings, but gestures; and gestures create the general rather than the particular. There are not ten ways of sitting down on a chair; the chair that will appear will be any chair, not a particular chair. If a fork appears between my fingers, there are not ten ways of using it; it is a completely general fork.

So once you have grasped this general aspect of all the accessories of a set, you can make decisions about it, you can carry it as far as you like, as Barrault often does, that is to say you can hold that the object itself need not be there since the object comes into being, so to speak, from the gesture of using it. Thus, a character's gesture of swimming will bring the river into being, and there will be no need for a cardboard river for him to seem to dive into.

You can also make stylized, schematized objects—this is the real meaning of "poor man's theater"[5]—because it is quite enough simply to indicate them, provided that the indication is a general one, and what we see of an object is always general. That, I think, is the real meaning of the appeal to the artificial, which means that the truly schematized setting which brings out the human presence is always a general setting. All we really need of a tree is that it should be a stylized tree.

But the setting, the actors, and the directions for the dialogue are a totally closed world, because we cannot enter it, we only see it, a unique world and one that is the very type of the human world, in short, of the world I live in but from which I am suddenly excluded; in other words, I am outside. Ordinarily, someone is simultaneously in the world, in its midst, and outside it, since he can look at it. But in the theater there is something that prevents this, for I am wholly outside it and I can only look at it. In short, all that is there is an immediate application of man's desire to be outside himself in order the better to see himself, not as others see him, but as he is. In the novel such efforts have produced works of fantasy such as Kafka's works and *Aminadab*.[6] Here the effect is immediately real, for I no longer exist except as pure sight and the world as presence is a self-bounded world of which I am pure witness; I no longer have any hands, since I cannot grasp the actor by the sleeve to prevent him from driving a dagger into his breast.

And so I think that the real origin, the real meaning of theater is to put the world of men at an absolute distance, an impassable distance, the distance separating me from the stage. The actor is so distant that I can see him but will never be able to touch him or act upon him.

While there can be no doubt that this is one of the principles of theater, I think we should never underestimate this distance; whether we are author, actor, or producer, we should not try to reduce it, but should exploit it and show it as it actually is, even manipulate it. To my mind, Gémier, for example, was wrong, dramatically speaking, in his staging of *The Taming of the Shrew*,[7] in which he reduced the distance between characters and audience by making the characters pass through the aisles of the orchestra stalls; if we see a character passing through the orchestra aisles, we are really seeing the actor, not the character.

The performance—there is no getting away from it— has to take place on the stage, and we ought to bear in mind that this is what accounts for the spectator's own desire for distancing and accounts for the pleasure he has always taken in the play within the play, the play on the stage, as in Italian comedy, in which another comedy was very often played out at the back of the stage and the characters were supposed to be watching it. Because that produced a second dimension of distancing, doubling the pleasure of those watching it—pure theater raised to the second degree.

But assuming that this is so, if we are to exploit this distance, we must discard any idea of naturalism in the theater; for how can you tell an everyday and individual story in a conceptual setting, in a setting that is necessarily conceptual, however much you accumulate signs, however realistic you try to make the decor itself? Apparently it simply cannot be done.

And further, if we are at a distance from the setting, we are equally distant from the man himself, which means that the man before us, acting in front of us, is someone whom we never come to know except by his actions; the only way we have of knowing a character is by his acts. And we do not have to concern ourselves with psychology, precisely because, in the first place, this brings us to the importance of miming in the theater and, in the second place, because of the very fact that we are looking at an act.

For the act is something that is *ipso facto* devoid of psychology; to begin with, it is a free enterprise—we do not, of course, have to discuss the nature and extent of this freedom here—but for this freedom to exist it must at least lie in the very elements of an act, which is a venture, has a purpose, is projected, is concerted. This, therefore, is what we primarily see in theater: people embarking on a venture and performing acts in order to do so. And, too, these acts always take us to a level other than the psychological, because there is a moral life: every act comprehends its own purposes and unified system; anyone performing an act is convinced that he has a right to perform it; consequently, we are not on the ground of fact but of right, since every individual in a play who acts because he is engaged in a venture and because this venture must be carried to its conclusion justifies it by reasons, believes he is right to undertake it.

This very fact brings us onto the true ground of theater, in which it is not what goes on in the actors' heads that concerns us, but watching a conflict of rights. Take the most moving scene in *Life Is a Dream*,[8] for example; it is not a psychological scene, but the scene in which the father, the king, who has deposed his son because portents in which he believed foretold that the son would become violent and barbarous, is confronted with the son, who has become barbarous precisely because of his deposition. The two confront one another twenty years later, and each maintains that he is in the right. And in fact each has right on his side: the son says, It is you who made me so violent, and the father replies, Your violence justifies what I did. It is precisely the conflict of these rights that makes the most moving scene in the play.

Of psychology there is none; the characters are too thoroughly engaged in saying what they have to say for us to learn anything about the father's or the son's tastes for this or that, and the spectator too, even while he is a witness, has a new attitude thrust upon him, that of a moral judge: he judges the cut and thrust; he says this one is in the right, that one is in the wrong. Dramatic surprise almost always comes from the way in which the person one thought at first to be in the wrong suddenly turns out also—but, of course, only in part—to have been in the right. In *Life Is a Dream*, for example, in the first two scenes of the second act we tend to find Segismundo in the wrong. When he enters to announce some news to an honorable courtier of his father's and suddenly declares, You made me commit this violence because you got rid of me, we suddenly realize that Segismundo is in the right.

The theater, therefore, seems to us a sort of ring in which people battle for their rights. But beyond this, the rights must interest us and consequently must be rights that are valid today—a point I shall come back to in a minute.

It seems to me that although it is always a good thing to revive plays of the past, it is even better that modern plays —and I say this all the more humbly in that I have not practiced what I am preaching—should not concern themselves with the past, should not concern themselves with antique myths which are hardly applicable to the circumstances of today. I believe that the conflicts of rights that interest and move an audience should be conflicts of modern rights and relevant to life as it really is today.

So here we have a set of factors wholly governed, as you see, by the very concept of distancing, but—and here we come to my real subject, here is where style comes in—if we have exploited this distance and if we also want specifically to present the characters to the audience, characters which are to affect it most closely, which are in fact itself ultimately, and they are what it wants to see, but at an absolute distance where they are out of its reach, what means are we going to use to achieve this?

There are some not very daring means of doing this, such as that for which Racine apologizes in the introduction to *Bajazet*, for failing to present characters far away in time, explaining that he has placed them instead far away in space, so that they are nonetheless distant and the requirements are therefore sufficiently satisfied. This is a shift to which Albert Camus and I have each resorted out of a sort of diffidence, he by situating *The Misunderstanding*[9] in Czechoslovakia— which is pretty far away and quite inaccessible these days— and I by situating my play in hell, an even more inaccessible country. But I must confess that it's a rather unadventurous solution, merely a sort of formal detachment.

Actually, I believe—and I think Camus would entirely agree with me—that the style itself, style as a whole, would suffice to secure this detachment. This style must, of course, be taken in the first place as a kind of bearing with which the characters are endowed. Camus has done this remarkably skillfully in *The Misunderstanding* by presenting a character whose role is essentially to keep things at a distance, a character who says, Don't touch me, and by his rigid attitude keeps both the audience and the other characters in the play at a distance throughout the role.

But apart from this, all contemporary dramatists have a problem: how, when we speak to an audience about their present-day rights, to develop a dramatic language that shall both be everyday speech and yet achieve the distancing. In short, how to do this with nothing in our hands and nothing in our pockets. Take a scene in Paris in 1944: a waiter or market gardener comes on stage and they have to have a conversation that distances them—not by elevated language, but by a kind of speech that creates a distance.

It would be a mistake—we must be quite clear about the problem—to use words in their conversation that are not the words used by everyone. There is a delightful scene in one of Salacrou's plays, *La Vie en rose*, which, he says in a note, no one has realized is by Henry Bataille[10]; he inserted it in his play and inserted it precisely for its style, and I don't think a more illuminating quotation could be had; it was this that saved me from the mistake of failing to use in a contemporary play words that everyone uses. Here is the scene:

> *Enter two elegant ladies*
> ODETTE How thrilling!
> ISABELLE Odette, my pet, I'm on the edge of something terrific and I'm terrified, I know, yes, I understand what's the matter with me.
> ODETTE He's told you lies, oh, take care, Isabelle, not to pick up Othello's handkerchief; do say you don't love him.
> ISABELLE . . . *(Reads)*

Now, basically what we note in a text like this is what is ordinary and everyday; the sentences are ready-made, like those we use all the time; they have no dramatic rhythm, no special rhythm, and the real difference, on the other hand, is the change from phrases like "the humiliation of a carnal caress" or "a great wounded shower"; these are far-fetched phrases, and what they are trying to do is to create the distancing by moral elevation. I believe that we ought to do just the opposite, as in the rest of Salacrou's play, where he goes back to the dialogue and uses everyday expressions like "landlord," "before ten," "stairs not done," and so on, and give the words a rhythm calculated to raise them to the dignity appropriate to language in the theater.

How can this be done, then? I can only give you the suggestions—and they may serve as a theme for our discussion—which I should like to take as rules in my own work, and they are these: first, a word is an act, one means among others of acting which a character can use so as never to refer to anything within himself. There is, I believe, a serious mistake in a play by a well-known American author, *Strange Interlude*:[11] characters enter and engage in dialogue, as in any play; but what is peculiar to this play is that from time to time they stand still, put on a rather strange expression, and pour out whatever is in their mind, as it were to themselves. They are trying to deliver a monologue like Joyce's interior monologue, but transferred to the stage.

It is a very serious mistake, I think, because the audience is not in the slightest interested in what goes on inside a character's head, but wants to judge him by everything he does. It is not concerned with some sort of slack naturalistic psychology; it does not want speech used to depict a state of mind but to commit. Speech in the theater should express a vow or a commitment or a refusal or a moral judgment or a defense of one's rights or a challenge to rights of others, and so be eloquence or a means of carrying out a venture, by a threat, for instance, or a lie or something of the sort; but in no circumstances should it depart from this magic, primitive, and sacred role.

The mistake in naturalism is that it depicts everyday things in words, that is to say in words about words.

In the second place, this language must be elliptical. This means that since language is an act, it cannot be dissociated from gesture; gesture finally becomes speech, just as speech becomes gesture, and it must therefore be elliptical in reading, if taken by itself alone. It is precisely this ellipsis that must continuously give language its rhythm, and it must be expressed in interrupted movement, which means precisely that some part of a script designed to be a complete expression of the actor's thought must always be omitted; it must be expressed by gesture.

Lastly, this language must be irreversible, that is to say it must be necessary precisely because it involves a commitment and because, as we have seen, foresight is required; at all times a sentence must be placed so that it could not be placed elsewhere than where it is.

Now, if we use these three means, will we manage to make the script move in a special way that will specifically be a way that gives it distance? That is to say, will we manage to make it precisely hard and imperative enough to put the actor out of reach if we use the most ordinary, the most banal words? No, not if the language stands alone, that is, not unless the actor too has grasped that this is how he has to act; a non-naturalistic language of this kind played in a naturalistic manner will certainly lose its character of rhythm because of that very fact, so that actors might well be given an education in this—and here is something on which a debate might be started—an education that they do get extremely well as regards plays that are not modern plays, but not as regards modern plays. In playing Molière or Shakespeare actors do give a rhythm to the sentence, but not with contemporary authors. But this is a problem that goes beyond the author's style. These are only a number of suggestions, and I should like the discussion to start from them.

Would any of you like to take over from me now and

speak against or in favor of what I have just said? Camus, I mentioned you just now, do you agree with me?

CAMUS   There is one point that needs clearing up, I think. Everything you said seems pertinent enough to drama and tragedy, but we might try to shift the reasoning to comedy, that would be interesting, that's harder, don't you think?

SARTRE   Comedy does have its own special problems, but I think that the gist of what I said remains true in practice, so far as I can see, at any rate, since the notion of distance holds good. And, in the second place, I was talking about plays in general rather than tragedies, for it seems to me that simply to inflate a play of some standing, a rather dense play, people call it a tragedy—a contemporary tendency that should be opposed. I don't think there have been any tragedies since the eighteenth century. I wouldn't call *La Reine morte*,[12] for instance, a tragedy, nor any other play of that kind; they aren't tragedies, but merely plays with a certain elevation, and I can't see how they differ basically from plays in which the comic element predominates, especially now that a mixed type has been virtually accepted.

Do you agree with my ideas about everyday speech?

CAMUS   What strikes me about the modern drama of the past fifty years is that everybody tries to speak naturally. A word out of the ordinary comes as a surprise to actor and audience alike, both of whom have been hearing a certain theatrical rhythm for the last fifty years. I'm sure you will have to be more specific about one point, though. There is some misconception about the term "natural." When one says that a script is not natural, or rather when one tries to specify the concept of natural, one gets the impression that natural means someone speaking naturally, as he does on the street. But that's not what natural is.

Kafka's heroes speak naturally, in a way, but they simply are not natural. I should rather say that the natural is a manner of speaking that is suited to a character or an atmosphere. And this immediately alters the problem. Is it quite certain that Berenice speaks naturally, when Madame de Z did not speak at Louis XIV's court at all as Berenice does?

SARTRE I quite agree. The discussion is starting on the wrong foot . . .

X. You have raised the problem solely from the dramatist's point of view, but that is only one quite small aspect of theater, a secondary one. You have passed over the director, the stage designer, in short, the whole staging, rather rapidly, but perhaps if we take that aspect, it will throw more light on the problem.

SARTRE I could speak of what I am learning about. There is a style in staging. But there are people here more qualified to talk about it than I am. Vilar, what do you think?

VILAR To begin with, what you were dealing with is outside my field. It seems to me that an author brings us things ready-made, and what we can do to serve him is not quite relevant to what you were talking about. It's all very well to talk about dramatic style from the author's point of view, but you must admit that the actor playing his part has a point of view about dramatic style, too.

SARTRE Is there any connection between the two, and how far can the player's dramatic style—

VILAR It's a matter of being sharp-witted and adaptable rather than intelligent. You, the author, provide material and we try to assimilate it, consciously or unconsciously.

SARTRE Do you think many actors concern themselves with the rhythm of a script?

VILAR It is imposed on them.

SARTRE I'm not so sure. I have seen cases in which very good actors, who rendered the character admirably as far as the action went, did not render the true rhythm of the sentences. I know of several cases in which actors interpolated phrases to make sentences easier to speak; I could quote you specific instances.

VILAR If they do not stick closely to the author's dramatic rhythm, they can't be the character, because one of the means you give them to be the character is, consciously or unconsciously, to follow the rhythm.

SARTRE   There is indeed a sort of reciprocal give-and-take agreement between actors and authors and between authors and actors precisely to try to speak naturally, as Camus said, that is to say, without rhythm, and so the actor tries to speak naturally, that is to say with a sort of give-and-take loose rhythm. You find the most typical instance in Tristan Bernard: a tap flowing with lukewarm water, a sort of burble of good nature. This lack of rhythm in Tristan Bernard practically amounts to a rhythm, and an actor who conforms to it will not have any sort of rhythm, whereas what he should do is to take a script and give it its movement, as he does with Molière or Shakespeare—though, since Shakespeare is in translation, the rhythm is the translator's rather than the true rhythm.

What would be interesting would be to try to transpose this to a play written today.

CAMUS   You'd have to get the play written first. But I would certainly like to defend the actors on this, for rhythm is not the first thing they have to care about in many plays; there are a great many other things too.

SARTRE   The fault is the author's originally, or more specifically the fault of the general naturalistic school of thought which prevailed at one time.

VILAR   One of the hardest things for an actor playing a role to do is to stick exactly to this rhythm. We have some actors here; I'd like one of them to tell us about this.

X.   About speaking exactly as everyone does, take one example: *Césaire*,[13] which Vilar has staged. A sailor is speaking; no sailor, of course, ever spoke like that, but the audience believed that no sailor could ever have spoken any other way, it swallowed it whole. Yet it was precisely the opposite of speaking as everyone does.

SARTRE   That was because there were two different elements in *Césaire*: Schlumberger's plays do, I think, have a rhythm; he's an author who writes with a rhythm and takes pains about it; but I do find that the words he used were not words that everyone uses. In other words, we found that we had something between the ideal I was suggesting to you a moment ago and the drama of Henry Bataille. The words were not words everyone uses, but the rhythm made them seem so; personally, I found *Césaire* fairly impressive in a way. Having said that, however, I must say that I think a hundred times more highly of Strindberg's *Storm*, which followed *Césaire*. I found that its use of words which were absolutely the same words as everyone uses created a quite special atmosphere.

VILAR   With a very few exceptions, Schlumberger does not use a sailor's vocabulary; he takes good care not to, but his speech is the same as everyone's, a very plain vernacular.

SARTRE   Yes indeed; perhaps the whole thing is made up of comparisons and allusions.

VILAR   It's not the language that is at fault, but some of the ideas expounded in it, which aren't those of a sailor. But the language is the same as everyone else's.

SARTRE   That means precisely that it did have a rhythm, and you rendered it extremely well, a rhythm precisely of actors' speech.

VILAR   Now, I'd like to ask you whether you think that dramatic style needs to be perfected to such a pitch that it becomes a prosodic language?

SARTRE   I don't think we have to go as far as rhythm in the strict sense, that is to say strict prosody. What we need, I believe, is a theatrical rhythm, which means a rhythm whose rules are not to be sought in prosody as such, but in the imperatives of action.

A break in the movement, for example, seems to me to be a property of theatrical rhythm; that is, you expound a theme in two or three fairly long sentences and then pass abruptly to another subject with an abrupt three-word interrogatory sentence. You can get rhythm of that sort, and it has nothing to do with prosody, in that you don't find a sequence of longs and shorts in it, or sentences with stresses —no, nothing like that.

VILAR   Don't you think that the prosodic range would give us far more means of expression, far more changes of expression than just prose? Would we like contemporary authors to take more trouble about the prosodic form? I don't mean the alexandrine or Claudel's verse form.

SARTRE   I don't think that has much to do with the actual content of a sentence. I am more inclined to think that rhythm should come from the way an author writes as well as from the subject itself, the situation itself. So I don't think we should use methods that are virtually predetermined.

VILAR   Racine has his own method of expression—

SARTRE   We do have the alexandrine, but I don't think we can go back to it, except in certain cases.

X.   Could André Gide's style in *Saül*[14] be considered a rhythmed style?

SARTRE   Certainly. That is a play which, precisely, is one of the kinds of play that gain their interest by distancing.

X.   From the words, from the vocabulary.

SARTRE   Vocabulary is a way of speaking that produces this sort of distancing in relation to both the present and the past, and it is, precisely, appropriate to authors who feel they have to find a rhythm they do not want in modern life and so situate their plays in the past, and this certainly does make for rhythm.

X.   Why do you hold that language must necessarily be everyday language, why do you insist so strongly on that?

X.   Take Shakespeare's sentence: "All the perfumes of Arabia will not sweeten this little hand."[15] It is part of Shakespeare's rhythm, but is it everyday language?

SARTRE   I think it is part of everyday language. It isn't a sentence I would call not everyday language. Perfumes of Arabia is exactly like perfumes of Chanel; it's a very fine sentence, it is uncommon, in a sense, but it belongs to the everyday. Whereas the sentence I mentioned just now, "I suffer from a great wounded shower" . . .

X.   "The ecstasy was divine in our arched brows" . . .

SARTRE   You yourself said that Shakespeare was a poet of the theater, a dramatist.

X.   But now I'm asking why you want everyday language brought into the theater at all costs.

SARTRE   I didn't say that. What I said was that we must take a language in which the words are the words everyone uses, but we must use these words with a rhythm, a significance, and a distancing which create a whole which is then no longer the everyday and natural at all.

X.   They are the words everyone uses.

SARTRE   Pegasus is not a word everyone uses; I hardly ever use it myself in ordinary conversation.

X.   Well, one doesn't often say "perfumes of Arabia" . . .

X.   You can attach non-everyday associations to everyday words.

SARTRE   Or rather sentences, or groups of words, if you prefer it.

COCTEAU   Don't you think that a dramatist's reflex is precisely to get a hearing by elevated speech? Surely that's the mark of a writer for the theater. If you take language from close at hand which can't be spoken at a distance, you haven't got a writer for the theater. We have been muddled by people who were not writers for the theater; we've had bogus theater, with a language of the theater which is a cheat. It sounds as if it has elevation, but it's a theatrical language, not a language of the theater. You get the same thing with poetry. Poetry in the theater is not poetic language, because poetry is something you can hear from a distance. Poetic language always falls short.

X.   A minor example: "Ah quelle cruauté à vous brasser du mal" in *Antigone*. The adapter took it upon himself to transcribe it as "à vous faire du mal," probably to avoid a word not used by everyone. Do you ban "brasser du mal," an expression that we certainly never use? It would be very interesting to know what expression we do use today.

COCTEAU   This is getting us into a linguistic discussion. The interesting point here is the viewpoint of theater. It is infinite, one has to achieve a special sort of elevation . . .

X.   "Effleureur" seems surprising in Bataille's play.

COCTEAU   Just details.

SARTRE   Yes, to a sixteenth-century author, but such problems don't concern us today. At all events, even if you defend "brasser," that is to say, an old word that has its charm as an old word in an old play, you can't expect me to use the word.

BARRAULT   I don't think our friend wants it used as an old word, but as a projection of the word in gesture. I like the word "brasser" because it gives me an idea for a gesture. Indeed, we might well start a digression here on style. I entirely agree that language should be elliptical. You have to hear it only once and hear it very fast, and so an audience should not be required to associate ideas. The language should be striking, not, shall we say, intellectual.

Stendhal's rhythm is a perfect rhythm to the eye, but impossible for the ear, or at any rate for every ear, it's no good for the teeth, the mouth, the tongue. I once had to say about Fabrice's escape in Stendhal that all the consonants had to be held in the mouth as a carpet layer holds tacks. The difficulty with Montherlant was also that his style is that of a literary man, not a dramatist. I think a dramatist should write with his breath, not his brain.

Mightn't we take this opportunity for a digression on the study of words as gesture, and, if we go far enough, a study of the consonants, for the word "brasser" gives me— it would even give a foreigner—a feeling of churning, of kneading. It's a word that gives me a physical impression, and I don't need any associations. That's why I go back to "brasser." The point of the digression would be that dramatic style might start out from what I might call a breathing out of a breathing in. I don't dare mention Claudel, because I know that will get me into trouble. But that was what Claudel was trying for.

SARTRE Without elliptical language, though.

COCTEAU Don't you think a great dramatist is always an actor? Racine was an actor.

BARRAULT A word always has to be breathed out so that it can be a transition to gesture, and this has sometimes led to a lack of smoothness in performances, in which there was invariably a break between the verbal and the gestic elements; there was never a transition, and that was because there was a sudden divergence of points of view. A light went up in the head, whereas a light had been switched on in the breast for expression in gesture.

SARTRE I believe that the dramatist should at least schematically suit the speech to the gesture accompanying it.

BARRAULT Claudel talked to me once about the word "voler" in the sense of flying. French uses "voler"—it hasn't any tonic accent, or rather, it gives you the soaring phase in the act of flying. English uses "to fly," that is to say, a lively movement. In the German "fliegen" you get the action of working. Three different temperaments are expressed regarding one and the same action, each of them taking a different phase in the action. These three words have a bearing on drama. So we might well consider the word not as idea but as action, as gesture, and that would lead on to studying all the consonants as gesture, and the vowels too. There would be a whole alchemy to study: consonant *c* with *a, e, i, o, u,* and then *d* and the vowels.

That is why gibberish could make an extraordinarily dramatic language; and it's wholly relevant to the case we are discussing because it perfectly explains the projection of ideas.

SARTRE You should add, however, for your audience's sake, that it should only be used from time to time.

BARRAULT   Of course, and consonance in certain circumstances.

COCTEAU   Speech in the theater is an act and speech is elevation. For modern plays I think the true language is a false natural language which should seem to be a natural language.

X.   I was meaning to bring up Claudel before Barrault did. I wanted to know whether you think Claudel was trying for a rhythm. He did not necessarily try to get a natural language, but do you think he has a style that can properly be called dramatic?

SARTRE   I think he does, but here we are dealing with the poetic, that is to say a type of theater which is not indeed contrasted with the kind of theater I was talking about; but I was, of course, thinking of nonpoetic theater. I meant a theater no longer concerned, precisely, with verse, rhythm, and a certain kind of beauty that is proper to what is commonly called poetry.

X.   Claudel makes fairly free use of words that depart from natural and everyday speech. Is he to that extent still relevant to dramatic style?

SARTRE   Precisely to the extent that he is not writing at the everyday level.

COCTEAU   You brought up the problem of the play of 1944. A courageous dramatist will write the play of today and find an elevated and harsh language to express what he has to say.

SARTRE   There's one play of Claudel's that I like less than the others, *L'Échange*,[16] precisely because the characters are contemporary.

COCTEAU   Language is supernatural in a way, the ideal language for theater. You are talking about something far more complicated, and the audience thinks it is hearing everyday language, but it is actually hearing something different.

SARTRE   You give an audience its everyday language, but with a sort of distance, and that makes a witness of it and intimidates it.

COCTEAU   There's also collective hypnosis when an audience becomes disindividualized; but when it becomes individualized again . . . You mentioned the noise of a seat creaking—yes, it's an awful moment when a lady starts to read her program or a gentleman squirms, that means there is a dull stretch, the play's not working, people become reindividualized.

SALACROU   That's no test.

COCTEAU   It's the danger of the mass mind.

SALACROU   The interest. But there are some very bad and very conventional plays that hold audiences spellbound.

SARTRE   True enough.

SALACROU   It's not a mathematical test.

SARTRE   It's a hint, all the same, even if a negative one. Suppose you write a play of a very lofty sort, but it bores the audience!

SALACROU   That's necessary, not conclusive, reasoning.

COCTEAU   You have to get used to a door opening for no reason and a lot of useless armchairs. A practicable door is essential.

SARTRE   Did you see *The Star of Seville?*[17] The decor was reduced to a minimum; there was simply an armchair right, a grille left, the far left of the stage, and a sort of low wall at the back. Depending on the scene, the lights picked out either the armchair or the grille or the wall, and the actor only had to start to speak for you to believe that you were in the throne room when it was on the left or in a garden when it was behind the wall. These were the only props, and I mention it because my illusion was complete.

COCTEAU   Economy is always necessary, and it was economical.

SARTRE   You need nothing more than an armchair.

X.   That is what Jean Cocteau tried to do in *Roméo et Juliette.*

COCTEAU   Yes, you only saw the essentials; the streets were constructed around them.

SARTRE   Here we come back to Barrault, who wants to economize even on a staircase.[18]

COCTEAU   The serious mistake in the theater is to use a lot of chairs and armchairs and unnecessary flowers. That makes for frightful disorder and a bogus naturalism.

X.   Why did you use a bronze by Barbedienne?[19]

SARTRE   It is named in the text as the bronze by Barbedienne; as to the bronze itself as decor, I can assure you it's not by Barbedienne. It's any massive object in the background; I believe it represents a naked woman astride a naked man. I don't anyhow think it's of any particular use.

COCTEAU   It's a bronze by Barbedienne because you can't lift it. It's in hell and you see a bronze by Barbedienne.

X.   Do you think there's a rhythm in Anouilh's *Antigone?*

SARTRE   I haven't seen it. Do you consider the conversation ended?

COCTEAU   Yes, I shall go and see your play.

Dullin and Spain

This article was written following the bad critical reception of Charles Dullin's revival of Calderón's *La vida es sueño* at the Théâtre de la Cité on April 1, 1944 (see note 8, p. 322, below), and was published in *Combat*, November 8, 1944. Dullin had produced Calderón's *The Physician of His Own Honor* (*El médico de su honra*) for the first time, in A. Arnoux's adaptation, at the Atelier in 1935 and Lope de Vega's *The Lovers of Galicia*, in Jean Camp's adaptation, at the Théâtre de la Cité in 1942.

The critics are unkind to Dullin. He worries and disturbs them; they admire him despite themselves; and since they do not dare to pretend that what he is trying to do lacks an element of greatness, they have decided once and for all to admire him only in retrospect. They never praise his current production, but the one that has just closed; and if he revives one of his former hits, you may be sure that the first performance was far better than the revival. This prevents them from seeing and commenting on the major features of his art. They, these frivolous and trivial critics, confide in

us that they did not like *Life Is a Dream*—though the public
could not care less whether they did or didn't—but they fail
to perceive that the play has its place in an enterprise on
which Dullin has been venturing for twenty years, to reveal
the true face of Spain. Dullin could have made his selection from a hundred comedies of intrigue and a score of
cloak-and-sword dramas among the works of Calderón or
Lope de Vega which would have furnished audiences with
a cheap diversion. He preferred three austere straight plays,
The Physician of His Own Honor, The Lovers of Galicia,
and *Life Is a Dream,* because all three demonstrate the
same desolate grandeur, because all three of them burn
with the dry flame of a flamenco. Don Guitiro kills his
innocent wife for the sole reason that she "might" be sus-
pected; Basilio, the aged king, puts his son Segismundo in
chains for life, for though he is innocent, a horoscope has
predicted that he will become violent; in both cases innocence is of little weight as compared with a sort of grim
loyalty to throne and family. In Don Guitiro's eyes, as in
those of Basilio and Segismundo, there shines the same arid,
unremitting passing, blanched by sun and dust, with the
melancholy grandeur of spending every moment meditating
its own ruin and the ruin of the subject of this meditation. A
sentiment bordering on despair, yet, unlike the passions
in Racine, proud of itself and deeply imbued with its
rights. Not one of them, even including the lord in
The Lovers of Galicia, is not perfectly certain, even in his
violence, that he is in the right: is not the woman he has
abducted a village girl living on "his" land? In raping
her is he not exercising his seigneurial right? The critics
gave a very bad reception to these three plays, especially
The Physician of His Own Honor. Dubech[1] called Calderón a savage and to reassure himself invoked Corneille,
who was at least polite. The disturbing thing was not, as
they thought, the barbaric violence of the passion; on the
contrary, it is the extreme lucidity of this passion which

knows that it is plunging toward disaster and is deliberately what it is. In short, the passion in Racine's tragedy—which our critics have always preferred—is tranquilizing because it is mechanical; it is not self-conscious, and we have an inkling that the exertion of a little will could halt it in time. The Spanish passion revealed to us by Dullin is steeped in right and will. It is the whole man engaged in an enterprise that he knows to be desperate, yet he will carry it to its utmost limit. This makes it akin to Greek tragedy, which is, of course, a conflict of rights. And it is a conflict of right that sets Segismundo at odds with Basilio in the splendid second act of *Life Is a Dream*, when Basilio says, "I had the right to put you in chains because you would have become violent," and Segismundo replies, "'I have the right to be violent, because you put me in chains." These conflicts cannot be appeased themselves; they appeal to a higher justice. In the three plays we have cited, the king plays the part of the gods of antiquity. His justice—whether he pardons or punishes—is pitiless. Pitiless to the criminal if he punishes; if he pardons, pitiless to the victim. In any case, this higher court appeals to honor, the family, the tribe, an oral and primitive body of laws acknowledged by the appellant. It comes full circle, for the royal judgment too is a passion and a will.

It is Dullin's great merit to have brought to the French stage this free and fatal world, which knows no rest, no relaxation, whose pitiless harshness is expressed in florid, even mannered, language. The critics' dislike of it shows that we know little about it, and Dullin's greatness lies in his ability to render it as it is, with its Castilian authority, its desert passions, its mannerisms, exasperating at times. If genius in staging lies in rendering the atmosphere and savor of a dramatic work, what shall we call Dullin's work, which has transposed to our stage and made us feel to the point of disquiet the savor of a foreign country far distant from us in space and time?

Forgers of Myths

(Forger des mythes)

This lecture was delivered by Sartre in New York in 1946, during his second visit to the United States. The following translation, by Rosamond Gilder, was originally published in *Theatre Arts* (vol. 30, no. 6, June 1946) as "Forgers of Myths: The Young Playwrights of France"; it has since been reprinted in the United States in various collections of essays on the theater. The notes for this edition are by the editors.

Addressed to readers who had little information as yet on what had happened in French writing during the Occupation and immediately after the Liberation, the lecture reproduces a number of ideas that Sartre had expressed in a less didactic form in the preceding pieces in this volume; but it also contains some fresh ideas.

In reading the newspaper reviews of Katharine Cornell's production of Jean Anouilh's *Antigone*,[1] I had the impression that the play had created a certain amount of discomfort in the minds of the New York drama critics. Many expressed surprise that such an ancient myth should be staged at all. Others reproached Antigone with being neither alive nor credible, with not having what, in theater jargon, is called "character." The misunderstanding, I believe, was due to the fact that the critics were not informed of what many young authors in France—each along differing lines and without concerted aim—are attempting to do.

There has been a great deal of discussion in France about "a return to tragedy," about the "rebirth of the philosophic play." The two labels are confusing and they should both be rejected. Tragedy is, for us, a historic phenomenon which flourished between the sixteenth and eighteenth centuries; we have no desire to begin that over again. Nor are we anxious to produce philosophic plays, if by that is meant works deliberately intended to set forth on the stage the philosophy of Marx, Saint Thomas, or existentialism. Nevertheless there is some truth attached to these two labels: in the first place, it is a fact that we are less concerned with making innovations than with returning to a tradition; it is likewise true that the problems we wish to deal with in the theater are very different from those we habitually dealt with before 1940.

The theater, as conceived of in the period between the two world wars, and as it is perhaps still thought of in the United States today, is a theater of characters. The analysis of characters and their confrontation was the theater's chief concern. The so-called situations existed only for the purpose of throwing the characters into clearer relief. The best plays in this period were psychological studies of a coward, a liar, an ambitious man or a frustrated one. Occasionally a playwright made an effort to outline the workings of a passion—usually love—or to analyze an inferiority complex.

Judged by such principles Anouilh's Antigone is not a character at all. Nor is she simply a peg on which to hang a passion calculated to develop along the approved lines of whatever psychology might be in style. She represents a naked will, a pure, free choice; in her there is no distinguishing between passion and action. The young playwrights of France do not believe that men share a ready-made "human nature" which may alter under the impact of a given situation. They do not think that individuals can be seized with a passion or a mania which can be explained purely on the grounds of heredity, environment, and situations. What is universal, to their way of thinking, is not nature but the situations in which man finds himself; that is, not the sum total of his psychological traits but the limits which enclose him on all sides.

For them man is not to be defined as a "reasoning animal," or a "social" one, but as a free being, entirely indeterminate, who must choose his own being when confronted with certain necessities, such as being already committed in a world full of both threatening and favorable factors among other men who have made their choices before him, who have decided in advance the meaning of those factors. He is faced with the necessity of having to work and die, of being hurled into a life already complete which yet is his own enterprise and in which he can never have a second chance; where he must play his cards and take risks no matter what the cost. That is why we feel the urge to put on the stage certain situations which throw light on the main aspects of the condition of man and to have the spectator participate in the free choice which man makes in these situations.

Thus, Anouilh's Antigone may have seemed abstract because she was not portrayed as a young Greek princess, formed by certain influences and some ghastly memories, but rather as a free woman without any features at all until she chooses them for herself in the moment when she asserts her freedom to die despite the triumphant tyrant. Similarly, when the burgomaster of Vauxelles in Simone de Beauvoir's *Les Bouches inutiles*² has to decide whether to save his beleaguered town by cutting off half its citizens (women, children, and old men) or to risk making them all perish in an effort to save them all, we do not care whether he is sensual or cold, whether he has an Oedipus complex, or whether he is of an irritable or jolly disposition. No doubt if he is rash or incautious, vain or pusillanimous, he will make the wrong decision. But we are not interested in arranging in advance the motivations or reasons which will inevitably force his choice. Rather, we are concerned in presenting the anguish of a man who is both free and full of good will, who in all sincerity is trying to find out the side he must take, and who knows that when he chooses the lot of others he is at the same time choosing his own pattern of behavior and is deciding once and for all whether he is to be a tyrant or a democrat.

If one of us happens to present character on the boards it is only for the purpose of getting rid of it at once. For instance, Caligula, at the outset of Albert Camus's play of that name,[3] has a character. One is led to believe he is gentle and well-behaved, and no doubt he actually is both. But that gentleness and that modesty suddenly melt away in the face of the prince's horrifying discovery of the world's absurdity. From then on he will choose to be the man to persuade other men of that absurdity, and the play becomes only the story of how he carries out his purpose.

A man who is free within the circle of his own situations, who chooses, whether he wishes to or not, for everyone else when he chooses for himself—that is the subject-matter of our plays. As a successor to the theater of characters we want to have a theater of situations; our aim is to explore all the situations that are most common to human experience, those which occur at least once in the majority of lives. The people in our plays will be distinct from one another—not as a coward is from a miser or a miser from a brave man, but rather as actions are divergent or clashing, as right may conflict with right. In this it may well be said that we derive from the Corneillean tradition.

It is easy to understand, therefore, why we are not

greatly concerned with psychology. We are not searching for the right "word" which will suddenly reveal the whole unfolding of a passion, nor yet the "act" which will seem most lifelike and inevitable to the audience. For us psychology is the most abstract of the sciences because it studies the workings of our passions without plunging them back into their true human surroundings, without their background of religious and moral values, the taboos and commandments of society, the conflicts of nations and classes, of rights, of wills, of actions. For us a man is a whole enterprise in himself. And passion is a part of that enterprise.

In this we return to the concept of tragedy as the Greeks saw it. For them, as Hegel has shown,[4] passion was never a simple storm of sentiment but fundamentally always the assertion of a right. The fascism of Creon, the stubbornness of Antigone for Sophocles and Anouilh, the madness of Caligula for Camus, are *at one and the same time* transports of feeling which have their origin deep within us and expressions of impregnable will which are affirmations of systems of values and rights such as the rights of citizenship, the rights of the family, individual ethics, collective ethics, the right to kill, the right to reveal to human beings their pitiable condition, and so forth. We do not reject psychology, that would be absurd: we integrate life.

For fifty years one of the most celebrated subjects for dissertation in France has been formulated as follows: "Comment on La Bruyère's saying: Racine draws man as he is; Corneille, as he should be." We believe the statement should be reversed. Racine paints psychologic man, he studies the mechanics of love, of jealousy in an abstract, pure way; that is, without ever allowing moral considerations or human will to deflect the inevitability of their evolution. His dramatis personae are only creatures of his mind, the end results of an intellectual analysis. Corneille, on the other hand, showing will at the very core of passion, gives us back man in all his complexity, in his complete reality.

The young authors I am discussing take their stand on Corneille's side. For them the theater will be able to present man in his entirety only in proportion to the theater's willingness to be *moral*. By that we do not mean that it should put forward examples illustrating the rules of deportment or the practical ethics taught to children, but rather that the study of the conflict of characters should be replaced by the presentation of the conflict of rights. It was not a question of the opposition of *character* between a Stalinist and a Trotskyite; it was not in their characters that an anti-Nazi of 1933 clashed with an SS guard; the difficulties in international politics do not derive from the characters of the men leading us; the strikes in the United States do not reveal conflicts of character between industrialists and workers. In each case it is, in the final analysis and in spite of divergent interests, the system of values, of ethics, and of concepts of man which are lined up against each other.

Therefore, our new theater definitely has drawn away from the so-called realistic theater because "realism" has always offered plays made up of stories of defeat, laissez-faire, and drifting; it has always preferred to show how external forces batter a man to pieces, destroy him bit by bit, and ultimately make of him a weathervane turning with every change of wind. But we claim for ourselves the *true* realism because we know it is impossible, in everyday life, to distinguish between fact and right, the real from the ideal, psychology from ethics.

This theater does not give its support to any one "thesis" and is not inspired by any preconceived idea. All it seeks to do is to explore the state of man in its entirety and to present to the modern man a portrait of himself, his problems, his hopes, and his struggles. We believe our theater would betray its mission if it portrayed individual personalities, even if they were as universal types as a miser, a misanthrope, a deceived husband, because, if it is to address the masses, the theater must speak in terms of their most general preoccupations, dispelling their anxieties in the form of myths which anyone can understand and feel deeply.

My first experience in the theater was especially fortunate. When I was a prisoner in Germany in 1940, I wrote, staged, and acted in a Christmas play which, while pulling wool over the eyes of the German censor by means of simple symbols, was addressed to my fellow prisoners. This drama, biblical in appearance only, was written and put on by a prisoner, was acted by prisoners in scenery painted by prisoners; it was aimed exclusively at prisoners (so much so that I have never since then permitted it to be staged or even printed[5]) and it addressed them on the subject of their concerns as prisoners. No doubt it was neither a good play nor well acted: the work of an amateur, the critics would say, a product of special circumstances. Nevertheless, on this occasion, as I addressed my comrades across the footlights, speaking to them of their state as prisoners, when I suddenly saw them so remarkably silent and attentive, I realized what theater ought to be—a great collective, religious phenomenon.

To be sure, I was, in this case, favored by special circumstances; it does not happen every day that your public is drawn together by one great common interest, a great loss or a great hope. As a rule, an audience is made up of the most diverse elements: a big businessman sits beside a traveling salesman or a professor, a man next to a woman, and each is subject to his own particular preoccupations. Yet this situation is a challenge to the playwright: he must create his public, he must fuse all the disparate elements in the auditorium into a single unity by awakening in the recesses of their spirits the things which all men of a given epoch and community care about.

This does not mean that our authors intend to make use of symbols in the sense that symbols are the expression either indirect or poetic of a reality one either cannot or will not grasp directly. We would feel a profound distaste today for representing happiness as an elusive bluebird, as Maeterlinck did. Our times are too austere for child's play of that sort. Yet if we reject the theater of symbols we still want ours to be one of myths; we want to attempt to show the public the great myths of death, exile, love. The characters in Albert Camus's *Le Malentendu* are not symbols, they are flesh and blood: *a* mother and *a* daughter, *a* son who comes back from a long journey; their tragic experiences are complete in themselves. And yet they are mythical in the sense that the misunderstanding which separates them can serve as the embodiment of all misunderstandings which separate man from himself, from the world, from other men.

The French public makes no mistake about this, as has been proved by the discussions engendered by certain plays. With *Les Bouches inutiles*, for instance, criticism was not confined to discussing the story of the play, which was based on actual events that took place frequently in the Middle Ages: it recognized in the play a condemnation of fascist procedures. The Communists, on the other hand, saw in it a condemnation of their own procedures: "The conclusion," so they said in their newspapers, "is couched in terms of petty-bourgeois idealism. All useless mouths should have been sacrificed to save the city." Anouilh also stirred up a storm of discussion with *Antigone*, being charged on the one hand with being a Nazi, on the other with being an anarchist. Such violent reactions prove that our plays are reaching the public just where it is important that it should be reached.

Yet these plays are austere. To begin with, since the situation is what we care about above all, our theater shows it at the very point where it is about to reach its climax. We do not take time out for learned research, we feel no need of registering the imperceptible evolution of a character or a plot: one does not reach death by degrees, one is suddenly confronted with it—and if one approaches politics or love by slow degrees, then acute problems, arising suddenly, call for no progression. By taking our dramatis personae and precipitating them, in the very first scene, into the highest pitch of their conflicts we turn to the well-known pattern of classic tragedy, which always seizes upon the action at the very moment it is headed for catastrophe.

Our plays are violent and brief, centered around one single event; there are few players and the story is compressed within a short space of time, sometimes only a few hours. As a result they obey a kind of "rule of the three unities," which has been only a little rejuvenated and modified. A single set, a few entrances, a few exits, intense arguments among the characters who defend their individual rights with passion—this is what sets our plays at a great distance from the brilliant fantasies of Broadway. Yet some of them find that their austerity and intensity have not lacked appreciation in Paris. Whether New York will like them is a question.

Since it is their aim to forge myths, to project for the audience an enlarged and enhanced image of its own sufferings, our playwrights turn their backs on the constant preoccupation of the realists, which is to reduce as far as possible the distance which separates the spectator from the spectacle. In 1942, in Gaston Baty's production of *The Taming of the Shrew*,[6] there were steps going from the stage to the auditorium so that certain characters could go down among the orchestra seats. We are very far away from such concepts and methods. To us a play should not seem too *familiar*. Its greatness derives from its social and, in a certain sense, religious functions: it must remain a rite; even as it speaks to the spectators of themselves it must do it in a tone and with a constant reserve of manner which, far from breeding familiarity, will increase the distance between play and audience.

.   .   .

That is why one of our problems has been to search out a style of dialogue which, while utterly simple and made up of words on everyone's lips, will still preserve something of the ancient dignity of our tongue. We have all barred from our plays the digressions, the set speeches, and what we in France like to call the *poésie de réplique*; all this chit-chat debases a language. It seems to us that we shall recapture a little of the pomp of ancient tragedies if we practice the most rigorous economy of words. As for me, in *Morts sans sépulture*, my latest play, I did not deny myself the use of familiar turns of phrase, swear-words, even slang, whenever I felt that such speech was germane to the characters. But I did attempt to preserve, through the pace of the dialogue, an extreme conciseness of statement—ellipses, brusque interruptions, a sort of inner tension in the phrases which at once set them apart from the easygoing sound of everyday talk. Camus's style in *Caligula* is different in kind but it is magnificently sober and taut. Simone de Beauvoir's language in *Les Bouches inutiles* is so stripped that it is sometimes accused of dryness.

Dramas which are short and violent, sometimes reduced to the dimensions of a single long act (*Antigone* lasts an hour and a half, my own play, *Huis clos*, an hour and twenty minutes without intermission), dramas entirely centered on one event—usually a conflict of rights, bearing on some very general situation—written in a sparse, extremely tense style, with a small cast not presented for their individual characters but thrust into a conjunction where they are forced to make a choice—in brief this is the theater, austere, moral, mythic, and ceremonial in aspect, which has given birth to new plays in Paris during the Occupation and especially since the end of the war. They correspond to the needs of a people exhausted but tense, for whom liberation has not meant a return to abundance and who can live only with the utmost economy.

The very severity of these plays is in keeping with the

severity of French life; their moral and metaphysical topics reflect the preoccupation of a nation which must at one and the same time reconstruct and re-create and which is searching for new principles. Are they the product of local circumstances or can their very austerity of form enable them to reach a wider public in more fortunate countries? This is a question we must ask ourselves frankly before we try to transplant them.[7]

People's Theater
and Bourgeois Theater

This interview was conducted by Bernard Dort after the first performance of *Nekrassov* and was published in *Théâtre populaire* (no. 15, September–October 1955) under the headline "Jean-Paul Sartre on the theatre." It contains Sartre's first recorded references to Brecht.

DORT Does the expression "people's theater" mean anything to you, and if so, what?

SARTRE People's theater . . . Yes. The expression does indeed have a real meaning. Perhaps even too much of one, since in point of fact, to me it means *all* theater. The problem, then, is not whether theater should be a people's theater—it can only be that—but whether, at the present time, this people's theater, or just theater, exists, and if so, how.

Here, in fact, we stumble on a contradiction. There are theaters, but no theater. Let us take, for example . . .

DORT The Théâtre National Populaire?

SARTRE Yes, the TNP . . . In my view, the TNP does not represent people's theater. This is not meant as a criticism of what Vilar is doing, but simply as a statement of fact.

Vilar himself is not what I am talking about; the point is the situation of the TNP.

To begin with, the TNP is a subsidized theater. That means a theater which puts on plays which it has to select from the repertory and, even so, select with a great deal of caution. Plays which were not written for the masses of our time. Plays which certainly were once part of a genuine people's theater—I am thinking of Shakespeare—which were written for the people of the period, but have now become cultural forms, are part of the bourgeois cultural heritage.

DORT   So you think that putting on plays from the traditional repertory—even in modern productions, even, so to speak, with the patina scraped off them, as in the production of *Le Cid*—is not relevant to a real attempt at people's theater?

SARTRE   Yes. Staging *Don Juan* or Racine is fine, it is useful, but it is *irrelevant*. For a people's audience the first thing you have to do is to produce its own plays—plays written for it and speaking to it.

And this brings me to the second set of reasons for the "failure" of the TNP, the question of the audience. In point of fact, the TNP does not have a people's audience, a working-class audience. Its audience is a petty-bourgeois audience, a public that would not go to the theater, or only very seldom, if it were not for the TNP with its relatively cheap seats—but not a working-class public. There are workers who go to the TNP, the TNP has given performances for workers; but the TNP does not have a working-class public. Even when it travels and performs in the working-class suburbs of Paris.[1]

The point is that workers are remarkably reluctant to go to the theater. Take my own experience. *Nekrassov* was welcomed unreservedly by the Communists, the CGT and the TEC.[2] Their papers wrote about it, seats were set aside for them at cheaper prices . . . Well, the workers came very slowly, little by little. To the workers the theater is still something ceremonious—something that partakes of bourgeois ceremony. They mistrust it, and when they do go to it, it is a lot of trouble; seats are expensive, even at the' TNP; there are the children to be looked after, the theaters are far away, in the center of Paris . . . and the workers are tired; if they want to relax, they go to musical comedies. This means that you must give them a theater of their own, overcome their mistrust (a mere hint is enough to turn them away from the theater. For instance, take Büchner's *Danton's Death*: the Communists came out against it and no one went to Vilar's performances in the suburbs. Whereas just the opposite happens with the bourgeois: the theater is their own preserve. When *The Devil and the Good Lord* went on the road and the bishop thundered against it from the pulpit, everyone was there and heard him, and they all met again the same evening at the theater) by dealing with *their* problem in the theater—the political problem.

This is no criticism of the TNP itself. But it is a revealing case. There is no real people's audience; what you have to have first is plays written for it.

The only example of people's theater I know of in France is Claude Martin's tour of the factories with the play about Henri Martin.[3] The play was slapdash and stereotyped, true enough, but it raised a political problem and talked about what the workers and the party were talking about, it was performed before workers at their workplace: that was the essential thing.

In this sense there is a people's theater in the U.S.S.R. —but not everywhere. In Leningrad, in Moscow, in the big cities the theater audiences are petty bourgeois, just as in France. But alongside that theater there is a theater near each factory in the Houses of Culture, a theater with an audience of workers. And in any case, there is an important difference as compared with our own situation. This people's theater does not make for segregation in any way. And it is performed by actors from the large cities (who have to give a specified number of performances in the factories each year). And the problems dealt with in the new plays are problems in the context of what the workers are concerned with. The theater in the U.S.S.R. is *educational*; it is not very good, it might be better. The essential point, however, is that it really *speaks* to this audience of workers . . .

Basically, the solution here might perhaps be to have fifty, a hundred TNPs.

DORT   Yes, but there is still the problem of the repertory, of tradition. Don't you think that another prerequisite for a people's theater is a complete change in theatrical style, a break with the theatrical tradition?

SARTRE   A change, yes. A break, perhaps not. Anyway, a discarding of the traditions of the bourgeois theater and a return to the theatrical tradition, the prebourgeois tradition. For the bourgeois theater alone has not been a people's theater. The entire tradition of the theater was a people's theater before the advent of the bourgeoisie.

Under the Old Regime the class struggle was just as savage as in our own time, but the structures of the city did not reflect it; everyone went to the theater and the theater was for everyone. But from the nineteenth century on, the city has been the city of the bourgeois. They place the theaters in the center of the city, in the heart of their citadel. The theater then becomes a class theater, the theater of the bourgeoisie.

The theater might of course have reflected the concerns of a class before the nineteenth century; but it was not, it had never been, exclusively a class theater.

DORT   What about our classical theater?

SARTRE   Yes, I was going rather too fast. Our classical theater is a people's theater only to a certain extent. There is a break between Corneille and Racine, a political and social

change, the emergence of the absolute monarchy. But that
was only a passing phase. The eighteenth-century theater
(with the exception of Marivaux, who is a sequel to the
seventeenth) becomes a people's theater again. Yes, Voltaire, even Voltaire's tragedies, was people's theater. Like
Corneille. The break lasted only from 1660 to 1730.

DORT   But for a revival of the tradition, wouldn't you now
need to invent another set of subjects? Wouldn't we have to
distinguish between theatrical structures—those of the traditional people's theater—and theatrical subjects?

SARTRE   Of course. The subjects for our people's theater
will have to be new. Its audience has changed, and now we
must talk to this audience about itself. The traditional people's theater, as I have already said, has become a repertory
theater, a bourgeois cultural fact.

What we need now is to place human conflicts in historical situations and show that they are determined by them.
Our subjects must be social subjects, the major subjects in
the world we live in, those we have become aware of.

I do not say that a people's theater cannot be a psychological theater. I only say that it cannot be at present.

DORT   You once defined what you meant by the theater of
our time: *a theater of situations.* You wrote:

> But if it's true that man is free in a given situation and
> that in and through that situation he chooses what he will
> be, then what we have to show in the theater are simple
> and human situations and free individuals in these situa-
> tions choosing what they will be. . . . The most moving
> thing the theater can show is a character creating himself,
> the moment of choice, of the free decision which commits
> him to a moral code and a whole way of life.

Do you still assent to all the terms of this definition?

SARTRE   Yes and no. Yes, because I do not see any reason
not to show in the theater freedoms which in fact demystify.
And while I agree with Brecht—Brecht's contribution to

the theater seems to me of capital importance, especially as a concrete example of a modern people's theater—that every theatrical performance must be demystifying, I think that if we really want to achieve this aim, we have to do something more than simply be critical. That would mean relying too much on the audience—which is possible only in Brecht's case, because his audience has already been politicized. But we have to make our audience—an audience which might be quite likely not to react to a purely critical play—share in the real demystification of certain characters.

Take Henri Martin. There you have a character who strips away mystification; a freedom at work, a freedom pregnant, humble, committed to an act with a limited purpose—all he has to do is to demonstrate against the war in Indochina—a freedom which thus serves its purpose. And again in the Henri Martin case you have another character, Heimburger, the negative, as it were, of Henri Martin. A character who is the wholly mystified individual, a man whose freedom is swallowed up, twisted by circumstances— something like what I was trying to do with the character of Heinrich in *The Devil and the Good Lord*, someone completely destroyed by his situation, someone who no matter what he does invariably does harm, because he is in a false position.

So we can conceive of a play in which, given a certain historical and social situation, we are presented with the whole range of mystifications and demystifications possible in the context.

And this is what I failed to take into consideration in the definition you quoted to me: the limits of freedom. For this demystifying freedom which the theater should show us if it is to be effective cannot burst on us like the flash of an explosion. It is, essentially, limited within definite bounds. It is the freedom to say Yes or No in a specific case, such as a strike or a revolt, or some such thing, and this Yes or this No is the point from which the dramatist must build, the aspect of his character that he has to bring out. Just that. He must show how the fact that his character says Yes or No creates the character, its density, its objective reality.

DORT But aren't you afraid that, precisely because of the way the performance works in the theater, the audience—a bourgeois audience—may not identify itself with this freedom, appropriate it for its own benefit?

SARTRE Perhaps . . . but to prevent this, the action in the theater must be very plain, very specific, and above all we must change the audience.

As far as I am concerned, I now have nothing more to say to the bourgeois.

But the real problem is probably not the structures, or even the subjects, of people's theater, but its technique—in the broadest sense of the word—or, if you like, its language. I mean by that not so much knowing what language to speak, but the part language has to play in theater of this kind.

Take the scripts of the plays that were performed on carts all over the place in the nineteenth century; take, too, the Elizabethans, Marlowe especially, there you have a rapid language. No classical drama ever achieved a rapidity like that. That is what we have to recover. And I do not know whether Brecht managed this; I do not find his dialogue—of course, this may be due to the translation—rapid. The action in his plays takes place in front of us and the language is carried by the action as a seagull by the wave. It is not decisive. In a deeper sense, in relation to the structure of his critical drama, Brecht is right; but dramatically?

Yes, as far as I personally am concerned, this is the main problem: to find a combination of speech and action in which speech shall not seem superfluous, in which it has an inherent power, quite apart from any eloquence. It is in fact the very first requirement for truly effective drama.

DORT Well, since you have brought up the problem of

language in the theater, can you explain to us your position as regards what is roughly called our avant-garde theater, a theater in which authors have concerned themselves primarily with problems of language?

SARTRE You want me to talk about Beckett, Ionesco, and Adamov? I must make it quite clear that I have no intention of judging them, but am simply trying to place their works in relation to the people's theater we have just been talking about.

I must point out at once that their plays are profoundly, essentially, bourgeois in content. Take Beckett. I liked *Waiting for Godot* very much. I go so far as to regard it as the best thing that has been done in the theater for thirty years. But all the themes in *Godot* are bourgeois—solitude, despair, the platitude, incommunicability. All of them are the product of the inner solitude of the bourgeoisie. And it matters little what Godot may be—God or the Revolution . . . What counts is that Godot does not come because of the heroes' inner weakness; that he cannot come because of their "sin," because men are like that.

And it is the same with Ionesco. All these writers are outsiders. Of foreign origin, they are external both to our language and to our society. So they look at them from outside. Ionesco's whole work is the proverbial society of union among men, but seen in reverse. And these writers' problem is the problem of integration—in this respect they are the only dramatists of our time (they shatter the bourgeois theater in which this integration is taken for granted beforehand)—but the problem of integration as such, of any integration at all, of their integration with any sort of society; while they are nonpolitical in this sense, they are also reactionary.

Adamov is a rather different case. I would go so far as to say the only one from whom something may be expected in the way of people's theater. Because he has changed. I did not like his *Tous contre tous*, which was a wholly negative work, a work which, denouncing any form of social life as oppression, ended up by making a law of oppression and so justifying it. *Ping-Pong* is different. Here Adamov is beginning to write positive drama. In it we feel the author's deep compassion for his characters, a real understanding of them—and he makes the audience share this compassion. Hence the possibility of a real criticism . . . Only, Adamov has not yet gone far enough. Society only appears in *Ping-Pong* right in the background . . . *Ping-Pong* is still on a very idealistic level, and in essence the question in it is still the question of the relation of men among themselves.

And there is another problem: is this theater, especially Beckett's and Ionesco's, accessible to the masses? Would this destruction of its own content by itself, which is its deeper movement, be understood by the masses? I fear not. And I certainly do not see that Adamov, the Adamov of *Ping-Pong*—

DORT   While we are on the subject, nearly three years ago you mentioned to me a performance you were thinking of putting on at the Vél' d'Hiv' with Fernand Léger. Have you dropped this idea, or do you think it is still possible . . . and desirable?

SARTRE   The project did not come to anything for purely personal and practical reasons. Léger and I were all for it. We badly wanted to do it. But it could not be done. As to whether it was desirable . . . I could only have told you afterwards.

In any case, it was not really theater. It was to be a festival, a festival of peace, and it could only have been done once, with actors who were to contribute their services free of charge.

In any case, people's theater should not be confused with theater for the masses. In some factories in Moscow they put on intimate plays before less than two hundred and fifty people. But the place where they are performed and the content of the plays leave no room for doubt that it really is genuine people's theater.

DORT Yes, indeed festival ought not to be confused with theater. It has been too often. And I was going on to ask you whether you think that the Vél' d'Hiv', which is a place remarkably suitable for mystification (as I realized when I went there to hear Billy Graham preach), is the sort of place that should be used for theater, that is, for a demystification?

SARTRE That is a problem, certainly. But to come to Brecht. And here I must again note the difference between us. I personally am fully convinced that any demystification must be in a sense mystifying. Or rather that if a crowd has been to some extent steeped in mystification, you cannot trust to that crowd's critical reactions alone. You have to give it a countermystification. And to do that the theater must not renounce any of the sorceries of theater. Exactly as the Jesuits worked during the Counter Reformation— those Jesuits by whom our friends the Communists have been schooled.

In this sense you might almost say that Brecht is too "formalist." Or rather, that though he is not so for his own audience, for politicized crowds, he would probably be so for us, for a public so lacking in backbone (to put it mildly) as ours is. But nonetheless I admit that Brecht has been the only dramatist to raise the problems of theater in their true terms, the only one who has understood that any people's theater could only be a political theater, the only one to have pondered a *technique* of people's theater.[4]

DORT One more question. What do you think, from this point of view, about *The Crucible*?

SARTRE I thought very highly of Rouleau's production. As to the play itself, what worries me is the ambiguity of its conclusion. It converts a specifically American phenomenon into something universal, which consequently means nothing except that intolerance is to be found everywhere and that everything always comes to the same.

The mistake was no doubt getting Marcel Aymé to adapt the play. In consequence, a whole violent, highly emotional side of the play disappeared. The stress was no longer on the "witches"; the whole relationship between the particular case and the social situation was blurred.

The real issue is a conflict between the older emigrants and the new, between rich and poor, for the possession of land. There is practically no trace of this left in Aymé's adaptation. All we see is a man persecuted for some obscure reason, and the whole of the ending of *The Crucible* is disconcertingly idealistic in tone. Montand's death and his acceptance of it would have meant something if we had been shown them as an act of revolt at the heart of a social combat. But this social struggle became unintelligible in the production of the Théâtre Sarah-Bernhardt, and Montand's death appeared simply as a purely ethical attitude rather than a free act performed to stir up scandal and as an effective repudiation of his situation in the only way left to him.

Miller's play with the whole point left out in this way, emasculated in this manner, seems to me to be the very image of a mystifying play, because everyone can find what he likes in it, because every audience will simply find in it a confirmation of the attitude it already has. Precisely because it fails clearly to bring out the real political and social implications of the phenomenon of the witch-hunt.[5]

DORT Or because the play as presented to us conceals rather than reveals what Brecht calls the "social gestus" of the witch-hunt phenomenon?

SARTRE Exactly.

Brecht and the Classics

Published in the booklet "Hommage international à Bertolt Brecht," the program for the Théâtre des Nations, April 4–21, 1957. The Berliner Ensemble had visited Paris for the first time since Brecht's death in 1956 with *Galileo Galilei* and *Mutter Courage*. The Bochum Schauspielhaus presented *Die Dreigroschenoper* and the German version of Sartre's *The Devil and the Good Lord*. Sartre attended the performance in honor of Brecht which opened the German series at the Théâtre des Nations on April 4, 1957.

In some respects Brecht is one of us. The density and originality of his work should not prevent the French from rediscovering in it their ancient traditions, which were buried beneath the romantic and bourgeois nineteenth century. Most contemporary plays try to make us believe in the reality of the events taking place on stage, but are not greatly concerned with their truth. If they can keep us in suspense until the final revolver shot and if it really startles us, what does improbability matter? The play "gets" us.

And the bourgeois admires actors not so much for the precision of their acting as for a mysterious quality that might be called their "presence." Whose presence? The player's? No, his character's; if he is Buckingham in the flesh, we let him talk all the nonsense he wants to. For the bourgeoisie believes only in particular truths.

Brecht was not much influenced, I think, by the great French classical writers nor by the Greek tragedians on whom they modeled their work; his plays recall the Elizabethan drama rather than the classical tragedies. Yet he has in common with the French classics and the classics of antiquity the use that he can make of the context of a collective ideology, method, and creed; like the classics, he situates man in the world once more, that is to say in the truth. The relation between the true and the illusory is therefore reversed, for, as in the classics, the event represented itself reveals its *absence*, for it happened a long time ago or never existed, and reality dissolves into pure appearance. Yet these false appearances reveal to us the true laws governing human behavior. Yes, for Brecht, as for Sophocles and Racine, Truth exists, and the dramatist's function is not to *tell* it but to *show* it. And this proud enterprise, to show men to men without resort to the dubious enchantments of desire or terror is most undoubtedly what we call classicism. Brecht is classical in his care for unity; if there is a total truth—which is the true object of theater—it is the total event that blends social strata and persons and lets individual disorder reflect collective disorders whose violent development throws light on the conflicts and the general disorder by which they are determined. This is the reason why his plays have a classical economy; admittedly, he does not trouble to unify by place or time, but he eliminates everything likely to distract us. He does not wish to move us *too much* to leave us wholly free at all times to listen, to see, and to understand. Yet it is a terrible monster he speaks to us about: our own. But he deliberately speaks of it without terrorizing us; you are about to see the result: an unreal and true image, aerial, intangible, and multi-colored, in which violence, crimes, madness, and despair are subjected to a calm contemplation, like the monsters "by art imitated" of which Boileau speaks.

Does this mean we shall sit there unmoved while people shout, torture, and kill on the stage? No, because the murderers, the victims, the torturers are simply ourselves. Racine, too, spoke to his contemporaries about themselves. But he was careful to minimize things by showing them through the wide lens of the opera glass. He apologizes in the preface to *Bajazet* for putting recent history on the stage: "My tragic characters," he says, "must be looked at otherwise than as we generally look at characters we have seen from so close at hand. It may be said that respect for the hero increases with his distance from us. . . . Placing the action in distant countries in some sort remedies an undue proximity in time." This is a good definition of what Brecht himself calls the "distancing effect." For the respect mentioned by Racine in connection with the bloodthirsty Roxane is primarily and exclusively a means of breaking down bridges. We are shown our loves, our jealousies, our dreams of murder, and we are shown them cold, separated from us, inaccessible and terrible, all the more alien in that they are our own, in that we believe we control them and yet they develop beyond our reach, with a pitiless rigor that we acknowledge even as we discover it. Such, too, are Brecht's characters: they astound us as if they were natives or savages, and our astonishment grows no less when we find that they are ourselves. These grotesque or dramatic conflicts, faults, cowardices, shabbinesses, complicities, they are all our own. If only there were a hero, at least; the spectator, whoever he may be, likes to identify with noble characters who bring about the reconciliation of opposites and the destruction of Evil by the Good to the benefit of themselves and everyone else. Even if he is roasted alive or cut in pieces, he strolls home if it is a fine night, whistling and reassured. But Brecht does not put heroes or martyrs on the stage—or if he does tell the story of a new Joan of Arc, she is a child of ten and we shall have no opportunity to identify with her; on the contrary, heroism, closed away in childhood as it is, only seems the more inaccessible. The fact is that there is no individual salvation; the whole of society must be changed; and the dramatist's function is still the "purgation" of which Aristotle spoke. He reveals to us what we are: at once victims and accomplices. That is why Brecht's plays move us. But our emotion is a very strange one: it is a perpetual disquiet—since we are the performance suspended in a contemplative calm—since we are the spectators. This disquiet does not disappear when the curtain falls; indeed, it increases and it blends with our daily disquiet, the disquiet we ignore and live with in bad faith, in evasion, and it is he who illuminates it. Aristotle's "purgation" is called by another name nowadays: realization. But was not the calm and austere disquiet aroused by *Bajazet* or *Phèdre* in the soul of some lady in the audience in the sixteenth century, when she suddenly discovered the inflexible law of the human passions, equally a realization —in another age and in another social and ideological context? This is why I think that Brecht's drama, this Shakespearean drama of revolutionary negation, is also—though its author never deliberately intended it—a remarkable attempt to renew the classical tradition in the twentieth century.

Theater and Cinema

Notes for a lecture
delivered at the sanatorium
at Bouffémont on May 6, 1958

One of the fairly large number of lectures on the theater
delivered by Sartre is extant in the form of his notes,
and is of special interest for its form and for the ideas
expounded in it (contrast between theater and cinema,
and a definition of Brecht's drama). The text given
here closely follows the manuscript, but does not show
all the breaks; some bridge sentences have been added
for smoother reading.

1. Theater is a social art which produces collective facts.
Its character derives, therefore, *as much* (or more) from the
section of society controlling it as from the author . . .

Whereas in a film we have actors and action ready-
canned, so to speak, theater is a true event, a jam session,
an event at once ordinary and unique.
2. But in most societies nowadays this event has a structure
peculiar to itself, not *everywhere* perhaps, but *today*. I
shall call this *presentation*.

The audience takes part in a *social event*; but for this
very reason it does not take part in *the story which is being
related*. This is *presented* to it. You get more participation

in a film than you do in a play. You have the film directly before you.

The actors are live, but:

(a) In film the actor is *closer*: close-ups, the naked face, Example: Robert Aldrich's *Kiss Me Deadly*.[1]

(b) The film actor dominates the audience; he is above it. The audience is flattened: low-angle shots. In the theater this "superman" aspect, the sensation of the actors' size and weight, does not exist.

(c) *Guided vision.* I am made to see what they want me to see; our perception of things is *directed*.

In the theater, by contrast, you look at whomever you want to. This is why it is *so hard* for actors to control their faces while someone else is speaking.

The theater, therefore, has *more freedom*.

(d) Consequence of absolute proximity in the film: a strict adjustment of person to part. Appearance merges with reality.

In the theater it hardly worries you for a moment to see Madeleine Renaud as a twenty-year-old widow. For what counts is not that she *is* a widow of twenty, but is *acting* here. Where *are* the beauty and youth? They *are not there*. What is there is the *significance of gesture*. It is not a presence, but a kind of absence, a kind of intangible ghost; the absent object is enveloped in the gesture; you believe it is still there.

A film is a landscape. The Californian desert in Stroheim's *Greed*[2] is a thing, a real and very tangible object, an environment. Later, there enter the characters who are to die there. In a sentimental film, landscape is a mood which creates its interpreters.

A film depicts men who are in the world and are conditioned by it. The opposite happens in theater: Beckett and mime. The decor in the film holds the man and destroys or saves him. In the Peking Opera the feel of a river, boats, danger, night is suggested by the action.

Theater, then, *presents* action by a man on the stage to men in the audience and, *through this action*, both the world he lives in and the performer of the action. This does not imply voluntarism; it means that *everything*, even failure, impotence, or death, must be signified as acts.

But what is an action?

1. An initial situation directly or indirectly endangers an individual or a social group.

2. The individual or the social group plan for a means to cause external changes so that the danger shall no longer exist.

3. The action is everything brought to bear on the external world and thereby on the individual or group themselves in order to achieve this end by specific means.

The aim is to show by the action of a human body upon itself the determining circumstances, the ends and means. In the theater action is gesture, but not in the film.

This is not a real action exerted on real objects, but a gesture of presentation presenting the action as its primary meaning and through it the world (in perspective) as its secondary meaning. Puppets. Everything, even youth and beauty, derives from gesture and is appearance.

(*a*) The play within the play.

People are acting a comedy to a supposed audience; here the comedy itself is appearance.

(*b*) Genet and *The Maids.*[3]

Even though Genet denounces illusion, he would like to maintain the character of pure presentation. Here you get the individual himself as appearance presented to real individuals who exist as performance.

Hegel and "pathos."

Action in the theater reveals the feelings. Hermione's hatred, jealousy, and desperate love appear in the act by which she sends Orestes to kill Pyrrhus.

Speech is the clearest gesture; that is, the clearest representation of the act is speech. But you must realize that in theater speech is necessarily the presentation of an act. Eloquence and theater.

Theater, therefore, is a presentation of a man to men by means of imaginary actions.

Result: a *distance*. Personal example: *The Victors* had too much violence in it. But this distance in presentation endows the universe presented with a different sort of coherence. It is out of your reach, you cannot act upon it or stop it. Thus it shows us that we have no power over it.

I can join with others, raise an uproar against a play and prevent the actors from coming onstage, but this is merely preventing something real, an economic and social fact. Just as I can smash a record.

But I cannot smash the symphony[4] or the dramatic object. Its originality is due to this.

Though there is no participation, there is at least a discovery, at times the anguished discovery, of someone beyond our reach rushing on his fate, and we can do nothing to stop him. In the film we *are* the hero, we are part of him, we rush on our own fate.

In the theater, we remain outside and the hero meets his fate before our eyes. But the impact on us and our feelings is all the stronger in that the hero is also ourselves, even if outside us.

Brecht's plays

Brecht's aim is to show modern man to us, his contemporaries, through gestures presenting action by him.

(*a*) Distancing (or alienation effect). Exploiting a contradiction: the man presented is myself, but without power over myself. That is, making us discover ourselves as *others*, as if other people were looking at us; in other words, achieving an objectivity which I cannot get from my reflection.

In film nowadays, participation excludes observation and explanation. In theater, just the reverse.

(b) Choice of subject: epic theater.

Replacing the conflicts of the classical drama by contradictions.

This person, then, presented to us is ourself as social man. But he is also presented to us removed from his context. This enables me to understand my contradictions, that is to say, those of my time, through a face which is alien to me and does not affect me.

As Brecht sees it, our inner contradictions and the contradictions between us and other persons are never accidental; fundamentally, they express the contradictions of society.

The action of the individual characters, therefore, must present our world to us as rent by social contradictions. Or, in short, as individuals and individual actions, they must *demonstrate* the major social currents and their significance. Hence theater is epic. It is never the enterprise of a single individual. It is the enterprise of society through him.

Example: the maidservant in *The Caucasian Chalk Circle* is given not speech but gestures to present love. Maternal love is a permanent explanation, but it has to be found, not felt.

The Author, the Play, and the Audience

Conversation published in *L'Express*, September 17, 1959, headlined "Two Hours with Sartre," at the time of the production of *The Condemned of Altona*. Sartre's interviewers were Françoise Giroud, Robert Kanters, François Erval, and Claude Lanzmann.

Why did you write The Condemned of Altona? *I don't mean this particular play, but why, if you had something to say, did you choose the theater as the medium in which to say it?*

In the first place because I have a problem about finishing my novel.[1] The fourth volume was to be about the Resistance. The choice was easy enough at the time—though it needed a good deal of perseverance and hard work to stick to it. One was either for or against the Germans. It was black or white. Nowadays—ever since 1945—things have become complicated. You need less courage to choose, perhaps, but the choices are far harder. I cannot express the ambiguities of our time in this novel, since it would be about the situation in 1943. And yet this unfinished work bothers me; I find it hard to start another one before I finish it.

Do you feel that you reach a wider public through the theater than through the novel?

If a play is a success, the author reaches a wider public, for the time being at least. Afterwards, I don't know . . . At any rate, a play that runs for a hundred nights in a large theater and is a hit has reached an audience of one hundred thousand. A hundred thousand readers is quite exceptional.

You have already had a circulation of far more than one hundred thousand in pocket books. And each book has more than one reader.

Of course. You can read a play as well as see it. The pocketbook edition you mention has already published several of my plays. There are also road companies and revivals.

But you have to remember that it's not quite the same thing. A book's success is not necessarily measured by the number of copies it sells. I know of excellent books whose circulation has never exceeded three or four thousand, yet they have influenced a whole generation, indirectly at any rate. Kafka is not a best-seller in France, but the whole of my generation of intellectuals would not be what they are without him. A play is an expensive business and has to show an immediate profit, and it must therefore either be an immediate hit or else disappear for good. That means that the author's relation to his public is different. A book gains its public gradually. A work for the theater has necessarily to be "theatrical," because the author knows that he will be applauded or hissed at once. It's like an exam you can only take once and never again. More and more a play is coming to be something like assault on the public; if it fails, it recoils on its author. In the United States and—for some time now —in France, if the criticisms are bad and the box office slack, a play is taken off after a few performances. A book can speak in a murmur; drama and comedy have to shout. This may be what attracts me about the theater: the assault and the heightened tone and the risk of losing everything in a single night. It forces me to speak *in another way*; it makes a change.

What do you think your audience expects from your drama?

Well, I am wondering about that. The theater is so much of a *public interest, the interest of the public,* that a play is out of the author's hands once the public enters the theater. My plays, at all events—whatever their success or failure—have almost all passed out of my hands. They become *objects.* Afterwards one says, "I didn't mean that," like William II during the 1914 war. But when you've done it, there it is.

That's obviously true of films, at any rate if films ever do have a meaning of their own. The public distorts their meaning or discovers another meaning. But with plays, can't the play-wright take a hand, change the staging, pull it together in places, give it a different direction?

No. What you suddenly find when you come to watch a play is that the devil takes a hand. It would be too facile to put it down to the director or the actors. A play has to be able to be revived, to be produced abroad, so it must be able to stand being acted by actors who do not quite get inside the characters' skin. Each part and the play as a whole should have a fairly definite margin for variations. What counts is something else. First, the unexpected interrelations which arise within the acts and scenes between a thousand things—gestures, attitudes, the characters' behavior, the time and place of the action, the scenery, the lighting, and so on. You can do something about all these, but nothing that is very effective; an *object* is created, with its objective characteristics, and they get away from you.

In *The Devil and the Good Lord* I had most of the scenes taking place in the evening or at night. One day I noticed, as I was watching one of the final rehearsals, that the sequence of these nocturnal scenes made it a night play. Now, that is exactly the sort of thing that an audience discovers—and likes or dislikes—before the author does, even if it is not wholly conscious of its discovery.

I also remember a scene in *The Victors*. Troopers of the *milices* were torturing people of the Resistance in 1944. What I was trying to do was not to show the physical reality of torture but the relations between these two groups and the conflicts between them. And we—Vitold, the actor and director, the other actors, and myself—got on very well. The rehearsals had been good-tempered. Vitold never had time for dinner and always took advantage of the moment when he was led offstage to grab a sandwich and bolt it. He had to shriek with pain in the wings, and he always had his mouth full when he shrieked. But that never prevented us from "believing" in the scene. And then, at the dress rehearsal, some of the audience found that moment unbearable. I discovered *through them,* and I confess I was astounded, the true value of classical discretion—you must not show *everything.* You know what some painters say nowadays, that a picture is *primarily* an object. Well, a play *in performance* is primarily an object. An object with an organization entirely of its own. But it's the audience that works with the author to bring about the transformation.

Do you always agree with the transformation?

No. But what can I do about it? An audience is primarily an assembly. That is to say, each member of an audience asks himself what he thinks of the play and at the same time what his neighbor is thinking. When I go to the theater and listen to a play in which some lines perhaps shock people, who nevertheless do not share my views, and I feel that as I sit there I do not have my full freedom of judgment, I am embarrassed *for them.* They themselves would be less shocked if they were not thinking of other members of the audience who are of the same party or the same social circle or the same faith as they are. From this variable reaction arises an alien reality for which no one is wholly responsible. Here the press comes in. It *does not*, as people believe, *create* this line of thought, but interprets and crystallizes it. Playwrights tend to blame it for turning some of the public away from their plays. But this is a misconception. The drama critic of a daily or weekly paper is in fact the skilled representative of a fraction of this public. He is only listened to if his judgment is on the whole confirmed by his readers' ideas. In other words, it is as if he *divined* the opinion of the people who will read him, precisely because he himself is one of them.

When *Dirty Hands* was produced, François Périer and André Luguet were greatly—and very rightly—applauded. There was some hesitation about the play itself, whether it was or was not anticommunist. The critics both of the left and of the bourgeois press waited. And when the former at last decided it was directed against their party—which I had not intended in the least—the latter acclaimed it as a weapon of war and so proved them right. After that, the play took on an objective meaning which I have never been able to change.

But haven't you had an opportunity since then to tell people what you really had intended?

I did, but I was wasting my breath. Intentions don't count in the theater. What counts is what *comes out*. The audience writes the play quite as much as the author does. And, of course, there is the element that affects an audience, the particular time, its needs, the conflicts it itself is aware of. For instance, people imagined that *Coriolanus* was an antidemocratic play, and the fascists went to applaud it at the Théâtre-Français around 1934. Whereas recent performances of it at the Piccolo Teatro in Milan have brought out just the opposite—the play's critical attitude toward and examination of dictatorship as a mystification of the masses. Though, of course, it is obviously not democracy but legitimate and hereditary monarchy that Shakespeare was really contrasting with the dictator.

Have these metamorphoses always happened?

More or less, I suppose. But at the great moments in the history of the theater there was a real homogeneity of author and audience. For the audience was more or less consciously experiencing in its own life the contradictions that the author was putting on the stage. There can be no doubt that *Antigone* represents the conflict between the great aristocratic families in the course of their breakup and the *city* which is establishing itself by limiting their power, as, indeed, Hegel observed. There can be no doubt that the Athenians felt deeply *concerned* by the conflict between Antigone and Creon. The theater, therefore, had a *united* public. Just as in seventeenth century England, when the language was being continually enriched and the absolute monarchy was establishing itself, it was the *English nation* that was becoming aware of itself through the Elizabethan drama.

Nowadays, the audience is drawn from too many different social groups and sometimes has too many conflicting interests for anyone to be able to foretell how such a diversified public is likely to react. In any case, the theater belongs, by and large, to the bourgeoisie. It's the bourgeois who support and fill the theaters by acquiescing in the constant rise in box-office prices. There are so many inner contradictions within the middle classes, and even within the ruling class, that part of the audience would probably be shocked if the drama showed an image of our society that pleased other parts of it. The result of this compromise is that the theater seldom shows the changes in man and the world, but rather the image of man as eternally unchanging in a universe that never changes.

A striking example is the way the audience laughed at

scores of points in *La Petite Hutte*.[2] Now, what is *La Petite Hutte* about? Supposing we change all the circumstances of the bourgeois triangle—that is, wife, husband, and lover. We put them on a desert island; and what happens? The triangle remains, one way or another. Nothing has changed. Nothing changes. And the audience is delighted. There is another play about a lot of people shipwrecked on a desert island, a British play, *The Admirable Crichton*.[3] Crichton, the servant, becomes the master of the rest of them and wins their respect because he is "the better man." Does that mean that the world can change? No. When a ship appears over the horizon, Crichton chooses to go back home in it and revert to his lowly status. The relations between the characters revert to what they were. The sole result of this Robinson Crusoe episode is that the masters have become better people because of their man's virtues. There'll always be an England. That was the point of the play. But we all know that the world changes, that it changes man and man changes the world. And if that is not what the basic subject of any play should be, the drama no longer has a subject.

Isn't that exactly what Bertolt Brecht deals with in all his plays?

Exactly. It is often claimed that he means to give a Marxist interpretation of the world in its entirety. That isn't quite true. Of course, he is a Marxist, profoundly so. But as a dramatist, personal dramas are nevertheless what he is interested in. What he intends to do is simply to show that there is no personal drama which is not wholly conditioned by the historical situation and at the same time no personal drama which does not react on the social situation and condition it. That is why his characters are always ambiguous. He brings out the contradictions in them, which are the contradictions of their time, and he wants simultaneously to show how they make their own fate.

I am thinking of Brecht's Galileo. In Brecht's play he is

shown as wholly conditioned by the moment at which he is living, a moment when emerging science is at odds with the traditions, beliefs, and interests of the Church and the aristocracy. And the very man who embodies science is the first to play it false. Why? Because his physical courage fails, but above all because he has not understood that his lot was not cast with the great ones of this world, but with the part of society which conditions science because it has need of it in order to develop. At that time it was the bourgeoisie. Once he has chosen the camp of the prelates and princes, Galileo refuses the support of the bourgeoisie. So Galileo is responsible for his fate. He makes it. But at the same time his error is only explicable at a time when the man of science was in some sort the servant of the lords and prelates and when he consequently did not know who he himself was, even while he was creating what would transform his situation.

How did Brecht manage to prevent his work from being changed by his public?

First of all because, despite all its problems, all its deeper contradictions, all its inner tensions, the public in East Germany is relatively unified. This society in the course of construction—whatever one may think of it—furnishes an audience for the theater which has anxieties and hopes in common and does not come, as in France, from all sorts of different levels. This is demonstrated by the fact that we have only come to understand the art and meaning of Brecht's plays because he first had his successes *elsewhere.*

But Brecht's plays were written before this unified society came into existence.

Yes, but his real successes came after it did.

Are you sure? Brecht was a success in Germany long before Hitler, under the Weimar Republic. And later, in New York, during the Nazi period. He is having a great success at the present moment in Western Germany, Switzerland, and London. So he transcends that unified public of his.

Quite true. But look at the difference between the Brecht of today and the Brecht of the time when *The Threepenny Opera* was being performed in Paris. Nowadays we know what Brecht is. But when we saw *The Threepenny Opera* with Simone de Beauvoir before the war, we only saw what is usually called a social satire.[4] It was very amusing. It was delightful. But Brecht's real intention was entirely lost on us. More than twenty years ago after I'd seen the play —and here's a prime example of a play being changed by its audience—I thought it was purely anarchist, for the bourgeois are all corrupt, the chief of police is a crook; but on the other hand, the play shows us the masses as beggars and their leaders as thieves who deceive them. I entirely missed the positive aspect of this two-edged criticism, as indeed the whole audience did at the time.

All the same, Pabst's film of it was viewed in France as "leftist"; that was the general view of The Threepenny Opera.

Because the bankers and the police were the butts. But a right-wing author, too, can satirize bankers. It all depends on how it's done. Such misconceptions disappeared once Brecht could deal directly with his audience. He decided to let the audience join in the game, and since the audience collaborates with the author in any event, he gave a direction to this collaboration. A play is an animated image of man and of the world as an image presented to him. The question is the relation between audience and image. I believe that what Brecht was trying to destroy was the participation which is the ordinary bourgeois drama's—not the classical drama's—relationship with the audience. *Participating* in the performance means, for instance, more or less identifying with the image of the hero as he faces death, or with the image of the hero in love. It means fearing that the lover will be betrayed or that the hero will end up by being killed.

Participation is the experience of an almost carnal relationship with an image, not merely a knowledge of it. Just as you cannot really know someone you fall in love with, someone for whom you experience a violent passion.

If you "participate"—and this is what troubled Brecht —you change what you participate in.

It has even been claimed, and quite truly, that a bourgeois can in fact participate in a play with a true hero, a revolutionary who transcends the contradictions within himself and overcomes them through his death. Why is this? Because it will not disturb the bourgeois. Because a bourgeois can, after all, identify with such a hero. Just as people can say, "Personally, I'm in favor of Algérie française, but I have every respect for the FLN militant who faces death heroically," so a spectator may say, when a leftist resolves the contradictions within himself and dies heroically for a certain sort of society, "I'm against the sort of society he wants, but I can't help seeing him as the image of a man who has succeeded in reconciling conflicting parts of his nature. I too have these conflicts—though of a different sort—and this story shows me that they can always be overcome." He will go away satisfied. He will have understood that in any society and in any situation personal contradictions can be resolved, and consequently, while he rejects the *substance* of the play, he will be attracted by the formal design of heroism. In this sense, the positive hero of Soviet plays does not *disturb* the bourgeois spectator.

Brecht believed that overcoming a difficult and contradictory situation was never a purely personal matter, but that only an entire society within the current of history could transform itself. He wished the spectator to leave the theater feeling disturbed, that is, grasping the causes of the contradiction, but quite unable to overcome it by indulging in a flood of emotion.

People ought to be just as disturbed when they leave Tartuffe.

As I see it, the classics have a very definite link with Brecht; you find both withdrawal and distancing in them. I don't believe that people really are very much interested in Orgon's ultimate fate, or Elmire's. Tartuffe is certainly repugnant, but he is not a horror. He does not really disturb you much. You laugh, but in moderation. It's mainly in the distancing that the power of the play lies.

What Brecht wanted and what our classical dramatists tried for was to cause what Plato called "the source of all philosophy"—surprise, making the familiar unfamiliar. Incidentally, Voltaire used this method in his tales. All you have to do is to present characters from another world. Then you can laugh at them, because you tell yourself as you leave the theater, "Why, that world is my world!" The ideal in Brecht's drama would be for the audience to be like a team of ethnographers suddenly coming across a savage tribe and, after they had approached them, finding that they were in fact exactly like themselves. It is at such moments that an audience comes to collaborate with an author: when it recognizes itself, but in a strange guise as if it were someone else; *it brings itself into being* as an *object* before its own eyes, and it *sees* itself, though without playing itself as a role, and thus comes to understand itself.

You were saying a moment ago that the mainspring of a play should be Plato's surprise. Do you think that is all that's needed? Are there no other links between spectator and stage? Wouldn't that be rather a frigid performance?

No doubt. But that was not what Brecht wanted. All he wanted was that the spectator's emotions should not be blinkered. After all, his wife, Helene Weigel, who was also one of his best interpreters, reduced audiences to tears in *Mother Courage.*

To "show" and simultaneously to "move" would be ideal. I don't think Brecht would have considered that contradiction an insuperable absurdity.

It all depends on the perspective you take when you want to tell a story. Either you take the eye of eternity—things are so, they will always be so, woman will always be the Eternal Feminine, and so on. If so, you fall back on the drama of "human nature," which I call bourgeois. Or you look at it as a sign of the beginning of a movement or the continuation of a liquidation. That is to say, from the historical point of view, or better, the point of view of the future. In *The Doll's House*,[5] which dealt with the emancipation of women at a time when it was barely thinkable, Ibsen chose the perspective of the future; it was from the point of view of the future that he saw the collapse of the domineering and vacuous husband and Nora's liberation.

An imminent, a very near future. Do you see this incorporation of a near future in your own plays?

I haven't given it much thought so far. I made some attempt at it in *The Condemned of Altona*. The whole play is constructed from the point of view of a future which is at once true and false. The condemned man's madness consists in avoiding a sense of guilt as he considers himself the witness of a vanishing century and appeals to a higher court. Naturally, everything he says is stupid, he is not narrating what the century really is; but I want the audience somehow to feel as if it were up before that court. Or, quite simply, up before the centuries to come.

Our century will be judged as we judge the nineteenth or eighteenth century. It will take the place in history which in some sense it will make for itself, and it will call for a morally objective judgment of the men of this century. I

want the audience to feel, by means of my character's confused ramblings, that it stands before that court.

Castles in Spain, of course. But if it could be done,
it would give the audience an impression that it is shifting
into the past. I want to give the feeling of our age as this
century goes on. Just as people say at the end of every year:
1959 was "not so good," let's hope 1960 will be better.

I want the audience to see our century from outside,
as something alien, as a witness. And at the same time to
participate in it, since it is in fact making this century. There
is one feature peculiar to our age: the fact that we know we
shall be judged.

Epic Theater
and Dramatic Theater

This lecture by Sartre was delivered on March 29, 1960, in the main hall of the Sorbonne under the auspices of the Paris Students Drama Association (ATEP), headed at that time by Ariane Mnouchkine. The lecture was recorded by Sylvère Lotringer, now teaching at Columbia University, who most kindly let us have the original tapes. It is published in full here for the first time in English.

We have taken care to keep the conversational and impromptu tone of the lecture, but have removed a few repetitive passages which added nothing of interest. The tape was transcribed by Maya Rybalka.

Some fragments of the lecture were published in *World Premières/Premières mondiales* (11th year, number 9, June 1960), and were translated into English by Rima Rell Dreck, under the title "Beyond Bourgeois Theatre," in *The Tulane Drama Review* (vol. 5, no. 3, March 1961). For further information see *The Writings of Jean-Paul Sartre*, volume 1, note 60/349.

You are aware, of course, that the distinction I am drawing between epic theater and dramatic theater is not my own, but was drawn by Bertolt Brecht himself in the course of arguing that his theater was epic theater and dramatic theater was bourgeois theater. He was right on both counts, but the problem I want to deal with here is whether we can conceive of a dramatic theater that is very close to epic theater and is not bourgeois theater.

You know what Brecht's epic theater is, you know what he is chiefly trying to do—to demonstrate, explain, and compel the spectator to judge rather than participate. He wants to show the individual act together with what he calls the "social gestus" which determines the act, to show the contradictions inherent in any behavior together with the social system that gives rise to the contradictions, and all this within a representation of the act . . . [*About ten seconds inaudible*]

Alain used to say that a teacher should not engage the emotions of his pupils because they are good at listening carefully but bad at grasping things. Dramatic theater, on the contrary—let's take the theater we all know which tells the story of an individual, though hinting that there are ulterior implications. But before I go any further into this contrast, I must warn you that everything is in a muddle nowadays because we are passing through a period of bourgeois theater. The bourgeoisie has now been in control of the theater for about a hundred and fifty years. It controls it in the first place through the price of land, which rose so high in the nineteenth century that the workers, as you know, had to leave the inner city, and offices and bourgeois buildings are there now and all, or nearly all, the theaters too are in the center of town. The bourgeoisie also controls the theater through the price of seats, which has constantly to be raised if the theater is to show a profit. In France, it controls it through the traditional centralization, with the result that plays never reach the smaller towns, where they might discover contacts with different sorts of audiences, or else reach them through road companies when the plays are long out of date. And lastly, it controls it through the critics. To contrast the drama critic with the public is quite wrong. A paper's critic is a reflection of *its* public; if he talks nonsense, it's because the public which reads the paper will also be doing so; and there is no sense in contrasting one with the other. Certified wine tasters exist for the purpose of assuring you that the wine in the barrel is up to standard. Well, Monsieur Jean-Jacques Gautier acts as a taster for the readers of *Le Figaro*, and it's quite plain that Monsieur Gautier is wholly identified with the reader of *Le Figaro* and the reader of *Le Figaro* with Monsieur Gautier. Why? Because the reader of *Le Figaro* believes that Gautier has never deceived him, which means that he espouses his opinions on every subject whatsoever. [*Applause*] So, you see, it's a complete control, all the more so because there's only one thing that this bourgeoisie need do to sink a play—just not go to it. It's clear enough, therefore, that the bourgeois dictatorship over the theater has created a bourgeois theater. Is this merely dangerous, does it only mean an excessive limitation on its subject-matter, or has this dictatorship broken down the whole structure of what theater ought to be? That's what we are going to try to discover.

To begin with, if we are going to get out of the total confusion we are in about the theater these days, it would be best to take a different approach, to find some sort of point of reference so that we can grasp what a theatrical ceremony is. I'm not, of course, going back to Thespis's cart,[1] but I'm going to tell you about an experience I recently had at the National Theater in Havana.[2] They were staging some black religious dances with accompanying songs and tales. What was very special about it was this: that African religion has been preserved almost intact in Cuba because Cuba was under the Spanish Church. In

Saint-Domingue the French Church said, We'll leave them their religion provided they subscribe to ours; and toleration of this sort led to voodoo. In Cuba black people who were not Christians were persecuted; they went underground in religious secret societies, and their religion remained completely pure. The most curious thing is that the white people in the very poor districts have been attracted by the religion of the blacks and form a single religious body with them, and consequently practice their religious rites. And even some of the wealthy, too, some rich whites. These ceremonies—they are genuine religious rituals—have always been forbidden; they were never given any publicity and so there was no reason to put them on the stage. You have to think of them, too, as ceremonies celebrated by all the blacks in the poor districts; everyone knew the songs and dances which were being staged. So one very curious point arose right at the start: many of the black people who went to the performance were very much surprised when they were asked to pay for their seats. They said, "But it's a religious ceremony; you don't pay for admission to religious ceremonies."

So you see, the starting point was a sort of concept they had of religion; they had come because they were religious, and they wanted to take their part in this religion. But in the second place, it was in a theater, so that basically there was a first phase of distancing within the religious participation. For the first time, black people and white—myself among them—were sitting on chairs and watching this religion being danced in front of them, whereas ordinarily those blacks sitting there danced with them. So something very contradictory happened. To begin with, there was laughter and applause in the hall—a universal feature of the performances—and secondly, there was also a dance which, little by little, took hold of some of the black spectators and finally had them standing up where they had sat and dancing in time with the dancers facing them, so that, so to speak, they were doing the same as the blacks facing them. Why? Well, the remarks made by some other blacks sitting quite near me gave me a clue. They, these blacks, were saying rather contemptuously, "But we dance just as well as they do, I don't know why they chose them rather than us." And that's what all of them, more or less, must have been thinking, because the dance was something all of them shared. What had abruptly happened was a break. But because there was participation and they were dancing, and because it also was a performance and it was going on, they sat down again; and there was a strange sort of disjunction whereby they came to discover their image, so to speak, on the stage. Basically, what they were seeing was themselves dancing as they always danced, but at the same time themselves without the accustomed relation of real participation, the relation that sets them dancing when there is someone dancing their religious ritual beside them and a communion becomes established by the rhythm without their even, as it were, seeing themselves.

And this introduced a new form of communication, a communication, if I may put it so, through the less immediate senses—not touch nor even smell, but seeing and hearing —and this was something entirely new. This transformation affected even the actors, because they were not in the least like actors when they entered the theater. In fact, I went to see them behind the scenes, and they were people of all ages, chosen mainly because they were specially good dancers, though they were people who worked at all sorts of trades in the daytime; that is, they were people who were not actors by profession and indeed turned out to be rather mediocre as actors, but they were also people obliged to comply with a certain number of rules. For instance, the dances lasted for a specific time and no longer, and they had to come back and take a bow at the end of the dance. They began each dance in a surly mood, sullen because it was not coming right, and then, little by little, it began to

come, and usually, the audience facing them started dancing and thus made them, too, eager to dance. And it went
on and it went on, and toward the end, after dances that
often carried them away far further than they had meant,
they still managed to come back and take a bow, just like
actors. But immediately afterwards, they went into trances
of their own behind the scenes; and that's why someone said
to me at one moment, "Don't worry if the curtain doesn't
rise; two of the actresses are in a trance." So there was this
strange blend, this very profound blending, which made the
actor suddenly feel just as much separated from the audience by this break as the audience felt separated from the
actor—whereas normally he danced among them. The actor
sensed in the audience, so to speak, his reality as a dancer,
because he was doing something he did not understand, and
the audience sensed in the actors its own reality as dancer in
image. Thus there was a curious relation, a blending of total
participation with representation and distancing.

This brings us on naturally—and if I had not mentioned it, it would have occurred to you anyway—to the
psychodrama, in which there is a kind of spontaneity which
gathers force, gathers strength and expresses each of the two
actors, one of them the patient or subject lending himself to
the drama, the other the psychiatrist or auxiliary playing
with him, and in which there are curious relations of trans-
ference and countertransference; for in psychodrama you
get the blending of image and participation. For instance,
when you play a role which you perform with a fellow player
opposite a psychiatrist or psychologist who is assuming the
part of fellow player, you find yourself in a strange situation. This situation is not quite real, because you in fact
know very well that from the start you will never wholly lose
the notion that the person opposite you is playing a role,
that it's an imaged fellow player you have opposite you,
and on the other hand, you cannot help in a whole lot of
cases showing your true relations with that person because

you are in the grasp of something or other. This happens even with professional actors. Lebovici[3] tells us—he has written an article about it—that he was consulted by a mother who complained bitterly about her son, saying he was really unbearable; she herself seemed externally very gentle and very reasonable. Lebovici suggested to her that they should play out her relationship with her son as a psychodrama. She laughed and said, "'Listen, I'm an actress, so, you see, if I had to lie to you, if I had to tell you that I am really kind whereas really I'm nothing of the sort, I could act it very well." So he said, "Well, let's try all the same." And what happened, as you no doubt expected, was that the actress's surface technique simply disappeared owing to the very spontaneity of this double play, the completely ambiguous game which is representation.

On the other hand, if we now go back to the blacks, and if we remember that there were also white spectators who did not share their outlook, then you had another aspect of the problem, namely, that these blacks and their religion appeared as objects. Let us be quite clear, though, that I don't mean objects in any derogatory sense; I simply mean that we didn't have the religious link which supplied the twofold disjunction—distance and presence. Then what did we have? Well, we were seeing poeple who really and truly were performing dances that were part of their religion. We were less aware of the aspect of performance than of the objective aspect. As a matter of fact, other black people of much the same sort consented at various times to perform the same ceremonies among the Havana students for some ethnographers. So we ourselves were rather off-balance then, half being ourselves understood as object, but in a different sense, and half being understood as representation. So that in the end, inasmuch as this religion presented itself to us as an object in its entirety and at a much greater depth, we were able to regard it as *the* religion, no matter what creed we ourselves held. If we took the thing simply objectively, it was a score of Havana blacks dancing their religious dances for the first time. If, on the other hand, we took it as image, the thing had a still further dimension; for this religion we were seeing was an image at that moment, and we no longer thought that they were real believers who were performing; but now it in fact contested every particular form of religion, because it was all religions. There was this passage toward myth and at the same time a passage in another direction, toward object; and we were perpetually perplexed. So that, generally speaking, there is something of a dual relation in the theater between people and the representation of themselves; and sometimes, indeed, a dramatist may want to use this dual relation as an element in a play.

I am thinking of a play which is currently running in New York in an attic off Broadway.[4] I must admit that I am rather vague about it, because I only know what a friend has reported, but that's not important because the gist of it is true enough. It was a complete failure at first, but now all America is thronging to it. You go in and you see some characters lying about the stage, all huddled up, not saying a word. Nothing happens for a fairly long time, until at last someone comes in and tells them to get up, and they say, "No, not now, no, not now," and fall back. Finally, the author himself enters and says, "Listen, these are junkies; we asked them to act a play about drugs to get some money, because they can't live without their drugs, and now they won't do it." And the whole thing goes on and on; these people are told, "Listen, try and make an effort," and they say, "'Give us a fix, we must have a fix before we start." They wait and wait for the drugs, other people enter, and so on. The interest of the play seems to be, from what I've heard, that it is intended to show, instead of the romantic addicts you see in American films, that drug addiction really means sheer brute stupor. But its interest for our purposes is something else: it is the kind of publicity stunt to make people believe that these are real addicts. In point of fact, the newspapers say so, and during the intermissions people go around the audience taking up a collection for the poor junkies to buy their drugs afterwards. [*Laughter*] People actually pay up, and many of the audience go away none too sure whether they are addicts who are earning an honest penny or whether they aren't. Of course they are not addicts, because the police would never allow money to be collected for them like that.

But apart from that, what is interesting for our purposes is that the success of the play is due to the spectators' perplexity. Is it image, is it object? I mean this: if they are really addicts, then it is object, that is to say, the spectator is there watching three poor showmen who, with the best intentions but no success, have collected some addicts and made a show of them so that they'll get a little money. It's just as if you went to visit an asylum and saw some drug addicts or mental defectives, for instance. If so, you can regard them as human objects and you are a human object to them. Or else they are not drug addicts, but actors; if so, it's something else again and, as you'll see at once, it's the same as with the religion I was talking about just now. If they are addicts and if you are not an addict yourself, you probably have nothing in common with them; their stupor, their degradation will disgust you because you will say, "Personally I have nothing to do with those people." If they are images, if they are playing the role of drug addicts, then that takes on a universal aspect in a certain way, in a way which will have to be demonstrated; it becomes myth. After all, we have plenty of ways to boost a whole lot of things, such as amorous obsession, highly romantic as it is, and what does it amount to in the end? Brute stupor. [*Laughter*] We can see very well how a number of cases of this sort may come to be expressed in impatience, nerves, and so on, which will resemble the tics of an addict. We

can therefore make the transition on a certain level, but only
provided that it is presented to us as image. And, as you
see, here you have both aspects at once.

But these two examples, both of which lie a little outside quite ordinary sorts of theater, whether epic or dramatic, lead to a question we may ask ourselves at once: Why
do men live in the midst of their images? Because, after all,
we might very well not. You know that Baudelaire spoke
of "the tyranny of the human face."[5] It is sometimes so
tiring to yield to this tyranny all day long that why on earth
should one also have to look at portraits, for instance, in
one's bedroom, why would one go to see representations of
oneself on the stage, why does one walk about amid statues,
which also represent us, why does one go to the cinema and
still go on seeing oneself? People harbor a sort of tedious
obsession with themselves, all of you and I myself too, which
is rather surprising. If you think it over, basically it's not
so hard to account for. I believe people live amidst their
images because they do not manage to be real objects to
themselves. People are objects to others, but people or
groups of people are not completely objects to themselves.
Take an individual example: you can take it either in the
form of the apprenticeship to the looking glass and to the
image in the looking glass which is so important in early in-
fancy, or of the mistake made by an animal when it looks
at itself in a glass, or of the misperception of an adult who
suddenly sees someone in a glass in a dark room and doesn't
realize that it's himself. One approaches oneself as one
approaches an object, because one approaches oneself as
one approaches someone else. There you have objectivity.
Almost as soon as you recognize yourself, you are no longer
an object. For one does not see one's own face as one sees
others. One sees one's own face with a privileged element
or factor. Why? Because one takes a deep interest in the
person who is there and one cannot understand him simply
by looking at him, in an absolutely cold and formal connec-

tion; one understands him by a form of participation, so to speak. One cannot really see what one is, any more, you know, than one can hear oneself talk. You know the experiment in which you record someone's voice, and then if you ask him to choose among a dozen voices, he will very seldom pick out his own; the percentage of error shows that a constant factor is involved.

The way in which we hear ourselves speak is not exactly the same as the way in which we speak. Similarly, one does not see oneself, for a whole host of reasons. One cannot judge oneself; and consequently what there is in the glass is still me, but out of my reach, out of my experience, out of reality as far as I am concerned; it's something I can't lay hold of; it is not an object, but an image. And it is an image not because it's a reflection, for a reflection is an object; from the strictly physical point of view, the term "image" simply means a reality of the physical world, merely what is produced by certain light rays. It's an image because there's nothing we can do to it, simply because it is an image, or else we can only slash at it blindly. In other words, the reflection passes into the state of object when it is not recognized and of image when it is. Not because it is a reflection, but simply because it is out of reach. So, at that moment, given that I am incapable, that you are incapable, of making a set of objective judgments about any face provided it is your own, and if we assume that this judgment must nevertheless be made, one will apply to others. One will ask, for instance, of a sketch, a sketch drawn of someone else—I don't know whether you have read a book by Aldous Huxley called *Crome Yellow*, published some years back.[6] The hero is disagreeably surprised when he happens to turn over a blotter at some friends' house and finds a sketch of himself, his portrait by one of his friends; it's not even a caricature, just an unpleasant surprise. Here we have the sudden shock of objectivity. Only, at that moment, the immediate question is, Who drew it? What was his idea of what a man should be? Do I perhaps dislike what he likes? Perhaps he wanted to see me in some other way? Perhaps he has gone too far in one direction because he projected himself into it? In short, the drawing is no longer an object, precisely because of the impenetrability of things inherent in a drawing (that is to say, it's there and you cannot affect it except by tearing the paper); and this impenetrability finally blends into a sort of mystery of the person who drew it, an absence, and it becomes merely an empty object, a gap. In other words, you have made the transition to a portrait-image, because you can't see yourself as an object in a glass; and this portrait is itself an image, because there's nothing you can do to it. And precisely because people are perpetually objects to each other, because each of us perpetually feels objectified by someone, that is to say in the course of becoming object, as, for instance, I feel at the moment that there are a vast number of times all at the same time [*laughter*], well, precisely because one feels that one is slipping, that one is losing oneself in objectivity, one tries to recover this objectivity, and when one does recover it, one finds an image. An image is something not real which still belongs to you, which still belongs to me, but is distinct from me—for instance, a portrait. A portrait of me is part of *my* possessions, just as a portrait of you is part of *yours*; it belongs to some sort of an external subjectivity; yet seen from another angle, it's nothing, it's unreal.

And what I am saying about individuals naturally applies to any social group. Men cannot see themselves from outside, and the real reason is that in order really to understand a man as an object, it would be necessary—simultaneously and contradictorily—to understand and not to understand his ends, his purposes. Because obviously you cannot consider that you have a truly objectified man before you, someone about whom you can say that it is truly someone you know, unless you know him through understanding what he is looking for, what he wants, that is to say through his future, through the most personal efforts he can make to gain his ends. Though if that is the way you know him—through understanding, that is—it means that you have the same ends as he does; that is, however much you may disapprove of his behavior in other respects, the fact remains that you will not understand him unless you in some way share in his purposes. And if you have the same ends as he has, then you are in a completely enclosed world—or rather, if you prefer, not so much enclosed as bounded, bounded by itself—from which you will never be able to get out, given the fact that you will always come to the moment at which the same ends as yours will be shared by the person you are on the way to understanding and judging. If, however, you cease to understand his ends, and if he then becomes a being who no longer has any ends but is merely understandable, or at any rate explicable by logical causation, then you have lost the man and you have an insect. So that between this comprehension of a man, in consequence of which a man is never, after all, totally an object but only a quasi-object to other men, and this refusal to understand, to understand a war criminal, for example, which makes us regard him as an insect, there is no room for men to know each other completely as objects. One might be total object either for ants or for angels, but one cannot as a man be an object to men.

An engineer may consider a doctor as an object insofar as he is a doctor, but not insofar as he is a man; and precisely when he tries to think about him as a man, he shifts to the image. A typical example of these imaginary judgments is when people tell you—and God knows they do tell you—"Good God, how evil men are, man is evil, all men are evil," and so on and so forth. How do you mean? You're either inside or outside. If you are inside, and most of the time you don't think of getting there, your judgment is not to be trusted. If you are outside, you're

not a man, so what are you? It's absolutely impossible, therefore—unless you fall into the unreal—to phrase things
like this, which . . . well, you call them images as a matter
of politeness, but really they are idiocies. [*Laughter*] So
you do see—and this is what I wanted to show you—that
the function of art which represents man (for there are of
course arts which do not represent him) arises from a failure; there would be no art of this sort if men were real objects to each other. Arts exist because you never wholly
manage to see a man face to face; so you have images; and
when you have images, you have special relations to them,
relations of participation, like the blacks I was telling you
about. You participate in the unreal, which is performed
before you in a certain form, by a certain fiction.

Of course, there are a lot of different images of man,
and certainly there are films and photographs representing
him. What, then, does the theater give, for it's not enough
to say that it gives an image of man. To my mind the answer
is simple enough, for basically theater is gesture. And gesture is, as you know, carried as far as pantomime. And what
is gesture? It can't be exactly defined as something which is
not an act, for acts are often gestures too. But let's say it
is an act which has no purpose in itself, an action, a movement intended to show something else. "Make a gesture,"
one says to people when two of them are quarreling. What
does "make a gesture" really mean? It doesn't at all mean
"be reconciled"; it means "make a sign which will enable
the other fellow to come and apologize to you . . . He's
in the wrong, but after all, you can at least make a gesture." Thus, the gesture is not the act of reconciliation, it is
just a movement. And looking at it more generally, it is the
reproduction of an act by movements, even though the
purpose of those movements is not to get what you want, to
do what you mean to do. Take, for instance, drinking on the
stage. Formerly it was a complete gesture, since there was
nothing in the glass; for some years now, however, since

the price of seats has risen, there has been something in the glasses and, consequently, the actor performs the act of drinking. But in reality it is a gesture, since the real act of drinking would imply that the actor was doing it with the intention of drinking because he was thirsty, or because he was taking medicine, or for some other such reason. But here he is basically making the gesture of drinking—though he is in fact drinking—to show that the character he's playing is drinking; so that the gesture, no matter whether it is a real act or a series of movements, always refers to an act that he wants to signify. In other words, since gestures signify acts in the theater, and since theater is image, gestures are the image of action. And what no one has said since the theater became bourgeois, and what ought nevertheless to be said, is that dramatic action is the action of the characters. People still think that dramatic action means some broad movement, hurly-burly, clash of passions, and so on. No, that's not action, it's simply a lot of noise, it's just a tumult. Action in the true sense is the action of a character, or in other words, his acts. There is no image in the theater except the image of the act; and if you want to know what theater is, you must ask yourself what an act is, because theater represents the act and can represent nothing but the act. Sculpture represents the form of the body, theater represents the act of the body. And consequently, what we want to rediscover when we go to the theater is naturally ourselves, not ourselves as we are, more or less sentimental or more or less proud of our youth or our beauty, but ourselves as we act and as we work and as we encounter difficulties and as we are men who obey rules, I mean the rules governing these actions.

Unfortunately, as you see, we have now got very far away from the bourgeois theater, and before we return to this question of action, I must take a moment to explain to you why what I am saying to you in no way resembles what has been performed on the stage for a hundred and fifty years—with a few exceptions, of course. It's because the bourgeois theater *does not want* dramatic action. To put it more precisely, it does want dramatic action, but it does not want it to be human action, it does not want it to be the action of the men performing the play. It wants it to be the action of the playwright constructing the events. The bourgeoisie, in fact, wants to see a representation of its own image but—and here we understand why Brecht created his epic theater, that is to say, one which goes in an entirely different direction—an image which is pure participation. It absolutely does not want to be represented as both image and quasi-object, because when it is totally object, it is not always an agreeable object; it takes itself very specifically for the image that is presented to it without externalization, the image of a man as near, as close as possible to the way he sees himself in a glass and as far as possible from the way someone else sees him. The bourgeoisie, in fact, wants to see a representation of its own inside its characters' heads—often you don't see it at all—but because the bourgeoisie wants a representation of itself that is subjective, that is to say, it wants to impose its own image of man upon the theater, one that conforms to its own ideology, and not to have to seek for that image through the kind of world where individuals see each other or groups form judgments about each other, because then it would be challenged. So it is evident enough that it wants the same image on the stage.

No, the bourgeoisie thinks according to the rules of what I would call a pessimistic naturalism; and to explain to you exactly what I mean by bourgeoisie, let's be clear about it: I mean the people who go to the theater, who keep the theater going, the people who can and are likely to pay twelve or fifteen hundred old francs for an orchestra seat, the people who control the theater; I wouldn't say they are the two hundred families, but they are the three hundred best seats. [*Laughter*] And these three hundred best seats set the rules—without realizing it, of course; but at all events what they like is a pessimistic naturalism. Why naturalism? Because there must be a human nature, and that nature must be bad, and of course, one recognizes what human nature is, to the bourgeoisie, by the very fact that it is bad, since one always says "That's only human" when anyone has just done something beastly or cowardly. [*Laughter*] So this nature must be bad and it must be immutable. I'm not going to dwell on this, because you can easily see more or less how it works: if man is bad, the thing that counts is order, any sort of order, one's as good as another. And, too, nature is bad for a deeper reason. To an aristocrat who believes he is by nature superior to the inferior races called commoners, nature is good because it is his blue blood that has made him superior; but since the bourgeoisie made the revolution and believes itself to be the universal class, to declare that nature is good is now out of the question, because it has made it the equal of those to whom it believes itself to be superior. It has, therefore, to find some way out of this, some way of distinguishing itself. Distinction is a sort of minor nineteenth-century puritanism expressed in the exercise of a dictatorship over needs, real enough when it comes to exercising it over other people's needs, expressed in images or asceticism when it comes to its own. Needs are to be condemned, the needy are bad.

Fairly recently, I asked an American whether the law for making prison more humane (allowing prisoners to have their women in once a week) would be applied in America one day. He replied that things would have to change a lot, for it would mean recognizing sex as a need. [*Laughter*] We do recognize it as one, and we do not take our distinction that far, but with the need to eat, the need to sleep, and so on we aren't so very far off the Americans, all the same, are we? We have a whole lot of needs, a whole lot of things that we repress for ourselves because the needs of other people for them are not satisfied. This distaste for needs, this appearance of denying them, is precisely what I mean by pessimism. In other words, the bourgeoisie needs human nature simply in order to deny it. And moreover, if human nature is evil and eternal, it is quite obvious that no effort to make any sort of progress is required; or, to be fair, any progress there may be will be very slow. But in any case, obviously any description of nature will demonstrate that it will always remain the same in all circumstances.

But to act (which is indeed the specific object of theater) is to change the world, and changing it necessarily means changing oneself. The bourgeoisie has profoundly changed the world, and the world has changed in changing it, and it has changed itself—not for the better [*laughter*]—and now it does not in the slightest want anyone to change it [*laughter*], above all not from the outside. [*Laughter*] So, if it still changes, it is chiefly to adapt itself precisely to avoid changing [*laughter*], to keep what it has; and this being so, what it asks of the theater is to refrain from disturbing it by the idea of the act; the act is impossible. In the theater that is to the liking of the bourgeoisie there can be no action except the sort of action that is carried on by d'Artagnan, Porthos, and Aramis; the new element in such plays must only be a swift disturbance between two periods of calm—as it is, curiously enough, in Aristotle's philosophy. All was calm before the curtain rose, and calm returns, whether tragically or comically, before it falls on the last act. Between the two there is agitation; but it must not *act* on the audience, but *move* it; and you all know what any director who means very well but is rather out of his depth in such matters will say to you about a play. He says to you, "It must have action in it." Agreed, and we ask, "How will you get action?" And he answers, "Oh, by working up the passions." But action and passion, the active and the passive, in that definition, don't go very well together. And in fact the bourgeois theater has replaced action in its plays with passion. Action as it is now understood in the theater means a playwright's practical construction of a plot. There must be some action, which means that the consequence must be deduced in a very lively and very definite way from the premises, the audience must have some slight notion of what is going to happen, but only enough to guess at it, and so on and so forth, and of course there must be a beginning, a middle, and an end. Then you choose some passions, bring them together, they crumble into dust, and so they demonstrate the eternal sameness of human nature; and then it's all over, you drop the curtain because there's no one left. [*Laughter*] Or else the passion is unleashed for a moment and then order is restored.

A famous British play, *The Admirable Crichton*,[7] presents a lord disembarking on a desert island with his whole family after a shipwreck; and there is also, naturally, an admirably trained butler. They all stay on the island. Who gets by? The butler. So, we think we are going to see some action. Well, he finds wood for the fire, he fishes, and so on. This goes on for six months; one of the lord's daughters falls for him; then a ship finds them and the greathearted butler, of course, becomes a butler again and the lord a lord. Consequently, as you see, we have been agitated for a few moments; that is to say, we began with a family of aristocrats and we ended with a family of aristocrats; betweentimes there was a storm, a shipwreck, but it has changed nothing. The theater that presents you with these passions and shows you disturbances that have no consequences also presents you with instances of typical characters, such as the Eternal Feminine, and tells you that you can change all the circumstances without the character being changed in the slightest. You know *La Petite Hutte*,[8] in which we find the famous *ménage à trois* of our entire French bourgeois tradition [*laughter*] transposed to a desert island, and there it does exactly what it does anywhere else. [*Laughter*] So what was to be demonstrated is demonstrated: human nature does not change. You see how easy it is. All these bourgeois plays have always seemed to me to be chock full of philosophy; only the bourgeois don't recognize it because it's their own. [*Laughter*] They only see it when this philosophy is someone else's; if it's their own, well, they believe it's the truth, and they say, "How well that is put." Consequently, you get the idea that, anyway, either nothing changes, or the unfortunate people who by their passions have set fire to some bourgeois institution or other are blasted and disappear, or else the best of them have yielded to something that was an aberration and returns to the fold.

There is an old play by Maurice Donnay—I forget whether it was called *The Suffragettes* or *The Insurgent Women*[9]—a lot of plays were written against the feminists. You have a group of women, all of them ridiculous except one, and she—she has just got her divorce—plunges head over heels into feminism. Another man appears and gets on better with her than her husband did; she quite naturally gives it all up, and you of course realize that she became a feminist because she felt lonely; and as soon as the second man marries her, you see her become a good housewife and mother. The story shows you how this type of theater absolutely insists on explaining things by causes and refuses to explain them by purposes. No one who wants to get out of the bourgeois order for moral or political reasons has the slightest chance. He is said to be embittered, or he has failed to pass his exams, [*laughter*] or he is a member of the intellectual proletariat, or else he is in love, or he is mad [*laughter*]; and therefore, of course, such people only have to be reasoned with, or if the case proves hopeless you cut off their heads, or if they are women in need of a husband, well, you give them one. [*Laughter*] But things are always accounted for by the past, by determinism.

So, you see, the purpose of this theater is to deprive acts of their purpose and hence of their significance, to replace the forces of action by what is most impervious and most false in whatever has been thought of man—that is, passion in the sense they understand it, something that has no understanding either of others or of self and that will always lose itself in seeking to save itself. Brecht once said —and it is one of the reasons for which, he explains, he decided to write drama of another sort—that he could not enter a theater nowadays without feeling he had got into a lunatic asylum, because, he says, you see people on the stage writhing about and wringing their hands, and in the dark of the house you also see people, absolutely tense, wringing their hands too and writhing about like the actors. He considered that participation was a relation of madness, that is, he judged that there was not enough distance between actors and audience, that there was far too much effort to move the audience and affect them and not enough effort to show them things; in other words, the relation was far too participatory, there were too many images and not enough objectivity. I think he is right; the bourgeois audience is mad, not because it participates, but because it participates in an image that is an image of lunatics. Obviously, most of the comedies and dramas you can see nowadays (I mean in the principal Paris theaters which produce plays imported from America as well as French plays) are plays in which the characters are mad. They are mad because their reactions are mad, and the reactions are mad because they have deliberately cut off all the characters' heads, deprived them of will, deprived them of action, deprived them of common sense, deprived them of any concept of the future, and have invariably made them out to be victims of their own childhood; they keep going back to childhood, and the result is that they deny all human action.

So you are dealing with a perfectly incredible theater; it is devoted to pessimism, and some plays are perhaps even more pessimistic because of their kindness or even compassion than they would be if we were shown people hating each other and whetting knives. I am thinking of *Patate*,[10] for instance, which I find a remarkable play inasmuch as the bourgeoisie recognized itself in it. In it we see two friends. What do they do? One seduces the other's adopted daughter and the other tries to blackmail him to revenge himself for twenty years of humiliation. They are friends, that's bourgeois friendship. The bourgeoisie said, "That's just how things are, isn't it?" These friendships are made up of rancor, spite, envy, jealousy, dirty little tricks. [*Laughter*] We are given all that, things are taken to a point at which the abscess is about to burst. What will they do, will they fight, will they at least have that much courage? Not a bit of it; the play has a happy ending; they were too cowardly to do anything like that; so, you see, it has come full circle. They are capable of trying to cheat one another, and each of them is capable of slandering the other to his wife, but they are not capable of really settling the scores between them. And as the note of compassion has to be struck, the women get the sympathetic roles, a few tears are shed, and that turns the trick; with due compassion the human race stands condemned. For there you have friendship, there you have the man of the universal class, there's the truth. The only relations between two men of thirty-five to forty, old schoolfriends as they are, is this blend of loutish behavior, envy, and jealousy; and that's what is called friendship.

Now, this whole bourgeois theater should also account for the theater of decent people in general when placed in a difficult situation, the theater to which Brecht objected. I am thinking chiefly of what has been called expressionism. Epic theater largely arose from a reaction against expressionism. There had already been a reaction against it called *Die neue Sachlichkeit*,[11] but it had not done too well, and expressionism was more important at the time. What was expressionism? Well, people wanted none of it, didn't want the expressionists. They were semi-outcast petty bourgeois, intellectuals who were pretty well disgusted by what was going on, but though they did view the drama as an adversary action, as a conflict, they did not have the means, the ideological tools—the time wasn't ripe—to understand that these were individual conflicts in which the whole of society is engulfed. They did not understand Gide's remark that the more individual you are, the more universal you are. They started straight off with the universal and got this pessimism, man against the world. What man? You could not ask them that. What world? You could not ask that either. Drama, struggle, world and man brace themselves one against the other, and in the end, invariably, because there must be an end, it is the world that devours man. Well, you'll say, that's too bad; but don't deceive yourself, we in France still have expressionist theater. *Tête d'or*,[12] for instance—I read somewhere that Jean-Louis Barrault had said, "It's man at grips with the materialist world"—is precisely the typical expressionist play, and indeed, we have a whole lot of contemporary plays which are reviving the expressionist themes without realizing it, in perfect good faith. For instance, Beckett's theme in *Waiting for Godot*,[13] that's a remarkable play, it's the best play since 1945, in my opinion, but I must admit that I find it both expressionistic and pessimistic.

There are two men, two tramps on the road, waiting for Godot. Godot is what you will, it could be a little respite or a rise in pay just as well as God. It doesn't matter, it's Godot; they are waiting for him, and he does not come. By the end of the first act he has not come; in the second act Beckett has the extraordinary nerve to start with the first act and play it through all over again, and it comes off admirably, and by the end of the play Godot has still not come. Why? No one knows, of course, but one gets the impression from everything they say that he did not come because they were too slack, too weak. Or perhaps he did come and they were too stupid to recognize him. Or perhaps he only exists in their heads, because they are weaklings, and if they were strong enough, there would not be a Godot. But the fact remains that it will all go on and on like that indefinitely; they will be waiting for Godot all the days of their lives and Godot will never come. The play is far superior to all the expressionist plays, but it is an expressionist play all the same. And it's a play whose content is, in a way, something that is agreeable to the bourgeois.

Similarly, too, another fairly recent play, *Rhinoceros*,[14] is an expressionist play; you have a man who becomes a rhinoceros. Well, why not? But what is this man who becomes a rhinoceros? We must note that many of Ionesco's people, or at any rate his most striking characters, have to do with elementary schools. I don't see any very particular reason why elementary schoolmasters should be exclusively privileged for admission to the category of rhinoceroses. I also find that when all's said and done, it's a denunciation of woman's frailty, because the woman leaves the man she is living with and flings herself on the rhinoceros. I can understand that well enough. But that said, what does becoming a rhinoceros mean? Does it mean becoming fascist or becoming communist? Or both? It's quite obvious that if it pleases the bourgeois public so much, it must be because it's both [*laughter*]; it's quite impossible to draw any moral from Ionesco's play except to suppose that some great misfortune, some great danger of becoming like beasts, is threatening the world, that there's an awful danger of contagion and, besides, women are all fascinated by these stupid great beasts with a horn for a nose, rhinoceroses. It's any danger you like; it might just as well be annihilation by the atom bomb. And why does anyone resist it? We ought at least to know, but we are told absolutely nothing. A person resists simply because he is there, because he represents Ionesco; so he says, "I resist," and he stays there among all these rhinoceroses to defend man all by himself, though we don't really know whether there might after all be something to be said for becoming rhinoceroses, for there hasn't been anything to show that, has there? After all, you have to be one or the other.

I don't mean that these plays are badly written—for one of them, as I say, is first-class—or dishonest; all I mean is that you always have a right to speak evil of the bourgeois as man, but not as bourgeois. There you have the whole matter in a nutshell: pessimism must be total, it must be a pessimism of inaction which dooms all the individual's potentialities, all his hopes, to failure. But if the pessimism is only a moderate one and simply says, "Things aren't too good," "Our ruling classes might be doing better than they are," and so on and so forth, well, that's not drama, but subversion. [*Laughter*] What I mean to say is that you must not imagine that pessimistic theater is nonbourgeois theater; the whole of the theater I've just been talking about, the theater of laisser-aller, of laisser-faire, of failure and evil, is bourgeois theater, that's what the bouregois goes to see every day, that's what moves his tender feelings. If we want to know what theater is, however, we must look for its significance from the other end; we have indeed to begin by positing that if action is truly central to theater, it means that dramatic action is the narration of an action or the dramatization of an action—one or more actions by a few individuals or by a whole group—I need not go into that at this point—but in any case an action. And an action means that people are wanting something and are trying to get it. It matters very little whether they succeed or fail in this, that's not of the slightest importance with regard to optimism or pessimism. The real point is that they must be making a try at it on the stage, and this is what we need to see. And when the action is of this sort, everything within it is also action. That is the essential point to grasp: that within a true theater of action nothing can exist which is not implicit in the action.

To give you an example to start with, objects in the

theater are objects created by the action using them. There is no such thing as a dialectic of object and man, as I used to be told; there is no such thing in the theater because a dialectic means the action of man on object and the reaction of object on man; and there is no such thing—not, I mean, where an image is involved. In films, yes. In a film you can see a man drowning, you can see the water fill his mouth, you see his head disappear, you see bubbles, you have the impression that he has been drowned by the water. Of course that's all faked, but you have entered a system of illusions, of reflections, or whatever you want to call it, and consequently you see the water drowning a man. I believe that if you look for the essence of film, you will find that it is to show you man through the medium of the world, whereas the theater shows you the image of man in action. There is, therefore, more potential for dialectic treatment in the film, far more. But in the theater a mime like Barrault, for example, can conjure up the illusion of a river simply by the action of swimming, and if he wanted to drown himself, he would have to make his drowning conjure up the water to drown him. This means that it does not matter in the slightest whether you have properties on the stage or not; that's an old actors' experience.

In a play I wrote,[15] there is a moment when a female character enters with a newspaper and gives it to her brother, saying, "Read that!" He reads it and a lot of complications ensue. A third character, another woman, enters and says, "Oh, you've given him the paper, you're moving rather fast." Some time ago the actress who gives the newspaper forgot to bring it on stage with her and the scene was played without it. There was nothing else the actors could do, so they carried on. "Here's the newspaper," she said, there wasn't one, there was some scrap of paper she had torn off a set. He replied, "Ah, yes, that's very important," and tore the tiny scrap of paper up as he threw it away. Thereupon the third character entered and said, "I see you have given him the newspaper." The other said Yes. The audience took it without raising an eyebrow and understood perfectly well what was going on; the fact that no one raised an eyebrow wasn't at all because the audience was in a stupor, but just the opposite, this happened because they understood perfectly well. They said to themselves, They've forgotten the newspaper, and there was no need for it; the illusion itself was provided by the gestures made by the actors. Basically, properties are no use at all, absolutely no use, not ever. You can never give any explanation in a play by using an article at hand; that's not the director's business. It is never any use except for a few minor effects. The only way that things come into being is through gesture; the gesture of stabbing brings the dagger into being. That said, there's no question, of course, of doing away with properties altogether; for there is no particular need to re- quire an audience to make an effort to accept a further superfluous illusion by having a clenched fist stand for a dagger. But the fact remains that you can reduce properties to basically nothing. We saw that very well demonstrated by the Chinese Opera a few years ago.[16] With almost nothing you can conjure up a river and a boat; if you have as much art as the Chinese actor who played the part of the ferry- man, you can conjure them up very well; and very fascina- ting it is to see it done, too.

I have seen something even better than that; I have seen, in the full blaze of the footlights—perhaps some of you saw it too, though a lot of you are too young to have seen it—I have seen two actors of the Chinese Opera create night wholly by pantomime. It was an extract from grand opera; a character, an officer, was sleeping in a room at night and the cunning innkeeper came into the room to murder him. Both were skilled swordsmen. The officer realized that there was someone in his room, leaped out of bed, and drew his saber, and they started fighting, groping about in the dark, slashing about all over the room, but never where either of them was. They never found one another, and from time to time there were surprising incidents, they were back to back or one astride of the other; it was an action with conflicts and contradictions which only made sense if it was happening in the dark. The result was that everyone saw the dark. Incidentally, this is what accounts for the fact that very white images of saints are bought here for the voodoo cult in Haiti, where they serve black goddesses, but without their color being changed. Though white, they are seen as black. So, you see, action in this case has a tremendous power.

The real problem is quite different, and it is no use trying to clear it up from outside. The problem is how real contradictions and a real dialectic of object and act and man can be properly created in the theater. It is one of the hardest things to do, and it has not yet been done, because, since the object follows the action, it has so little tensile strength. In the film it generates action; in the theater it ensues upon action, is generated by it. The whole problem of the dialectic of work is a very real one. In a film you can narrate the life of an engineer, an engine driver, as documentary, without boring anyone. Can you imagine it on the stage, with a cardboard engine [*laughter*], with flares you shoot off when the engine starts? You do see engines like that at the Châtelet, of course. You see that it can't be done; and yet what should theater be talking about if not work? For after all, action and work are the same thing: this is the true inner contradiction in theater, and this is why the problem has not yet been resolved. It is not enough to show, as epic theater does, the contradictions that generate actions which, basically, are not quite actions, because they bear the marks of their origin. What we need to know is how work can be rendered in theater other than by having someone say, "Good work, lad." This problem has never been solved; intellectual work in particular has always been horribly badly shown on the stage, whether literary work (where you saw poets composing verses off the cuff) or scientific work—even, I must admit, the science in Brecht's *Galileo*. These extraordinarily difficult problems are obviously facile enough in bourgeois theater because, since it does not deal with them, there's no problem.

The point I wanted to make was specifically that action is central to a play, that language is action, that there is a language peculiar to theater and that this language must never be descriptive. And that it must never be simply local color as an accompaniment to action in sound; that language is a moment in action, as in life, and it is there simply to give orders, defend things, expound feelings in the form of argument for the defense (that is, for an active purpose), to persuade or accuse, to demonstrate decisions, to be used in verbal duels, rejections, confessions, and the like. As soon as it ceases to be action, it bores us. And above all, the whole world must be encompassed by theater—sun, moon, stars, rain, wind, absolutely anything you want, all nature, all towns, but never in descriptions, almost never by words. By action. No matter how, by action. And this concept of language obviously leads on ineluctably to the concept of a language as irreversible as action itself. A real action is irreversible; it becomes more and more radical as it goes on; even if you want to reverse and go back to the start, you cannot, you have to go on to the end. It is the radical movement of action that becomes schematized in theater. You simply must not be able to place a single one of the sentences or pieces of dramatic prose spoken by an actor or a character in front of another or another in front of it just as you like. If there really are any equivalents, you must omit one term or both, but in any event there must never be a check to the movement. You must find what an action is, grasp which way the action is going, and the way it goes is the way it goes on becoming more radical, unless of course the person engaged in it dies or unless there is a sudden clash with something else wholly external to it and purely a matter of chance. But action in itself is taken to its final end, it is irreversible, the narrative must be irreversible.

But, that said, you are surely going to ask me is there nothing else but action? Don't you have passions? Aren't people going to love or hate in this sort of theater? Is theater really as grim and cold as the theater you are talking about? To which I'd reply, Not a bit of it; all the characters will be indeed impassioned, but in the good, not the bad, sense of passion. The bad sense of passion means total blindness to oneself and others, with the result that you simply commit one stupid act after another and get farther and farther away from your own interest by massacring everybody around you without the least idea of what is happening to you. One talks of a sudden stroke of passion, when what it really is, is a sudden stroke of stupidity, isn't it? I have never met people who were really like that; I've met people who were stupid—and so have you—but stupidity and passion did not necessarily go together, and usually, as a matter of fact, the more passionate they were, the less stupid. [*Laughter*] For what is passion? Does a jealous man, for instance, emptying a revolver into his rival, kill for passion? No, he kills because he believes he has a right to kill. He has suffered an injury to his right because, for instance, at a given moment, if he was married, he undertook obligations before the judge or the priest and he kept them; if he did not marry, if he is just living with someone, he has made sacrifices for the woman and he conceives that he ought to be rewarded for them. In short, jealousy implies a right; if you have no right over the person with you, you may be very unhappy because she does not like you any more, because she is deceiving you; but there will be no passion.

Generally speaking, it is impossible nowadays to draw a distinction with respect to any of us between individual man and social man; and social man is at the bottom of all our passions in the form of a claim. Envy is a claim and a sense of right; it is an extremely unfortunate passion, but it is also a sense of right. Envy is myself who am worth what I am worth; why do I not have what he has, when he is worthless? At bottom there is always this idea of right which comes precisely from the fact that passion is a way of finding oneself in the right, of referring to a whole social world of claims and values to justify the fact that one wishes to keep, take, destroy, or construct something. Passionate people invariably spend their whole time reasoning; they often bore you stiff with it. Pirandello saw this very well; a character in his plays who is in the grip of passion talks the whole time, because passion expresses itself in words, calculations, seeking out evidence. That's why I say that passion is far less stupid than is usually thought; it is rather that someone is trying to see as lucidly as he can. What is it that has him in its grip? His right, which he refuses to relinquish. "It's my right, I stick to that," you know the old refrain. He will maintain his right unto death. In other words, the passionate man must go to every length, gradually become more and more radical as he goes right on to the end; he is capable of absolutely anything to maintain his right. Just as Vailland once said, "Italians are jurists," well, I believe that the passionate are jurists, and if they are, passion sets in when a right is infringed. Consequently, passion is reciprocal; it is an act in the sense that it is a social claim manifested by an individual resolved to challenge reality to the very end. Once he is resolved, he must consider himself injured by someone else, and that other person must consider himself injured by this right. And in point of fact, passion only exists in the form of conflicting claims, in a complex society with a whole lot of structures, a society in which people represent different things.

You know the *Antigone* as well as I do, and you will certainly have read Hegel's passage on the *Antigone*,[17] which is absolutely clear on the subject. You know that the city was already established and stabilized when Sophocles wrote the *Antigone*. [*Short interruption owing to changing tape*]

". . . members of my family, because I only have to do with them and they only have to do with me." The leader of the city says, "No, there are no great families any more but only citizens, and you, as a citizen, may not bury a man who betrayed the city and fought against us." So you see that here you have a conflict which had once existed. But was it still a living issue at the time when Sophocles was writing, or did he feel that it was dead as far as he was concerned, but was still familiar to his public? I have no idea, but I am quite sure Hegel was right in saying that this was the deepest meaning of the play and that everyone realized it. Here we have the combination of the passionate with the social element, and both of them are notably emphasized. For what is Antigone, after all? The determination to carry out the burial at all costs, because that is her right and duty; or, to put it more concisely, we can sum it up in the phrase, "She claims the right to perform an absolute duty." Antigone has this right, and she has the right not to derogate from this duty, because she judges that this duty is good; it is, so to speak, the survival of the *genos* which is being liquidated by the city, and this being so, you can see what her passion is. Her passion is her refusal to compromise. You can't imagine anyone more impassioned than Antigone, for though she is offered life if she will make some concessions, she absolutely refuses in order to carry things right through to the end; she is radical and, at a given moment—and this is one of the interesting things in the play—she so to speak radicalizes Creon, because he had no intention to begin with of causing a scandal by killing Antigone; little by little she drives him toward it, and in the end he becomes as implacable as she is. Consequently, after a certain point in the play you have two passions and a story which develops because it is a dual action taken to its worst, that is, to its most radical (the most radical may, of course, be the best, but that's not the point). One of the most interesting features of ancient classical theater is that each person represents *one* term of the contradiction, never two. Here you have the family on one side and the city on the other, but there is no character, as there would be in a modern play, who is a member of one of the great families and yet is attracted by the establishment of the city, or conversely, a citizen with links with the great families—who would therefore embody the contradiction within himself. That is a form of drama which was unknown in the period of classical tragedy; there the characters each represent *one* form and only one, or one term of the contradiction, and they embody passion inasmuch as they are made up of it and only of it. You can see that there is no synthesis in the play; the contradiction is not transcended. The *deus ex machina* is something quite different; here he represents Sophocles himself. Antigone's complete disappearance and the series of plagues that strike Creon show that Sophocles' audience found both of them in the wrong. This means— though this is not of course the most interesting point about the play—that the poet was in favor of a moderate solution: gently bring the aristocrats to heel (there is no question of this being at all hard to do, because you see them fighting on both sides of the ramparts), bring them to heel, find some sort of accommodation, but do not destroy their customs; take care not to go too far and do not prevent their daughters from burying them; that's roughly the solution he suggests. Fortunately, this solution is not expressly stated in the play, but appears only in a negative form; for the two rights and the two actions entirely disappear. The misfortunes which befall Creon are of no great importance, although they provide some very fine scenes; the play is ended to all intents and purposes once Antigone has been killed; the action is completed, and the rest is simply about the gods avenging Antigone.

But if a right represents the simple form of dramatic

action in Greek tragedy, we must now look at what is new
in the theater which has been growing up alongside, but not
among, the bourgeoisie for some time now: the fact that
contradiction can nowadays be a property of the individual
character. Action is not now made up of a single contradiction; there are series of contradictions within a character,
that is to say he encompasses within himself perpetually,
let's say, an Antigone and a Creon, or a Don Quixote and
a Sancho Panza, or else, like the judge in *The Caucasian
Chalk Circle*, a rogue who has no respect for anything and
yet is someone with a kind of vulgar common sense who
administers justice when it can be done almost as burlesque.
We can see a whole lot of plays nowadays in which all these
contradictions are combined in a single person. Nowadays,
on the stage of drama, of the sentimental play, people have
several passions; an action is something far more complex
than burial was in Antigone's case. In her case the action
called for dauntless courage, extraordinary obstinacy, but
the action was simple. What is to be shown today is that
actions (1) arise from contradictions, (2) reflect these
contradictions, and (3) set up further contradictions. There
you have it; and you can see that this provides plenty of
things to say, plenty that one can find to do in the theater.
A man—or a group of men—only acts insofar as internal
contradictions are the driving force of his action; he thereby
severs himself from them, and consequently these initial
contradictions will give the actual meaning and purpose of
the act he wishes to perform; and from a different angle,
by severing himself from them he throws light on them.
This dual point of view—transcending contradictions to
achieve an end, but of course still continuing to embody
them, and then reverting to clarify them—is the first element. But the second element is the fact that this action
itself, which arises from the contradictions in consequence,
must itself be contradictory; which means that, basically,
there are several of them at the same time, assembled and

inseparable because a number of elements are pressing forward simultaneously.

Take Brecht's *Galileo*. You find that the protagonist is simultaneously a scientist of genius who is making great advances in science and a character expressing the precise level of scientific development which was possible at that particular time—not merely its technical and practical development, but also the people on whom it was dependent. Clearly, it was dependent on aristocrats and lords, so that Galileo's money, power, and working tools were dependent on a class, or sector of society, which was simultaneously very much opposed to letting research go beyond a certain point, in other words, which regarded scientific research as primarily technical and practical and was contemptuous and above all rather afraid of the advancement of knowledge. Thus Galileo's contradiction is that he is simultaneously the man responsible for scientific progress and, for that very reason, the man who betrays and denies it. Brecht makes it quite clear that it is not a question of deciding whether he is guilty or not, but of showing in a play the contradiction in Galileo's action—the twofold aspect of discovering an interpretation of the law of gravity and of rejecting and refusing it; simultaneously raising the level of science by a very important discovery and casting it at the feet of two or three petty princelings and a pope who was actually a scientist himself. Is the contradiction valid, is the action valid? Yes, it's a dual action, because we are also shown in the play the personal interests of Galileo, who is something of a comic character and almost, in places, a cunning and sly one, because he doesn't have the kind of scientist's dignity that later ages were to attribute to him, because he has a streak of the mountebank and buffoon in him, because he is himself astonished at his little discoveries, because he tries to fake things a bit and to steal some money (and he is always like that when he has anything to do with his lords and masters). So, on one side we have this petty world of Panurges and on the other the continuous sequence of research and discoveries, and the way the two blend and the way science is betrayed in the end by the man because he is what science has made him; if science had not been at the level it was, if it had not been so backward, if it had not been dependent in practice on just a few people but had been an independent discipline not having to depend on them, Galileo would never have dreamed of betraying it.

A play of this sort can present you with the inner contradiction of a single individual, as indeed it will present you with the contradictions of the other characters in the play with whom he is surrounded. Take the pope I mentioned just now: the contradiction in him is just the opposite, because he is the pope but venerates science; and so this sort of timidity of the man of science confronted with the pope he has become leads him to yield to other forces and makes him, though a scientist, threaten a fellow scientist with torture. Hence, all these characters, the entire contrapuntal movement of their contradictions, can combine to give you a starting point, to show how someone bears witness to his act and passes sentence by his acts on what people have done to him. That's something of great importance, the fact that one changes by changing the world and because the world changes. There are many of Brecht's plays in which the world is seen changing man rather than man changing the world, because there is a sort of primacy which perhaps is given to the equally real fact that we live in a world of flux, and it does not ask us whether we want to change before it changes us. But there is also the reverse factor that we change the world—and that is one of the things which must be shown in plays—that things are no longer what they were before some action or other, but at the same time we change too. For example, it was the Revolution that changed royalists into republicans, and finally it was royalists who demanded the death of Louis XVI; they demanded it inasmuch as they had become republicans, but all of them had been thoroughly royalist at the start; all of them had been to schools like the Jesuit schools, all of them had been in favor of Louis XVI, all of them had belonged to a royalist bourgeoisie, and it was the revolution they had made which, by changing itself and by compelling the king to take certain attitudes, compelled them to radicalize their own attitudes and consequently made them revert to acting both as republicans and as ex-royalists. So you find that any member of the National Convention you choose turns out to be a rather curious character, a royalist who does not know quite who he is at any given moment and, later, realizes that he has become radicalized, and so goes on to the bitter end.

This kind of action is also a dramatic action, and if you have understood that the basis of a drama is the recognition of an absolutely certain and real fact, you can see that an action cannot exist unless it becomes radicalized. If it stops, it disappears; it must be taken to its end, for that is fundamental to drama, that is a dramatic action. What you have to do is not to confront passions with each other, but to confront people with acts, and the confrontation engenders contradictions which reflect social contradictions; and this action goes on to its end by wiping out the characters who were there at the beginning, achieving success in radicalization itself; for we simply must not be so much sunk in our bourgeois theater as to think that all actions are failures. So, if you have understood this, you will understand what a character is, for a character is defined positively by his situation and his action and negatively by his reluctance to take action; and this reluctance places him in a situation and can only be made to live through some sort of passion.

After all, what do we know about Antigone, or about Ismene, for that matter, a creature whom the critics are kind enough from time to time to find touching or charming or gracious or what have you? We know only one thing about her, that she would not go as far as Antigone; and that is enough to present a character, it's enough to show us a reluctance which we really do not need to know about and which may arise from causes far more remote. For dramatic purposes this defines her quite adequately; theater has no need of psychology. Indeed, psychology is a waste of time in theater because plays are long and the audience's attention can necessarily be held only for a brief span, and fine shades of meaning have no interest of any sort, especially in an action—indeed, they're not given very much attention in any psychological enterprise either. And since a play is in fact tantamount to launching people on an enterprise, psychology is not needed. On the other hand, what is needed is very precisely to trace the bounds of the position or situation in which each character may be set as a result of the precedent causes and contradictions which have led to it in relation to the main action. This is how we come to have a number of secondary and primary characters, all of whom will be defined through the action itself as an enterprise which must be an enterprise in common involving the contradictions of all the characters and each individual character.

In connection with this point and all the other points so far, we have not yet had to draw the distinction between dramatic theater—if we mean by that a theater which is intended to be rid of the bourgeois concept of human nature, that is, individualism and pessimism—and epic theater. In both cases we certainly have to bring out the dual aspect of all individual acts, that is to say that each individual is only an expression of what Brecht called the social gestus, the totality, the social totality, of the contradictions within which the person concerned lives. For instance, as you know, Brecht admirably displays the actual contradictions of war in the contradictions of Mother Courage, for she is a woman who dies of war and lives by war. War does her all the harm it can, but she cannot live without war; she is happy when war starts up again and she is miserable when it continues, and Brecht made an admirable choice in choosing that slant to examine war and the contradictions of war. And in the end, it is *she* who *is* war, not at all as a symbol, but as a living contradiction which can do only one thing: lead us to consider all the contradictions of war.

So far, so good, we all agree, but the real problem arises elsewhere; it arises as soon as we ask whether the object thus created—the play—should be represented to the audience as object or image. What I mean is, must we really, on the pretext that the bourgeoisie has used it as a weapon, get rid of participation, which is the deepest essence of theater, the very movement which creates the psychodrama as well as the black facts of which I was telling you? Or if we do not completely get rid of it, should we at least reduce its share and give a larger share to explanation and teaching? Or else, again, should we look at it from a different angle and finally refuse to rid ourselves of participation? What in fact does happen in epic theater? Epic theater's aim is to show us the individual's adventure insofar as it expresses the social gestus and also to show us, in what I would prefer not to call a didactic way—though Brecht did in fact write some didactic plays—but, shall we say, in a very ostensible way, the implications and reciprocal correlations of which a system is composed and which involve people in systems— systems that must of course be interpreted in the light of a far more comprehensive system, the modern capitalist system, for instance. Let us take as an example Brecht's *The Exception and the Rule*. A merchant in the colonies hires a guide; he loses his way and is dying of thirst; the guide is not much better off, but he gets up and fetches a water bottle and hands it, out of habit or perhaps generosity—at all events, it will be the exception—to the merchant, who becomes frightened and kills him; the merchant reaches home, and the guide's wife, hearing about it, takes him to court for killing her husband. The case seems to be going badly against the merchant, when the court at last recalls that after all we do these natives so much wrong that it is quite natural that they should think only of revenge, especially as men are not good; consequently, how could a native finding himself all alone with an evil-minded merchant hesitate to kill him? Obviously, he could not. Consequently, the merchant believed that he was acting in legitimate self-defense when he killed him. The rule, the play says, is that a native ought to want to kill, to kill the people who exploit him. If this particular native was an exception, so much the worse for him, for no one could know that. The play is very amusing, but if you look at it, it is valid for one reason only: that we are dealing with a system of contradictions which come into being and combine, a sort of fallacy generated indeed by colonization itself, but in a world in which men are put not simply to adopt such fallacies and transcend them either by making them even worse or else by trying to resist them but finally yielding to them—in short, in a world in which men represent the lowest common denominator of this kind of circular fallacy, which is a basic structure of the capitalist world of the modern colonialists.

We have the impression that there is at a given moment a choice in Brecht, and that these people are insects. The proof is that in *The Caucasian Chalk Circle* he draws a distinction between the characters according to levels of reality. That political or moral or other judgments may be passed upon them is arguable, but why state *a priori* that because they are bad characters—for instance, the palace guards who play cards all day and think nothing of massacring people—some of them will have masks, whereas the two or three characters who are simple folk will not have them? In the light of the contradictions themselves and the way in which classes, or the proximity of certain classes, generate inner contradictions, we put forward people who are really only empty shells—they are eaten out from within and all we have to do is present them in masks. Then we get another category less proximate than the category in masks, but nevertheless not quite human, and lastly the maidservant and her betrothed, who are a true woman and a true man, almost without make-up, who act absolutely naturally, because they have a kind of fullness about them. But why, just because they do things that tend toward social usefulness and are consonant with their own nature and reality, are they more fully realized than the guards? They are people, they are neither fuller nor less full, they are human beings. This way of looking at things is too simplistic; it consists in saying that man changes into something abstract. It is one way of understanding Marxism, but it is not the right way; it is not true, for instance, that in a labor market it is the worker who becomes something abstract and the market which finally becomes something absolutely concrete. That, as I see it, is not at all what Marx meant—Hegel, if you like, but not Marx. It is precisely the worker, regardless of whether he is totally exploited and alienated or not, who nevertheless keeps his human reality. To introduce choices and to place reality in perspective is, ideologically speaking, an extremely dubious stance. It should not be accepted, for reality cannot be placed in perspective because it is not in perspective. On other levels it is; but man is man, no matter what he is, and is man just as all men are. None of them ought to be better or worse depicted than the others. If this is an aesthetic device, it must be based on something, and in this case it is not based on anything. So you see, it is not acceptable to put in small doses of reality or large doses of reality, or hierarchies and perspectives. Anyway, can anyone show that this method of getting rid of participation has any true philosophy to guarantee it?

That Marx is the great philosopher of the nineteenth century cannot be doubted. That Brecht read and knew Marx well there can be no doubt. But that there are five hundred different interpretations of Marx, each of them so passionately held by each particular reader of Marx that

he is prepared to fight you with bare knuckles for his interpretation, cannot be doubted either. Consequently, why say
that theater will be demonstrative if it is not sure of what
it is demonstrating? If the theater is to be confined to a
couple of reflections and is to present only a few rudimentary
thoughts, the simplest thoughts that are to be found in Marx,
I do not see any need to bring distancing in; if it is to go
farther, then let us be told what it is about and what we
have to be shown. We ought, after all, to know what is
being talked about; and over and above that, we must know
what sort of Marxism is meant. Who is to say that there
may not be a vast number of epic theaters, all of them with
different meanings? For the difference between dramatic
theater and epic theater on this level is that the author who
writes for dramatic theater speaks for himself and tells a
tale with his own interpretations, whereas the author of
epic theater is demonstrative and does not speak in his
own words. He removes himself as author at the same time
as he removes the spectator to make way for the spectacle
he is showing. And on this level, if we revert to the ideology to which I referred a while ago, image and object,
and if we even assume that we have taken every precau-
tion to get rid of whatever element of passion there may
be in participation, and that consequently the relations
between audience and actors are as distant and as stiff as
you like, that's all very well if you are dealing with a society
in decline, in which you take the point of view of one of
the classes, the class which is rising, or trying to rise or
going to rise, for instance; in other words, it's all very well
in a period in which Brecht can consider himself the spokes-
man of the disinherited classes and a judge exposing to
those classes what the bourgeoisie is. But let us now suppose that in East Germany, for instance, Brecht had also
been able to speak about East Germany. He was wholly in
favor of the regime. Obviously there were, as in all regimes, or perhaps more than in other regimes, things which

were not going well in East Germany. There were, for instance—and there will be in the future and there have
been in the past—officials or, say, militants who did not
take the view they should of their duties as officials or militants. Let us suppose that, after some scandal perhaps,
Brecht had wanted to explain to himself or to an audience
how there are contradictions in the socialist society too,
would he have used the same method? Would we have been
shown officials guilty of some small negligence or total
lack of imagination? Would we have seen them in masks?
Would we have seen the principal cause and the conflicts
of the hero or group of characters (who could be judges
or engineers or just anybody)? Would we have seen them
really from outside and involved in the absurdity of their
contradictions, or would we not have seen them, still with
their contradictions—for Brecht was an honest writer—but
from within, that is to say, sympathetically? In other words,
if we imagine the story of an official in the German Democratic Republic who has committed some faults or errors, or
of a group of officials whose errors demonstrate the contradictions of socialism, I am convinced that this character
would be treated in a play by Brecht in the light of the
ends he was aiming at—the same ends as Brecht's: that
is, the revolution still to be completed; the sympathy that
Brecht would naturally have for him would ensure that
this was a man he had understood. When you do not share
the aims of the social group which you are defining, you can
certainly create a sort of distancing and in consequence
show people from outside and even sometimes use a song
to reveal what they are thinking; but when you are a member of a society whose principles are the same as yours,
it's very much harder, and you have to say, "Yes, the poor
fellow is guilty, but you don't realize all the difficulties
there are; there are these contradictions and this is how he
felt them; he wanted this, he wanted that," and so on. Here
we are dealing with another sort of theater, a theater trying

to understand, and this is precisely where I find the difference between epic and dramatic. In dramatic theater you can try to understand, but in epic theater, as it is presented to us at the present time, you explain what you do not understand. I am not speaking about Brecht himself, but more generally. So we will say, if you like, that there is a very definite lack in epic theater, for Brecht never solved— in any case, he had no reason to do so and it was not his business to do so—the problem of subjectivity and objectivity in the context of Marxism, and he was therefore never able really to find room for subjectivity as it ought to be embodied.

A serious defect of dramatic theater is that it did after all emerge from bourgeois theater, emerged from the means created by individualism through individualist experiences, and is not yet suited to speaking about work. Nor, for that matter, is epic theater. Plainly, it would be a great pity to abandon either of these two forms of drama, a pity even that each playwright cannot choose—as, after all, he could choose in the eighteenth century either to write an epic or to write sonnets—that each author cannot ponder whether he would prefer to write an epic drama or a truly dramatic drama. In the circumstances, the best course seems to be to combine all the strengths that the coming theater may possess and pit them against the bourgeois plays we have at present, and to consider that there is no real conflict between the dramatic form and the epic form, except that the one tends toward the quasi-objectivity of the object, that is to say, man, and so toward failure—because you never will have man objectified—combined with the mistaken belief that you can present society as an object to the audience, whereas the other would tend too much toward sympathy, *Einfühlung*,[18] unless corrected by an element of objectivity and would be in danger of degenerating into bourgeois theater. Consequently, it is somewhere between these two forms of theater that, I believe, the problem rests today.

Interview with
Kenneth Tynan (1961)

This interview was first published in the London Sunday paper, *The Observer*, June 18 and 25, 1961, and was later reprinted, as "An Interview with Jean-Paul Sartre," in *Tynan Right and Left*, by Kenneth Tynan (New York: Atheneum Publishers, 1967). An incomplete French version, retranslated from the English, appeared in *Afrique-Action*, July 10, 1961. The full text from *Tynan Right and Left* (pp. 302–12) follows, with notes by the editors, and with minor stylistic changes.

Sartre's apartment in Paris is a working place, small and book-cluttered, on the fourth floor of a corner building in the rue Bonaparte, overlooking the Café des Deux Magots and the church of Saint-Germain-des-Près. Its owner, instead of the bleak, intimidating oracle I expected, is warm, lively, and instantly responsive; a quick, compact figure of a man, with suntanned skin, a condition rare in middle-aged intellectuals. (Or could it have been jaundice?) What follows is a condensation of an interview lasting some ninety minutes.

TYNAN   You once said that *Altona* was not the play you intended to write. You meant it to deal with torture in Algeria, but transposed it because you felt such a play could not be staged in Paris. Now Genet has written a play about Algeria—*Les Paravents*.[1] Do you think it will be put on?

SARTRE   I don't think so. It has been published, and it may win a literary prize, but that is another matter. Strictly speaking, there is no theater censorship in Paris, but there is self-censorship on the part of theatrical managements. They are afraid that the police may intervene and forbid a production on the grounds that it might cause a public disturbance. That is an economic risk that they can't afford to take.

TYNAN   Have you read Genet's new play?

SARTRE   Yes, and I find it very interesting. It's not the whole truth about Algeria; it's a version of the truth, seen through the prism of Genet's ideas and sensibility. In Genet's mind, one must embrace what is vile in order to achieve what is good. For myself, I don't believe that people should be taught that kind of heroism. But you will notice that it is exactly in keeping with his belief that judges should be as harsh as possible. According to Genet, it is only when man has been reduced to his lowest level—sentenced to death or life imprisonment, despised by the world as a traitor, etc.—that he can begin to rebuild humanity. It's a fascinating theory, but I don't think it really applies to the problem of a colonized people.

TYNAN   Would you say the same thing of *The Blacks*—that it poses a general problem in highly subjective terms?

SARTRE   Yes, I think so. Although many Negroes have found in the play a kind of resonance. I mean the way in which it shows the Negro poised between two cultures. Against his will, and almost as if it were a game, he participates in the culture of the white, and suddenly his own culture begins to take on the aspect of a game.

TYNAN   In your Sorbonne lecture,[2] you condemned bourgeois theater. Is the bourgeoisie to blame for everything that is wrong with contemporary drama?

SARTRE   The essential fault seems to me to be bourgeois. Look at the plays that are performed nowadays; you will see that the majority are worn-out psychological exercises, making use of all the old bourgeois themes—the husband with a mistress, the wife with a lover, the family who don't understand one another. But there is another problem that should be mentioned in connection with the theater, and that is the cinema. Today many people—not only directors, but ordinary spectators, and especially young intellectuals—think the cinema a better means of expression than the theater. And under the influence of the cinema, the theater has tended to withdraw from its own battlefield. It has given in to the enemy; it has multiplied its settings, and has tried, by stressing the visual element, to tell stories in a form that is more cinematic than theatrical. It has thus become easier to destroy. The same thing happens in politics: if a government shows signs of yielding to the opposition, in the end the opposition will seize power.

The theater is not concerned with reality; it is only concerned with truth. The cinema, on the other hand, seeks a reality which may contain moments of truth. The theater's true battlefield is that of tragedy—drama which embodies a genuine myth. There is no reason why the theater should not tell a story of love or marriage, as long as it has a quality of myth; in other words, as long as it occupies itself with something more than conjugal disagreements or lovers' misunderstandings. By seeking truth through myth, and by the use of forms as nonrealistic as tragedy, the theater can stand up against the cinema. Only thus can it avoid being swallowed up.

TYNAN   Isn't it true that there are a number of private symbols in *Altona*—for instance, the tribunal of crabs that Franz addresses?

SARTRE   Yes. Since my childhood I have always had a special aversion to crabs, and all kinds of shellfish.[3]

TYNAN   Including oysters?

SARTRE   I never eat them. For me, the fact that Franz eats oysters means that he is living on extremely unpleasant food. Once, in a moment of fatigue, when I was about thirty-two years old, I had some very disagreeable hallucinations connected with crabs.[4] Since then I have always regarded them as symbols of something inhuman. I can't imagine what these creatures think or feel—probably not very much! For me, theirs is a world completely opposed to the human world.

TYNAN   So this court of crabs is something you regard as frightful?

SARTRE   It is frightful to Franz, not to me. Since Franz is guilty, he makes his judges as frightful as possible. I believe that the tribunal of history always judges men according to standards and values which they themselves could never imagine. We can never know what the future will say of us. It may be that history will consider Hitler a great man— though that would astonish me enormously—and in any case, there is always Stalin! The point is that we know we shall be judged, and not by the rules we use to judge ourselves. And in that thought there is something horrific. Moreover, it has been said that progress is made laterally, in a sideways motion, rather like the movement of crabs. That was also part of my idea.

TYNAN   Jean Genet has said that he can't bear judges who "lean over amorously towards the defendant."

SARTRE   I agree in the sense that Genet is speaking from the point of view of the criminal. It is his revenge against society. Instead of saying, "It's society's fault, not the criminal's! Don't punish him too harshly!" he says the opposite: "We are enemies of society! Punish us as much as possible. If you don't punish us, you are contemptible. By punishing us you make us live in a harsh world and that makes us the more heroic." On this point I don't entirely agree with Genet.

On the other hand, there is a world in which I think judges should be wary of "leaning over amorously towards the defendant." That is the world of politics. I am opposed to the death penalty; but I think the rebel generals in Algeria should have been condemned to death, and reprieved afterwards.[5] In cases like this the crime is committed against society as a whole.

TYNAN   I recall that in your lecture to the Sorbonne last year, you said that the theater today had no need of psychology. But isn't the character of Franz full of psychological subtleties?

SARTRE   What I meant was that no situation should be analyzed exclusively on the psychological level. Take, for example, the conflict of a man with his wife. Unless we knew something about their work, their background, the society that formed them, the situation has no theatrical reality. Franz's problem is the result of many conflicting social circumstances—his father's business, the development of German capitalism, the rise of the Nazis, his father's collusion with Nazism. His problems and inner contradictions are created by historical events.

TYNAN   Talking about Franz's father, do you think his desire for power is purely a bourgeois impulse? Or is it a general human impulse?

SARTRE   I think the desire to retain power comes from already possessing it. Let me put it this way: the authority that a factory owner brings into his family life comes from the factory itself—in other words, from the power that the structure of capitalist society gives to its leaders. The capitalist is not, in himself, an authoritarian. But if one puts him in a position in which he must exercise authority, he will always want to exercise it: he is shaped by his social role.

Now in countries like Germany, and even more in

America, we have the phenomenon of capitalist enterprises in which management and ownership are beginning to diverge. Old Gerlach is a man who has had total authority over his business for nearly the whole of his life, and who sees that authority slipping away just at the moment when he is growing old. That is his tragedy. He has created his son in his own image, as a man born to exercise authority. But in reality even if Franz were not cut off from the world, even if he took over the business, he would merely be the owner, not the ruler. Power has passed into the hands of the technocrats.

TYNAN   But isn't it possible that a noncapitalist bureaucrat might seek power for its own sake?

SARTRE   Everything depends on the situation. No one is born with a desire either to seek power or to shun it. It's a man's history that makes him move one way or the other. And even then, he is seldom quite sure. There are many cases of men who thought they wanted power, only to discover when they reached the top of the ladder that they would rather be on the second rung or the third. It's not a question of instincts or inborn tendencies; what counts is a man's relationship with society, with his family, with everything around him.

[My next question gave rise to an interesting confusion. I intended to ask Monsieur Sartre whether he thought it was possible nowadays to create right-wing art. I mispronounced the phrase: instead of *la droite*, the political right, I heard myself referring to *le droit*—the law. Before I could correct myself, Monsieur Sartre had taken the question in his stride, and embarked on his answer. I append it herewith as a tribute to his mental agility.]

SARTRE   By all means, yes. The law *is* theater. For at the roots of theater there is not merely a religious ceremony, there is also eloquence. Consider the characters of Sophocles, of Euripides, even of Aeschylus—they are all lawyers; and we must remember that the Greeks loved lawyers. They come forward with a cause to defend. Others take the opposite side and plead against them. At the end, there is a catastrophe in which everyone is judged, and matters return to normal. The stage is the courtroom in which the case is tried. Antigone, for example, has a cause to plead—the cause of the great families, whose traditions and religious obligations are being threatened by the state. Creon, meanwhile, stands for another, newer cause—one which clearly does not appeal to Sophocles, whose sympathies are conservative. Creon is a primitive democrat, who says, "In a dispute between the state and the family, authority rests with the state." These are the two positions; and instead of Antigone and Creon, one might just as well have engaged two lawyers to put forward their respective points of view.

TYNAN   A socialist poet named Christopher Logue recently wrote a play about the Antigone legend.[6] His attitude seemed to be that Creon was right.

SARTRE   Naturally. That is the democratic point of view.

TYNAN   (*getting back to his original point*)   Do you think that nowadays there is such a thing as right-wing art?

SARTRE   I don't think theater can be directly derived from political events. For instance, I would never have written *Altona* if it was merely a simple question of a conflict between left and right. For me, *Altona* is tied up with the whole evolution of Europe since 1945, as much with the Soviet concentration camps as with the war in Algeria. The theater must take all these problems and transmute them into mythic form. I don't think a playwright's commitment consists simply in stating political ideas. That can be done through public meetings, newspapers, agitation, and propaganda. The playwright who usurps their function may perhaps interest the reading public, but he will not have written a play.

TYNAN   But could an author of extreme right-wing views ever succeed in creating a work of art?

SARTRE In my opinion, no. Because nowadays although the right may still be in control of events, to the extent that it still has power, it has lost the ability to understand them. It has surrendered most of its old ideals and has not replaced them; it does not understand the nature of its adversaries. The fact, for example, that General Challe could declare in court that the army in Algeria was riddled with communist infiltration—the fact that a man can say that proves to what degree of incomprehension the right is driven by its inability to face facts.

In the presence of so many accumulated misunderstandings, how can the right create a work of art? For a work of art, even if it is nonpolitical, must proceed from an understanding of one's era, it must be in harmony with the age. One can't imagine a modern play that could be at the same time right-wing and good.

TYNAN Which contemporary playwrights do you most admire?

SARTRE Brecht, incontestaby, although he is dead—and in spite of the fact that I do not use his techniques or share his artistic principles. Then, on a different level, there are certain plays of Genet. His work is a game played with mirrors and reflections, very beautiful and very expressive of its era.

TYNAN You once said that you admired *Waiting for Godot* more than any other play since 1945.

SARTRE That is true. I have not liked Beckett's other plays, particularly *Endgame*, because I find the symbolism far too inflated, far too naked. And although *Godot* is certainly not a right-wing play, it represents a sort of universal pessimism that appeals to right-wing people. For that reason, although I admire it, I have reservations. But precisely because its content is somewhat alien to me, I can't help admiring it the more.

TYNAN Are there any English or American playwrights who appeal to you?

SARTRE Arthur Miller, certainly. And Tennessee Williams

clearly has something, although his world is very different from mine, and his work is permeated with subjective myths. One of the troubles with the theater is that when a play moves from one country to another, it often takes on a completely different meaning. As the audience changes, the play changes.

I am disturbed by this question of transplanting works of art. I remember seeing a remarkable Mexican film: it told of a one-eyed child, who was an object of derision to other children.[7] According to the film, one-eyed people are considered comic in Mexico. The child prays to heaven for a miracle; his mother sends him on a pilgrimage, and they pray together. Meanwhile, a firework display is being held to celebrate the fiesta, and a spark falls into the boy's good eye, blinding him. Even in Mexico, according to the film, blind people are not comic.

Now is this story a savage joke at the expense of religion? Or is the author presenting his belief that, although miracles may be terrible things, they are still miracles? The answer must remain a mystery for those who don't know Mexico.

But in general, films are simple enough to travel freely. American films in particular are more popular here than any others. American plays, by contrast, never get acclimatized in France: they always fail.

TYNAN   Would you like to revisit America?[8]

SARTRE   Frankly, I would rather not. I wouldn't enjoy seeing people in the state of mind that exists in America today. It would grieve me to see people so restless, so uneasy. And to the extent that they were too violent, too full of oversimplifications, I would feel discontented. Nevertheless, I used to like America very much. Very much indeed.

TYNAN   You recently wrote a film script for John Huston about the life of Freud.[9] Could you tell me something about it?

SARTRE   Except in construction, the final script has little resemblance to what I wrote. The fault is partly mine, and partly Freud's. My scenario would have been impossible to shoot; it would have lasted seven or eight hours. As you know, one can make a film four hours long if it has to do with Ben-Hur, but a Texas audience won't sit through four hours of complexes. Hence the script was cut down to ninety minutes or so. I haven't seen the final version, and I don't know if I shall leave my name on it; that depends on the contract.

However, what we tried to do—and this was what interested Huston especially—was to show Freud, not when his theories had made him famous, but at the time, around the age of thirty, when he was utterly wrong; when his ideas had led him into hopeless error. You know that at one point he seriously believed that what caused hysteria was fathers raping their daughters. We begin in that period, and follow his career up to the discovery of the Oedipus complex.

That, for me, is the most enthralling time in the life of a great discoverer—when he seems muddled and lost, but has the genius to collect himself and put everything in order. Of course, it is difficult to explain this development to an audience ignorant of Freud. In order to arrive at the right ideas, one must start by explaining the wrong ones, and that is a long process: hence the seven-hour scenario.

The other problem was that Freud, like the majority of scientists, was a good husband and father who seems never to have deceived his wife, and even to have been a virgin before he was married. One hears rumors of previous escapades, but I ascribe them to the devotion of his admirers; the psychoanalysts don't want us to think that this man, who knew so much about sexuality, came to marriage utterly unfledged. In short, his private life was not very cinematic.

We therefore tried to blend the internal and the external elements of Freud's drama; to show how he learned from his patients the truth about himself. To take one instance, we show how the memory of the hysterical girls who told him their fathers had raped them provoked in him feelings of violent aggression towards his own father. And finally these two approaches—from the interior and from the exterior—meet in the discovery of the Oedipus complex.

TYNAN   Can one deal with Freud's life from a social viewpoint?

SARTRE   We have tried. There is one great problem that the analysts tend to sidetrack: Viennese anti-Semitism. It seems to me that Freud was profoundly aggressive, and that his aggressions were determined by the anti-Semitism from which his family suffered. He was a child who felt things very deeply, and probably immediately.

TYNAN   Do you think Freud's discoveries will be of permanent importance?

SARTRE   Unquestionably. Unlike some of my friends, however, I am not convinced that the basis of human activity is sexual. Whether it is or not, I don't believe that this substructure of sexual need reappears intact in the superstructure of the personality. It may reappear, but on a completely new level and in a completely different form; as any believer in the dialectical process must agree. It can no longer be reduced to itself.

One may say that a man's politics reflect his sexual impulses, but one may just as well say that his sexual impulses reflect an underlying sympathy with humanity that may later be translated into political terms. In any event Freud was the first to say something that seems to me of capital importance: that everything which makes a man has meaning.

TYNAN   There are no accidents?

SARTRE   There are no accidents! And Freud's second great discovery was that even in the matter of self-knowledge, human progress derives from human need. I regard Freud as an excellent materialist. He did not single out hunger, because he came from a background where that kind of need did not apply; instead, he chose sexuality, which is equally necessary—not in the sense that a man would die without it, but in the sense that the lack of it may drive him mad.

TYNAN   So you think it is possible to build a bridge between Freud and Marx?

SARTRE   Certainly. I think the Marxists have lost a great deal by cutting themselves off so completely from psychoanalysis, by refusing to accept it. Of course, Freud used his analytic discoveries to bolster up a great many historical theories that hold little interest for any sociologist, least of all for a Marxist. What matters is his demonstration that sexual desire is not simply sexual desire, but something that will encroach upon a man's whole personality, even affecting the way he plays the piano or the violin. That, I think, is a permanent contribution.

TYNAN   Many people, surveying your work as a whole, have remarked that in an age of equality you are the only playwright who creates outsize heroes, gigantic protagonists like Goetz in *Le Diable et le Bon Dieu*, Edmund Kean in your Dumas adaptation, and Franz in *Altona*. Isn't this something of a paradox?

SARTRE   There must be some personal reason; there are always personal reasons—as with the crabs in *Altona*! At bottom, I am always looking for myths; in other words, for subjects so sublimated that they are recognizable to everyone, without recourse to minute psychological details.

Let me give you an example. If I write another play, it will be about the relationship of a husband and a wife. In itself, that would be boring, and so I shall take the Greek myth of Alcestis.[10] If you recall, Death comes to seek out King Admetus. This doesn't please Admetus at all; "I have things to do," he says, "I have my kingdom to rule, I have a war to win!" And his wife Alcestis, who regards herself as utterly superfluous, offers to die in his place. Death accepts the bargain; and then, taking pity on her, sends her back to life. That is the plot. But my version would imply the whole story of female emancipation: the woman chooses the tragic course at a moment when her husband has refused to face death. And when she returns, she is the powerful one, because poor Admetus will always be the man of whom it is said, "He allowed his wife to die for him!"

TYNAN   But will ordinary people recognize themselves in characters like those?

SARTRE   I think so. I don't remember ever having had difficulties of that sort. *Altona*, for example, was supported by the *petits bourgeois*, not by the rich bourgeoisie who usually keep the theater alive.

TYNAN   And the proletariat?

SARTRE   That is another matter. In Paris, they never come to the theater except to see a comic opera or an operetta. Little by little, they were pushed out of the city during the nineteenth century, and they established their life on the outskirts. They hardly ever return; as a theatrical audience, they scarcely exist.

TYNAN   If *Altona* were presented in Moscow, do you think the public would support it?

SARTRE   Yes. Because in Moscow the working class—even perhaps the peasantry—is much further evolved than ours. Not because of modern Soviet literature, but because of the immense diffusion in Russia of nineteenth-century literature. These people really discuss things in their factories; they make their own choices, and care about the choices they make. They are devoted to educating themselves. Ilya Ehrenburg[11] told me that the soundest criticisms he received came not from the critics but from his readers. That isn't the case here.

TYNAN   Some years ago, I saw *La Putain respectueuse* in Moscow, very much lengthened and simplified. Were the changes made with your consent?

SARTRE   I didn't see the production,[12] but I agreed to an optimistic ending, as in the film version, which was made in France.[13] I knew too many young working-class people who had seen the play and been disheartened because it ended sadly. And I realized that those who are really pushed to the limit, who hang on to life because they must, have need of hope.

TYNAN   Is it true that you have abandoned your novel about the French Resistance?[14]

SARTRE   Yes. The situation was too simple. I don't mean that it is simple to be courageous and risk one's life: what I mean is that the choice was too simple. One's allegiances were obvious. Since then, things have become much more complicated; much more romantic, in the literary sense of the term. There are many more intrigues and crosscurrents. To write a novel whose hero dies in the Resistance, committed to the idea of liberty, would be much too easy. Nowadays, commitment is altogether harder to define.

TYNAN   The era of simplicity has passed: do you think we shall ever arrive at a new simplicity?

SARTRE   If our society can disengage itself from the cold war; if it can manage to shed its colonies in peace; and if there is an evolution of the West under the influence of the East, I see no reason why Soviet communism need be exported to the West. What I hope is that something will happen akin to the Counter Reformation that followed Protestantism—a movement in the other direction. Just as Catholicism has evolved its own kind of Protestantism, I look forward to a day when the West will become socialist, without ever passing through communism. At that moment, I seriously believe, simplicity will be reborn.

Myth and Reality in Theater

This is a lecture delivered in Bonn on December 4, 1966. It was taken down by J.-P. Berckmans and J.-C. Garot and was published in a Belgian monthly magazine, *Le Point*, in January 1967. As Sartre was speaking in French to a German audience, he had to slow down his delivery for the simultaneous translation and was therefore unable to reach the conclusions he had intended to draw.

Today, after the works of Ionesco, Beckett, Adamov, Jean Genet, and Peter Weiss and the success of Brecht's plays, which has spread far beyond the borders of Germany, we can no longer talk about the theater as we used to. Indeed, the real question is, Has the appearance of what is called the "New Theater"[1] caused a revolution in the theater? Not really; it is not a revolution, because these playwrights, with their quite different backgrounds and quite different aims, cannot be brought under any single head. They have been called the writers of the "theater of the absurd," but the title itself is absurd in the first place, because none of them regards human life and the world as an absurdity. Genet certainly does not; he studies the *relation* between images and mirages; nor Adamov, who is a Marxist and has written, "No theater without ideology"; nor even Beckett, about whom I shall have more to say a little later. What they in fact represent either through their inner conflicts or through their contrast with each other is a flare-up of the contradictions which are the very basis of dramatic art. For there is no art which is not a "qualitative unit" of contradictions. The novel itself is full of contradictions and mutually destructive presuppositions. The theater has contradictions of its own, which it has hitherto passed over in silence.

What has happened is that for years, for centuries, the theater combined the roles of theater and cinema for audiences that needed the film but had no inkling of what it could be, for it had not yet been invented. Contrary to the common assertion, the emergence of the cinema did not plunge the theater into a crisis nor did it injure the art of theater. It did in fact injure some theatrical producers by depriving them of part of their public, and it did harm a certain type of theater, specifically the type which was a substitute for the cinema, that is to say the bourgeois realistic theater—realistic in that its aim was the accurate representation of reality—and harmed it because after a certain date cinematographic realism seemed to have downgraded theatrical realism permanently (to someone seeing a film a tree is a real tree, whereas a tree on the stage always looks false). In short, the film showed up the theater's artificial tree as mere scenery and the false act as mere gesture. But that did not harm the theater—far from it. For the theater immediately pondered its own limitations and, like any other art, converted them into the prerequisites for its true potentialities.

After what Nietzsche called the Death of God and the death of inspiration—God-whispering-in-the-writer's-ear—

we had the critical novel of writers like Flaubert and the critical poetry of writers like Mallarmé, or in other words an art compounded of the artist's reflections on art. The emergence of the cinema, coupled with various social factors, made for the emergence of what we may call *critical theater* around 1950.

I regard all the writers whose differences and similarities we shall be discussing as representatives of *critical theater*. All of them are trying to convert the very inadequacies of theater into instruments for communication. Take unreality, for example: some of them may find the gesture in itself a specifically theatrical medium, inasmuch as gesture rather than act is what should appear in theater. It is precisely here that the work of each of them, as a reflection on the theater translated into a play contrasts with that of the others and even with some of their own, precisely because each of them chooses one or another of the contradictions of theater. Thus, by examining these writers, we shall see what kinds of contradiction exist in dramatic art itself and how each writer stands in relation to them. We shall, therefore, now have to discuss the inner conflicts in dramatic presentation.

The first conflict we find is that between ceremony and the single and irreversible form of presentation. Should theater, which had its origins in the masses in Europe and in ritual songs and dances in the East, keep its ceremonial character once it has been secularized, as Jean Genet wishes to do and as the French classics who wrote in verse did? If so, you have to communicate with the audience through the sympathetic magic produced by certain rites. Jean Genet's play *The Blacks*[2] is quite simply a Black Mass. Its effect upon a white audience is certainly disquieting—which is what Genet is aiming for. Slow incantations prepare us for a sacrificial act, which in fact is not performed, since it is the imaginary murder of a white girl. Nothing in fact happens. One of the characters says, "We shall have the courtesy, learned from you, to make communication impossible. We shall widen the initial distance between us by our ostentation, our manners, and our insolence, for we are players too." In short, the black rejected by the whites, incommunicable because of the whites' refusal to communicate, wishes to play out to the end the play-acting imposed upon him. He is, therefore, a theatrical subject both as himself and in life; he puts on the act and plays it because, according to Genet, the play-acting imposed upon him by the whites has became second nature to him. Thus, the choice of subject is reflective and critical; Genet did not go out to look for a good subject and a good plot, but deliberately chose to assert the power and limitations of theater by choosing a character who, according to him, can assert himself in life itself only through theater. And as their dramatic acting—the acting of blacks—is a repetition and exaggeration of the roles prescribed for them by others (the whites), which are unchanging, the form of the play and the ceremony are a single whole, since repetition is the characteristic of ceremony. What is being suggested to the spectator through this inflexible ritual, this playing out of a sacrifice which is not a sacrifice, is therefore the vanishing presence of the black, which conceals as much as it reveals the black truth. For the character who puts on the act on the stage because he is compelled to put it on in life partly reveals his truth by doing this, but also partly conceals it. We do not know what the player is in depth, and it is precisely this lack of knowledge, the notion that the actor is something other than an actor, which produces a disquiet, a malaise. The more the black plays what we wish him to play, the greater the depth at which we apprehend the menacing revolt, armed insurrection, and the affirmation of man through the liquidation of the colonizers who have been the executioners of the colonized blacks.

The fact remains that by identifying theater with ceremony in the persons of black actors (really actors, profes-

sionals from the black Les Griots company, yet falsely
actors, since the rhythm is imposed upon the characters they
are representing—fictitiously in revolt, since the blacks represent a concealed revolt, and really in revolt, since these
blacks were asserting the black personality against the colonizers), Jean Genet produces a play whose deeper meaning
is, as Georges Bataille has pointed out, the denial of those
listening to it. The ceremony magically possesses those hearing and seeing it and gradually teaches them to deny themselves.

This was one of the terms of the contradiction on which
I am now concentrating; but if we take the other term, Antonin Artaud—who wrote *Le Théâtre et son double* and was
long the director of the Théâtre Alfred Jarry[3]—has never
had so many followers as he has at present; a great many
of the younger writers in France and elsewhere are following his lead and regard him as the prophet of modern theater. Artaud does not much care for ceremony as repetition.
He holds that the primary characteristic of dramatic performance is precisely the reverse, its evanescence—a performance is an event, and if an actor has a lapse of memory,
the whole thing is abruptly brought to a halt—and its
uniqueness—every night it is unpredictable, the actors will
play well or badly depending on their own preoccupations
and depending, too, on the audience, for there are days
when, as Jean Cocteau says, "an audience shows genius"
and other days when the audience is terrible. So, depending
whether an actor acts well or badly, or even well one night
and badly another, and depending whether the audience is
interested in one part of the plot, one character, one aspect
of the play or another, the balance of a dramatic performance and its meaning change from day to day. From this
point of view, repetition is the characteristic of the cinema
rather than of the theater, according to Artaud. In the cinema the operator will run the same reel every night, the
actors will act with exactly the same talent (or lack of it)

and the only accidents that can prevent the showing will be technical; there will be no human relations between actors and spectators. As early as 1928 Artaud was so deeply impressed by this singularity and evanescence of performance that he wrote, "The theater will aim at being truly *an act*, subject to every twist and every turn of circumstance, and chance will always have its say. A production, a play will always be random and liable to revision, so that a spectator who goes back to see the play again a few nights later never sees the same performance."[4] The theatrical performance has, then, to be regarded as a nonrepeatable act. The ceremony, whose main characteristic is repetition, gives place to each day's singular adventure. The comparable thing in music would be the contrast between the jam session and the jazz record.

The essential difference between Genet and Artaud leaps to the eye, though both of them have their Brechtian aspects. Artaud remarks in the same context, "A performance will be as exciting as a card game in which the whole audience is participating,"[5] whereas Genet's aim was to put it under a spell while keeping it at a distance. In this sense, Artaud discarded the distance between actor and audience which both Genet and Brecht, though for totally different reasons, wished to preserve. Artaud's deeper reason—deliberately chosen by him—is that he assigns to theater the function of bringing out into the open by "the operation of magic" (to use Artaud's own terminology) the forces latent in the depths of each member of the audience—libido, obsession with sex, death, or violence; it must suddenly surge up in each of them. That is why Artaud was later to call his theater (a theater of which he only dreamed, for he was never to be able actually to bring it into being) the "theater of cruelty."

This contrast between Genet and Artaud expresses the two contrasting aspects of theater very neatly, because theater is both ceremonial repetition and violent drama renewed night after night; the world of theater holds us at a distance far more than the world of cinema does, yet we participate in it by identifying with one character or another. But the contrast goes further, and the further we pursue it, the more aware we become of yet another contradiction.

Artaud tells us, "I regard theater as an act." And sure enough, if we put ourselves in the playwright's or director's place, theater, the theatrical performance, is an act, a real act; for it is a job of work to write a play and a job of work to stage one, and the purpose of this work is to exert a real action upon an audience. Putting things at their lowest, taking the mass-consumer theater, the act consists in attracting as many people as possible and so producing a cash flow into the box office within the real economic channels of circulation. Putting them at their highest, the aim is to cause a definite change in the spectator's mentality, for at least as long as the performance lasts, if only by shocking him. But it is also true that if we put ourslves in the spectator's place, a play is something imaginary. That is, the spectator never loses sight of the fact that what he is being presented with—not even excepting historical plays—is something nonreal. The woman there does not exist, the man, her husband, is only in appearance her husband; he certainly does not really kill her. This means that the spectator does not believe—in the full sense of the word "believe"—does not believe in Polonius' murder. Otherwise, he would take to his heels or jump on the stage. But his belief itself is imaginary; that is, it is not a deep and vital conviction, but an autosuggestion which holds to the unformulated certainty that it is autosuggestion.

The result is that the feelings resulting from participation in the imaginary and the representation of the imaginary on the stage are themselves imaginary feelings, for they are both felt as things defined but not real—hence you can enjoy your fear if you go to what are called horror plays—and are not necessarily representative of the spectator's real emotional state. You know that in the mid-nineteenth century the stage performance of *Uncle Tom's Cabin* affected slaveowners to tears as long as the performance lasted, yet when the play was over, they continued to hold to their own manners and customs and their own ideas about blacks.

Owing to this further contrast between act and gesture, between real action and imaginary enchantment, the stances of modern playwrights and those who are often grouped together as "new theater" vary considerably. Thus, Genet thinks that the fact that a play of his is imaginary is not a defect but quite the reverse, a quality. What he has written about *The Balcony*[6] applies to all his other plays as well: "Don't act this play as if it were a satire on something or other. It is a glorification of the image and its reflection. Only if it is done in that way will its satirical or nonsatirical significance emerge." This radical stance parallels Genet's basic concern—man. To him the outlawed writer, the *poète maudit*, and the thief, outlawed *ipso facto* by society, the unreal and the evil, are one and the same. The adversary of the respectable who have doomed him from childhood to be nothing but imaginary, he revenges himself in his plays by presenting them with mirages that lure them to plunge headlong into the hell of the imagination's reflections which he has prepared for them. In short, his real intention as a writer is to compel the upright to become an imaginary villain for a few hours, and this gives him a twofold satisfaction. First, because he obliges the practical man sitting in his theater seat to become unreal, to slide into the imaginary into which he himself has plunged. Secondly, he compels the upright man to imagine people by identifying himself with Genet's characters and at the end of the play to feel guilt at his complicity with evil. There you have the point: in Genet's plays the imaginary is the spectator's compelled complicity with evil, the aim being to bring the upright under the spell of evil and to leave him still with his conscience at rest, but with a deep disquiet to which he knows no answer.

Brecht too engages with the imaginary, but for totally

different reasons. What he wishes to do is to show, to demonstrate, to make people grasp the inner dialectic of a process. Any true feeling harbored by the spectator, such as horror or fear, would hamper the communication of information. The spectator must be gripped by the action just strongly enough to perceive its mainsprings. *The Good Woman of Setzuan*, for example, is admittedly not a demonstration, but an enchanting fable which is not in the least frightening and does not evoke any violent feeling or sexuality or libido or anything of that sort, and which consequently enables the audience's reason—for it is to reason that the play appeals —to grasp through continuous amusement the fact that you cannot do good in a society based upon exploitation. So to Brecht imagination is simply a connecting link between reason and its object. That is why he does not hesitate to denounce it constantly on the stage as pure unreality. We are presented with stage devices and corpses which are deliberately shown as puppets precisely to prevent us from being instinctively horrified by them and to stop us from thinking of the resemblance of a live player stretched out on the ground to a corpse. Some of the characters wear masks, some do not; there are songs on the proscenium to present the characters' subjective feelings; there is a consistent refusal of emotion, a rupture, a cleavage in their very disorder. The difference between Genet and Brecht in this respect is that Genet makes the imaginary an end in itself.

This is the meaning of theater: its essential value is the representation of something which does not exist. Brecht uses this as a device. But there are two sides to trying to create the unreal. In one case the writer wishes for the feeling of unreality because that is what he believes in, as with Genet. In the other case, that of Brecht, the feelings are made unreal in order to prevent passion from prevailing over a reasonable conviction. On the other hand—and this is the other term of the contradiction—Artaud (who was a fellow-traveler of the Surrealists) is not satisfied with such results, as we have just seen; he regards them as petty. He requires representation to be an act. And he means act in the broadest and fullest sense, not just the work of producing an unreal object. The purpose of theater is to produce a veritable tidal wave in each spectator's soul. To that end, whatever element of the conventional—or, if you prefer, the classical—there may be in a play disintegrates; there is no plot in the strict sense, no scenery, and the surrealist effect to be produced is based on the principle that there is no difference between the real and the imaginary. It's an arguable principle, of course, but it does lead to reducing the fictitious element to a minimum and seeking for all the real means that really act upon the spectator. In *Le Théâtre et son double* he writes: "As to the musical instrumentation, the instruments will be used solely as objects, because the necessity to act immediately and profoundly upon the sensibilities through the organs involves finding absolutely unfamiliar qualities and vibrations of sound as accompaniment. . . . Special attention must be paid to lights and lighting, since the special action of light comes into play and the effects of the vibrations of light rays."[7] I could quote a score more passages which all show that the intention here is to discover means of directly conditioning an audience by real stimulants and inducers. We may well ask, therefore, why we should keep any semblance of fiction, as a general principle at any rate. Artaud wished to take the conquest of Mexico as a theme for one of his productions; but why would the general theme remain intact despite all the variations in its abstract unreality likely to occur from one day to the next, when real sounds and real lights are more effective in conditioning us? If theater is not an art but an act, as Artaud maintains, and if as an act it liberates the terrible forces dormant within us, and if the spectator is merely a potential actor who will shortly join in the dance with all the violence unleashed within him, then Artaud stopped halfway. If we are to be logical with Artaud's thesis, we should quite simply confront an audience with a *true* event and thus make belief total. The modern outcome of the theater of cruelty along these lines is what is known as the "happening."

The "happening"—which exists in France, England, America, and even Japan—is especially the occurrence of a real event. There is no stage; it occurs in a hall, on the floor of the hall, or in the street, or at the seaside; there is only a temporary difference, a difference in time, between the spectators and those whom we will now have to call agents rather than actors. The agents really do something, no matter what, but something provocative which causes a real event, no matter of what sort, to happen. Some performances exploit expectation or boredom to liberate forces. One of the commonest is a man entering—the agent—people look at him, there's no knowing what he'll do, he sits down on a chair, folds his arms, and goes on sitting for two hours. The sheer boredom of it provokes outbursts of violence among the spectators, tears of rage. One can also directly provoke the sexual instinct; for instance, there was a happening banned in Paris, in which a woman stood on the stage stark naked but covered with whipped cream and one could lick the cream off her. Sometimes the appeal is to the death instinct or the urge to violence. I saw a happening in which the throats of cocks were cut and the audience was sprinkled with blood—the interest never being in the particular fact, of course, because it is provided for in part beforehand, since if you are going to cut the throats of cocks, you obviously have to buy the cocks first, but in what really happens, which is the audience's reaction. The first reaction is almost invariably outrage, then conflict, for and against, with its train of violence; and then, in some cases, feelings such as sex or the removal of sexual inhibitions or the death-wish or whatever; and finally all the spectators and all the agents become welded in a single group. There was a case in Paris when a happening turned, for some unknown reason, into a demonstration against the Vietnam war, though no one had gone there with the slightest intention of demonstrating against anything.

The happening as a happening is a reality; it exists, it does in fact bring about some sort of liberation from complexes, and we can therefore regard it as a fact. The problem is rather what happens to representation as an appeal to an audience's free imagination. Isn't this conditioning by some factor, possibly with some added element of cruelty, the reverse of theater, or rather the point at which theater disintegrates? In most cases the happening is a cunning exploitation of the cruelty of which Artaud talked. In France, Lebel[8] subjects his audience to a form of sadism in which it is stunned by spasmodic flashes of light and intolerable sounds and is sprinkled with liquids, most of them causing disgusting stains; indeed, you have to wear old clothes to these happenings. On the whole, the spectators at the happening have reacted to the torture. Can we say that here we have transgressed the bounds within which the idea, the essence, of theater is contained? In England Peter Brook has tried to find a mixed form, a meaning between the happening and the performance, combining the two in the play he is currently producing called *US,* whose title is a provocation in itself because it means both "'us"—that is, us English— and "U.S."—the Americans; and its subject itself, so far as it has one, is also a direct provocation since it is the war in Vietnam. Only, the play has no meaning as a play; you can't really call it a play. The performance takes place on a stage before an audience; it is a sequence of scenes, words, and acts of violence with no connection between them other than the emotional context, confusedly based on two themes.

The first is the horror of the war in Vietnam; the second has more to do with the impotence of the left.

What we see is neither real—since after all it is being played by actors—nor unreal—since each movement refers only to the reality of the war in Vietnam.

And yet it is in fact the real that acts upon the audience, since it is the sounds, colors, and movements that finally produce either a trance or a stupor, depending on the member of the audience. The spectators are not asked to join in the performance; indeed, to some extent they are kept at a distance. They are, so to speak, assaulted by this deliberately disordered blend of interrupted sketches, breaking off just as the illusion is taking shape. And lastly, they are faced with a real event, a true happening, though the happening is repeated every night.

Someone on the stage opens a jar of butterflies, they fly out, and a hand holding a lighter or torch burns them. They are burned alive. This is obviously an allusion to the bonzes who set themselves alight and burned alive in Saigon. This happening is a happening because something really happens, for you have animals dying, and dying in agony. Yet it is not quite a happening, because the curtain falls, and the spectator, alone once more, leaves the theater in a state of confused despair compounded of stupor, hatred, and impotence.[9] There is no conclusion; indeed, what conclusion could there be? It's true that the Vietnam war is a crime. It's true that the left is wholly powerless to act. Is this theater? It is really an intermediate form where you can just as well say "It is theater" as "It isn't theater." Let's say, at all events, that if it is theater, it shows what we might well describe as the crisis of the imaginary in theater today.

Actually, if we look at things in this light, we find almost everywhere this strange and contradictory wish to present the public with a fiction that is reality. People attending these performances are aware of what is happening. Witness such experiments in documentary theater as *The Oppenheimer Trial*, which has just been put on in Germany and was produced by Vilar in France.[10] What is going on here is not a presentation of a reality transposed and reconstructed subjectively by a playwright, as with historical plays, but a repetition of the actual trial and of the words actually spoken at particular moments during it.

The result has been the reverse of what occurs in a happening. In the happening, the real ends by absorbing the imaginary. In the documentary, reality is converted into the imaginary; the imaginary devours the reality. One proof of this is that the play performed here in Germany and the play performed by Vilar were two totally different plays, as everyone knows.

Why were they different? Because they could not help reflecting the playwright's own perceptions. The trial of Oppenheimer lasted for days and days; so a selection of what was said had to be made. Now, selection is a writer's job; it's a choice, an option, it defines a character. What we saw in France and what you have seen here therefore have nothing in common with a reproduction of the trial of Oppenheimer. That was something else, and Oppenheimer himself becomes fictitious, for we never lose sight of Vilar, the famous French actor who is playing Oppenheimer. Oppenheimer at once ceased to be a real character and became fictitious, became Vilar's role. He was not seen as a real person, quite simply because Vilar was speaking French and the trial had been held in English. We were perfectly well aware of that. All the conventions that we are perfectly prepared to accept in real theater—where we see Englishmen talking to each other in French—they are all right, that's theater. But when it comes to presenting us with the Oppenheimer trial, all these people speaking French when they are expressing a real—and an American—situation become totally unreal; they cannot be Englishmen or Americans. So you had a sort of temporary illusion; as you looked at the object, you told yourself, "'This is a condensed trial, it's a trial that lasts for two weeks in illusion, but in representation in fact two hours." In reality, the trial in the play was rather a symbolic allusion to the trial: the "cipher" of the trial, the transposition revealing its abstract truth rather than a real reconstruction of it.

Thus, between the theatrical illusion, which is absorbed or devoured by the real, the sadistic action upon the spectator, as in the happening, and the represented real, as in the documentary, which, however, is devoured by the illusion, we see the crisis of the image.

In point of fact, right at the bottom of the happening there is a recourse to the image.

Because, at bottom, an event of any sort is symbolic of some other thing, for the real serves the unreal. I don't have the time to demonstrate this now, but if we at least assume it, we may say that even if this crisis had to lead to some degree of disintegration of theatrical forms, it does show the progress of reflection.

There is no longer any call to work with the indeterminate and confused principle of the playwright and the director of the past or the philosopher of theater of the past, who held that the essence of theater involved at its cruces a lack of differentiation between the real and the imaginary leading to the belief that a mirage presented and accepted as mirage necessarily appeals to the real feelings of an audience.

That is the Greek notion of catharsis. The complacency with which Gémier, around the turn of the century, scattered his actors around the house and had them file through the orchestra aisles and climb onto the stage clearly shows the innocence of the playwrights of that time. They simultaneously held that the place called the stage was an illusory place, a mirage, and that the character who was to get to the stage by way of the aisles would convince the audience of the reality of the performance because he brushed against them as he passed. But now all the dramatists of our generation no longer believe that theater is realistic, as we shall see shortly. For either you want reality, and if so, you must carry it through to the end, there's nothing for it but that—you evoke real feelings by real events; or you recognize the totally illusory character of dramatic representation, but if so, you have to exploit it as such—as a denial of reality (we shall revert to the meaning of this expression later) and not as an imitation of it.

The final contradiction—the most evident and the most basic—relates to the role of language in theater. The theatrical character is a human being or, as in *Chantecler*, an animal conceived anthropomorphically. Therefore, if he is the sum of human behaviors, regardless whether there is a plot or no, he must speak, since man is a speaking being. Language is therefore one of the means of stage expression. In the classical drama it was indeed the principal means; the great tragic actor in our classical tragedies hardly moves; he may even remain motionless for whole long speeches; the verbal incantation, inflection, rhythm, and rate of utterance, the marked caesura in the verse, the stress on a single word, render the situation, the passions, or the decisions. And further, in the French classics the world is wholly psychological; through his language Racine expresses only the psychological world. But the whole scene changes with the advent of the romantic tradition and the playwrights who drew on it.

These writers tried to encompass the whole world in language, all that is presented by nature, the world surrounding us—what you call the *Umwelt*—the furthest reaches of it and the obscure forces working within and outside us must be present directly or indirectly in the dialogue, as conscious signifier, as referent, or as subconscious superdeterminant of the message, or even as silence in this concept giving primacy to language. In France between the wars we had a type of theater called the theater of silence, its leading playwright being Jean-Jacques Bernard.[11] But it was in fact a very loquacious sort of theater, because the "theater of silence" really meant that language had appropriated silence. On one level, in these plays language expressed some superficial and humdrum aspect of life; in *Le Feu qui reprend mal*, for example, the husband and wife, the husband being a soldier returned from the war and his wife not finding him quite as he used to be; their conversations are empty and uneasy. But these conversations purposely refer to a subconversation. What emerges is that behind the empty words, in the silent pauses, there is the inaudible speech: "I know you don't love me any more"—"but that's not true; I need a little time; perhaps I do indeed love you less, and you too," and so on. Though unspoken, this whole conversation was wholly present like a verbal supersignification of the words that were spoken, their code, their real meaning.

Thus the theater of silence was panverbalism, the total conquest of the theatrical world by the word. Silence was no longer a matter of chance, as when one stops because one has nothing more to say or because one coughs or because one is waiting for someone to reply. Silence meant verbally miming a verbal content. Remaining silent was to bring the conversation to a climax just as the conflict reached its peak. In short, you could say that by the nineteen-fifties the theater had, so to speak, filled up its tank with words. Which means that everything lay in language. To some extent, no scenery was needed, and indeed many playwrights and directors discarded it, because decor is merely the illustration of what is spoken. Shakespeare's language, for example, always informs us about the external world. It is wholly unnecessary, therefore, to haul up a sun or use flashes of lightning when the stage direction is "lightning" or "thunder"; once it is said, it is represented. The visual element becomes superfluous because of the strength of the verbal element. Certainly there are forms of mute signification in theater; there are gestures—when a killing is done on stage, it must be seen to be done—but all of it (gestures, processions, colors, sounds sometimes) has only been an accompaniment to the word; theater was expected to say everything itself.

That is why modern theater has been the most apt to discard scenery. Barrault replaced the object by pantomiming which conjured it up and made it vanish again when his mime ended. He considered that quite sufficient. In an adaptation of a novel for the stage[12] he had in one scene to enter his lodgings, pass in front of the porter's lodge, and climb the stairs to his room on the third floor. Quite obviously, the porter's lodge and the stairs become wholly unnecessary once he is in his room, and consequently inert and a nuisance. Miming a few words to the invisible porter and miming climbing the stairs was more than enough. The world is produced by mime and expressed by theater. But the new theater is in fact emerging from a conflict about speech. Actually, the sovereignty of speech in the theater accentuates the imaginary; when mimed or spoken a tree, rain, the moon exist only as completely unreal allusions. They cannot act physically and really upon the audience's active faculties in any way.

Now, if we take Artaud and his search for ways of reaching into the spectator's inmost depths by real means of conditioning (carefully devised sounds and lights), obviously he was likely to give language only a secondary function right from his earliest writings on the theater. In his "Théâtre de la cruauté"[13] he says that he will use words less for their significatory value than for their real force. If I tell the story of the death of Pompey on the stage, as Corneille did, I reduce the emotive force of the words because I dilute it in an imaginary tale. According to Artaud, when a word charged with force and power is spoken at the right moment under a certain light in a particular voice produced by free association from a nonsignifying verbal assemblage—such as the word "murder" or "mother" or "blood" or a sexual word—it can directly assault the spectator and force his subconscious verbal organization up into the full light of day, as in psychiatric treatment. This is an extreme attitude toward language. There is a clear contrast between the theater of Claudel, who prides himself on being more or less the organization of "intelligible dust," as he puts it, and the attitude of Artaud, who subordinates speech to real action.

The contemporary theater has produced mixed solutions because of the rather different matters with which it is concerned. The origin is doubtless the conviction which has slowly been making itself felt that, as Lacan puts it, "the Freudian subconscious is structured like a language." To put it briefly, they set out more or less explicitly from the same notion as Artaud's, but the concept of language as the "masked face of our destiny" is growing stronger and stronger. It might be said that Heidegger's remark, "Man behaves as if he were the creator and master of language whereas it is language that is and remains his suzerain," would apply to many contemporary writers, whether they know the remark or not. If we substitute "character" for "man," we shall understand many of the experiments in modern theater. In the theater of discourse, even if the character does not tell all, even if the conversation refers to a subconversation, the writer behaves as if he and his heroes were masters of language. They say or indicate what they consciously wish to say. But if, as many people believe, language is the master of man and forms his person and his destiny, and if the laws of language are not practical recipes for communicating and expressing ideas, but are seen to be prehuman necessities shaping man in the fashion of physical laws, then the playwright will no longer consider speech the sovereign instrument which the hero is completely free to use as he pleases, but will on the contrary wish to show it as the master of man. To Ionesco and his followers language is primordial and is no longer the hero's chosen way of expressing himself at all. On the contrary, they wish to show it developing inhumanly through man, imposing its laws upon him despite the speaker's effort to signify something, depriving him of his own signifiers and driving him by sheer verbal force to acts which he had no intention of committing and which will simply take form to predetermine him in proportion as the speech continues to take form. In *The Lesson*[14] the teacher murders his pupil at the end of his speech, which he certainly did not intend at the beginning of it. Language in Ionesco's early plays is therefore the hero, the protagonist. It is sovereign in the exact degree to which this theater dethrones man. These are, therefore, plays of language, but you can see how far Ionesco differs from Claudel. There are still characters in them, imaginary characters, but they are purposely colorless, for they are simply what is said by and through them.

The theater is losing its anthropomorphism and is starting on what is now called by one style of writing in France the "decentering of the subject." We now have only a single object before us, language or speech. Is this object real or imaginary? Is it the way of Artaud's act or Genet's mirage? Ionesco seems to be something intermediate. He is trying to reveal language by letting it speak for itself, but at the same time he pushes it to absurdity, even though this absurdity proves logical. Hence, he proclaims language as inhuman. Take the first long speech in *The Bald Soprano*,[15] in which a woman gives a list of what she has eaten and talks of the English dishes she has had—since she is English and in England—and says she has had English sauce and ends by saying, We drank English water. Now, it's quite clear that it's both perfectly logical, since all the dishes are listed in English—including English water— and perfectly absurd, for though she is in England, water is generally regarded as a universal element. The way in which the language runs is driven to the absurd by its logic through the woman, contributes to making it unreal and to showing us by exaggeration and an unreal language that true language—the same language but without the exaggeration—contributes wholly to the enslavement of man.

The theater of the direct, the classical theater converted into the theater of the bourgeoisie, contained contradictions of which it was unaware. So while the plays differed in content, all of them referred to the same forms of theater, comedy, tragedy, melodrama, and the rest. Now that the new theater, critical theater, has discovered these contradictions as repetitive ceremonies/ singular events/ enchantment by the same mirages/ real conditioning by act/ glorification of the imaginary/ sadism of reality/ mastery of language by man, and panverbalism/ language-as-man's-destiny, or a simple and invariably treacherous device for a conditioned subjectivity, the writers who adhere to this new theater no longer differ solely in their content, but chiefly in the terms of the contradiction for which they have opted. Does this mean that the theater is in a state of disintegraion? No, merely that it is dedicated to self-examination and the exploration of greater depths.

Far from expressing a decomposition and dispersal in disorder, the disintegration of a new medium represents the dialectical synthesis of the real contradictions of an art. If we view all these contradictions comprehensively and if we take the sum of the contemporary plays representative of them, we in fact encompass all theater; not all theater with the obscure contradiction concealed in it, but rather all theater as a dialectical process which, through its contradictions, makes for unity and progress and may at any time reconstitute the integrated synthesis by the emergence of a work which has been generated by and has transcended its contradictions. If, too, we look at all the plays in the new theater together, we find that they have several things in common. These are negative, indeed rejections, but rejections from which we can, I think, derive an intimation of a future unity. In essence, there are three forms of rejection in the contemporary theater: a rejection of psychology, a rejection of plot, and a rejection of realism of any sort.

All of these playwrights reject these three for the same reasons. In rejecting psychology they are rejecting the predominance of the bourgeoisie, for psychological drama is basically ideological, holding, as it does, that man is not conditioned by historical and social factors, that there is such a thing as psychological determinism, and that human nature is the same everywhere. These playwrights, regardless of whether they are political or nonpolitical, reject this simply because they consider that all that counts is the fundamental—no matter whether it is language or being-in-the-world or the social factor in the deepest and broadest sense of the term "social," so long as it is not the verbal play of psychology. The rejection of psychology implies a desire to reach down into the forces latent deep within us either through the imaginary or through the reality of an assault upon them.

Far from being in any way afraid of shocking audiences, all the authors I have mentioned deliberately try to shock them, since the result of shock should be some sort of relaxation of inhibitions. I believe that Beckett was speaking for all of them when he exclaimed as he heard the whole audience frantically applauding the first night of *Waiting for Godot*,[16] "My God, there must be something wrong, it isn't possible, they're applauding it!" Because in fact all these playwrights, regardless of whether they believe in the imaginary or the real, maintain that, strictly speaking, audiences ought not to accept a play until after they have been shocked to the core.

This, indeed, is the reason why they reject the convenience of plot. There is no longer a plot in the sense of a well-constructed anecdote with a beginning, middle, and end; there is no plot any more because they believe that plot means diverting and distracting the audience's attention from the essential. The purpose of plot was to please. They do not want to please; they want a subject, that is to say a developing total theme rather than recipes for constructing an anecdote within a tale. They are not in favor of discarding the whole idea of construction, but they try to construct the subject within a tight frame; their construction is basically concerned with time—which is the raw material of drama. Their purpose is not to tell some trifling tale, but to construct a temporal object in which time will mark out what is the subject in the strict sense by its contradictions and structural components. Lastly, they reject realism, because realism is at bottom an entire philosophy for which they have no use. In the first place, it is a philosophy which seems to them bourgeois, and in the second place, they do not accept the notion that reality is realistic. In fact, reality is realistic at the conversational level. In other words, we adjust to the real when we chat about insignificant matters. At the level on which they want to work, which for all of them (no matter whether it is comic, tragic, or simply blackly humorous) is the level of the subterranean forces or, if you prefer it, the level of the human adventure, on that level the essential conditions of the human adventure are no longer realistic because we can no longer really grasp them. We cannot grasp a death, we are still incapable of thinking death through, even if we are convinced, as I am, that it is no more than a purely biological process; for even if it is, the sudden absence, the interrupted dialogue, is a thing that cannot be realized. Consequently, if we wish to speak about life, we cannot speak about it as realists. And if we wish to speak about birth, our birth, something we have never consciously experienced and yet something which has made us what we are, here again realism has no meaning since we cannot realize our birth.

These three rejections of the world show that the new theater is in no way absurd, but is returning, through criticism, to the great fundamental theme, which is, after all, man as event and man as History within the event.

The Actor

In the first volume of *L'Idiot de la famille* (Paris: Gallimard, 1971), Sartre has to elucidate the existential status of the actor in order to explain one of the stages in the making of Flaubert the writer. Here and in the following piece, "The Comic Actor," we reproduce four selections which together make up an original restatement of the "paradox of the actor" which Sartre had already discussed in his adaptation of *Kean*.

Affirmation is common in plays. Characters may make mistakes, affirm things in a fit of passion, fake their testimony, but nonetheless they see and say what they see, and everything they do is an act. I have come to the conclusion, however, after attending many rehearsals, that most actors are incapable of *representing* affirmative behavior on the stage. In private life they are just as prone to affirm or deny as the members of their audiences, that is to say, every minute of their lives. But as soon as they come on stage, action gives place to passion. If you are to listen to them, they are enduring what they are saying; they will use every sort of device to convince—warmth of tone, impetuosity, the un-controlled violence of desire or hate—except certainty of judgment based on evidence. This when expressed is an invitation to reciprocity; being free itself, it appeals to the freedom of others, but the actor wishes to convince by *contagion*. He has hardly said, "The weather is breaking up," before we become aware that we are entering the world of weeping and gnashing of teeth. He *does not know* that the weather has broken; judging by appearances, he feels some sort of misery in his bones which wrings the words from him like an outcry. There is only one way of accounting for this strange behavior: that every dramatic work is phantasmagoric; however deeply the player is committed to his role, he is never wholly unaware that his character is unreal. He may well say, of course, after the performance that the play is true, and he may even be right. But it is a different kind of truth; it relates to the playwright's deeper intention and the reality he is trying to achieve through images. In short, the whole of Hamlet as a play by Shakespeare delivers a truth, but Hamlet as the hero of the play is a phantom. Regardless of his own opinion about the basic meaning of a drama, the actor is bound to reproduce the total work, word for word and gesture by gesture; and this means that he moves in an imaginary universe, which may be true as a whole, but is not true in detail. The Truth is there, however, the word is spoken in the play, and the error of one protagonist and the lie of another are revealed to the audience. But what is this really save *imitating* the stupidity of the one and the turpitude of the other? On the other hand, affirmation, certainty, evidence, never appear on the stage; we merely see imitations of them which may or may not be convincing. They are, indeed, *invariably unconvincing*, for only a debased image can be presented of the *fiat*.[1] This does not imply that the player lacks talent, but that the material is at fault. Since representation strictly excludes praxis of any sort, the resolute will is replaced by transports of feeling, or in other words, the will has to be depicted by its opposite. If a prince says, "I am a prince," that is an act; but if Kean says he is the prince of Denmark, that is passion filled out by gesture. Discourse in the theater gives no hold to verbal acts; the memorized speech flows along and can neither promote nor receive them. Kean is not Hamlet, and he knows it and knows that we know it. What can he do? Demonstrate it? He cannot. The evidence is integrated in the imaginary whole even before it has been provided. Hamlet can, if he wishes, convince the gravediggers or the soldiers he meets on the road, but he will never convince us. The only means he has to ensure that the play shall exist *through us* is to infect us with it. It is a contagion through the emotions, in which the actor lays siege to us, enters us, excites our passions by his feigned passions, draws us into his character, and dominates our heart with his. The more closely identified we are with him, the closer we shall come to sharing his belief, even while our own remains imaginary. However deeply felt, it is neutralized; and in any case it is *belief* and nothing more. The actor will not attempt to do without the pathetic register—which is also the register of Faith—for if he did so, nothing would remain save a frigid interest. It is here that an experienced actor will be careful to avoid delivering as truths observations or speeches with any universal reference, for they may concern us directly. Hamlet's soliloquy, a somber meditation and an inner pause for reflection, a perplexed ruminating of obsessions, brooding uncertainties, and flashes of illumination, should properly be murmured in monotone, in a dull, uninflected voice, for he is *voicing* his passions and has withdrawn to a distance; and his concerns are ours—life, death, action, suicide. Everything is generalized: to be or not to be. Who is asking the question? Anyone, if we are to go by the words alone. It may be *me*, in my present reality. But if the doubts and arguments apply universally and are likely to take on the nature of a sermon, even for a single moment, and to be applicable to me or to be a reflection on man's common condition, the whole thing falls to pieces, just as when an actor in a film suddenly turns his gaze on the house and seems to be staring straight at us. The *act*—for staring is an act—destroys the fiction; Hamlet dies and all that is left is a man in a doublet bringing us a message from Shakespeare. Every player of the role, reasoning in this way, tries to *singularize* the soliloquy; he is bound to see to it that we do not find that the words may be addressed to us, so he tries to confine us within the character and to imprison us in a world of belief: no, no, there is not a trace of truth in all this—or if there is, you will have to await the end of the play to find it—but merely anguish, no more, and it hardly concerns you, for what have you in common with a Danish prince as seen by a seventeenth-century Englishman? The sentences you hear are not even subjective observations, the evidence of a courageous lucidity. They spurt out in spasms from *experienced* sufferings as blood spurts from a wound; all in all, they are designed to embody, far more than to express, Hamlet's anguish. The soliloquy will therefore be *acted*; and we shall be lucky if the prince refrains from rolling about on the boards or spares us his sobs. When the actor knows his job, we remain captive to Hamlet till the curtain falls. Captives to belief, for it is belief that, in the full blaze of the footlights, masks from us the universality of the truths which the author darts at us like arrows. Believing is not acting; we are paralyzed, and this restrains us from going out to meet the ideas winging their way toward us. We have only to *suffer* them, so that we do not have to recognize the praxis of thinking in them. The player of the role himself has not needed to reflect; from his very first line he enters into belief and emerges from it only with his last line, or sometimes even slightly later. He does not think; he feels. Is thinking—as has often been said—a handicap to a player? It is worse: it is an impossibility in the practice of his craft, even at rehearsals. The reason why the best actors deliver affirmative lines so badly is that nothing is known, everything believed. Everything is doubly alienated —from the author, who is free to impose the lines, beliefs, and passions, and from the spectators, who can maintain their faith and carry it to the limit or else suddenly lose grip of it and awake, solitaries, confronting horrified sleepwalkers.

(Pp. 167–70)

No one can act a play without permitting himself to be totally and publicly devoured by the imaginary. The imaging act as a general principle is the act of a consciousness focused on an abstract or nonexistent object through a form of reality which I have elsewhere termed an *analogon*,[2] functioning as a symbol rather than a sign, that is to say, as a materialization of the object on which it is focused. Materialization here does not mean realizing an object, but precisely the reverse: unrealizing the material through the function it has to perform. When I look at a portrait, the canvas, the patches of dried pigment, and even the frame compose the *analogon* of the object—the man now dead whom the painter used as both model and, combined in an indissoluble unit with it, work—intentionally totalizing the appearances gathered around this illustrious countenance. With what are improperly called "mental images" the imaging intention treats my body's part-attributes (such as phosphenes and eye and finger movements or the sound of my breathing) as *analogon*, and I am partly unrealized by it, for my organism is still the existent real which is detached from being at only one point.* With an actor things are entirely different, for an actor's aim is to make an absent or fic-

* In another sense, however, the unrealization must be regarded as total in every case. But that is not the point in this case. (*Note by Sartre*)

titious object manifest through the totality of his individual-
ity, treating himself as a painter treats his canvas and pal-
ette. When Kean walks the boards at Drury Lane, he gives
Hamlet his gait; his real movement downstage to upstage
disappears, no ones notices it any longer, and besides,* the
comings and goings of this wiry little man are meaningless
in themselves and have no conceivable purpose other than
to wear out his shoes. But the audience and Kean himself
are absorbed into the prince of Elsinore's gait as he strolls
about soliloquizing. And this applies to the actor's gestures,
voice, and physique. The spectator's perception unrealizes
itself into imagination; he is not observing Kean's mannerisms, gait, and "style." Diderot is right that the actor does
not really experience his character's feelings; but it would
be wrong to suppose that he is expressing them quite coldly,
for the truth is that he experiences them *unreally*. Let us
concede that his real personal feelings, such as stage fright
—"you exploit your stage fright"—serve him as an *analogon*
and through them he aims at the passions that he has to
express. The player's technique is not based on an exact
knowledge of his body and the muscles he must contract to
express a particular emotion; more or less complex and more
or less conceptualized, it consists primarily in using this
analogon for the imaginary emotion which he must experience fictitiously. For feeling in the unreal is not *failing to
feel*, but deliberately deceiving oneself about the meaning
of what is being felt; indeed, the player clings to the unack-
nowledged certainty that he is not Hamlet at the very moment when he is publicly *manifesting himself* as Hamlet and
for the purposes of demonstration is obliged to convince
himself that he is Hamlet. Here the audience's partisanship
supplies him with an ambiguous confirmation; for on the
one hand, it consolidates the materialization by socializing

---

* Let us put it this way: the general anxiety to *render* Hamlet
finally becomes an obsession, so that any and all circumstances of real
life are seized upon as a pretext for derealization. (*Note by Sartre*)

it ("What is going to happen? *What will the prince do* after this new stroke of fate?"), and on the other, it turns the player of the role back upon himself in that he holds the house in suspense and knows that he will be applauded in due course. But from this very ambiguity he derives a fresh incentive, which in turn serves him as an *analogon* of his personal emotions.* Moreover, a role always encompasses automatic reactions (habits acquired during rehearsals) controlled by an unremitting vigilance, which, whether expected or unexpected, are nevertheless set in motion at precisely the right moment, surprise him, and readily lead through the unreal into the spontaneous imaginary, provided that he can direct them even as he abandons himself to them. It is this vigilance that enables him to say after the curtain falls, "I was bad tonight" or "I was good," but these judgments apply both to Kean, the flesh-and-blood individual whose job is to amuse the audience, and to a Hamlet who devours him; and from one day to another they will be profound or mediocre to a greater or lesser degree. Thus, to the true actor each new character becomes a temporary *imago*, a parasite living in symbiosis with him even when he is not on stage and at times unrealizing him when he is about his daily business off the stage by dictating attitudes to him. His most effective defense against madness is less his inner certainties—he is little given to reflection, and if his role requires him to rise to reflection, his real Ego also serves him as an *analogon* of the imaginary being he is embodying—than the heartbreaking conviction that the character takes everything from him and gives him nothing in return; for though Kean may offer *his being* to Hamlet,

---

* I do not claim that the unrealization is continuous. The merest trifle (such as giggles on stage or an aside under the nose of the audience to the actress playing opposite him) suffices for it to give place to cynicism; but that is all that is needed, too, to pass from cynicism to exaltation and an unrealization of its exploitation. The reason is that this takes place within a general project of unrealization in which the incursions of the real are mere incidentals. (*Note by Sartre*)

Hamlet will never offer Kean his, since Kean *is* Hamlet, frantically, entirely, *heart and soul*, but with no reciprocity, that is, with the sole reservation that Hamlet *is not* Kean. Which means that the player sacrifices himself to the existence of an *appearance* and as an alternative becomes a medium for nonbeing.

This does not necessarily mean that the actor has chosen unreality for its own sake. He may have wished to lie in order to tell the truth, like the actors trained by Stanislavski and his school—even though this wish itself may be suspect. At any rate, without a detailed knowledge of his life, there is no way of judging his basic choice of alternatives. Even if his choice is "realistic," however, it involves a certain preference for total unreality far more definitely than a writer's or a painter's choice does. The sculptor's material is external to him, is in the world; what his chisel unrealizes is the block of marble; the novelist's material is language, the signs traced by him on the page: both can claim to be working unremittingly at being themselves.* The actor cannot, for his material is his person and his aim is to be some other person in unreality. Every actor, of course, acts being what he is. But Kean, Kean acts being what he is not and what he knows he cannot be. So each night he recommences a metamorphosis which he knows will stop on the way, always at the same point. And it is from this very incompletion that he draws his pride in the fact that he would not be admired for "being" the character so well unless everyone,

---

* What supports him in his effort to be unreal, and perhaps even when he is not making an effort, is his "stance"—a set of postures, motions, and attitudes suggested by the author or the director. You often hear the actor playing a role say during rehearsals that he *does not feel* the suggestion: "Act that sitting? Say that moving upstage? No, my friend, I *don't feel it*." The *feeling*—the attitude helping out speech—here represents a connecting link between real sensations (kinesthesia, coenesthesis, postures) and their exploitation by the imaginary; if he gets up to speak, suddenly springing from the armchair will predispose him to feel in the unreal the indignation that caused the character to spring to his feet. (*Note by Sartre*)

starting precisely with himself, knew that he was not. So that not everybody can make a career on the boards; the basic requirement is not talent or natural aptitude, but a certain *constituted* relation between the real and unreality, without which a player would not even think of subordinating being to nonbeing,

(Pp. 662–64)

A statue is an imaginary woman; this Venus is not and never has been. But the marble exists as an *analogon* of the goddess, and how can one distinguish between the beauty and purity of the material and the form that vampirizes it? The sculptor who designed it and realized it with his chisel at the cost of very real effort also exists or existed. In short, Venus is not, but the statue exists; for it is known, appraised, has a definite price, is possessed by some person or institution; if it is to be sent abroad for an exhibition of its maker's works, its weight and fragility are known and practical steps will be taken. I am designating this strange object here for the first time by a term which will frequently be used in what follows, "a real and permanent center of unrealization." In point of fact, it has an individuated being and has not remained a rock in the mountains of Carrara simply because it has been given the function of representing a certain nonbeing; but conversely, as soon as this nonbeing itself is recognized as something determined by the social imaginary, the whole object is *instituted in its being*; and society therefore grants it an ontological truth inasmuch as the being of this object is regarded as a permanent incentive to derealization by unrealizing this block of marble into Venus. The object is an aid to unrealization, but unrealization makes it a necessity, for if the unrealization is to take place, the object must come into being. In this context the imaginary is anything but fleeting, vague, or devoid of contour; indeed, in itself it possesses the strength, imperviousness, and defined bounds of the marble block. The compact and inert being of the stone exists for the purpose of derealizing itself publicly by derealizing its beholders, but some element of its immutable consistency and radiant inertia thereby passes into the Venus or Pietà; the woman of stone is the ideal of being, the representation of a thing-for-itself which seems to be the dream of a thing-in-itself. The sculptured stone therefore certainly possesses, as a mineral without which a common unreality cannot be attained, the *maximum of being*, if we think that in social intersubjectivity *being* once instituted is being-for-others.

I have taken the simplest possible example, for here the being is the practico-inert aspect of the imaginary, something impenetrable, semi-enclosed, and universally recognized, a piece of merchandise with a *determined* and fixed outlet in its midst, a function, value, and demand. But I have taken it simply by way of approach to the status of the actor. What complicates matters here is that the actor is not just a lump of inorganic matter which has absorbed human work, but a living and thinking man whose immersion in unreality is an unpredictable blend of rehearsal and invention each night, in which at the worst he comes close to being an automaton and at the best transcends the habits he has contracted in "trying out" an effect. Be that as it may, he resembles the statue in that he is a permanent center, real and recognized, of unrealization (permanence here being a perpetual recommencing rather than an inert subsisting). He musters and commits his whole self to make his real person the *analogon* of something imaginary called Titus, Harpagon, or Ruy Blas. In short, he derealizes himself every night in order to draw five hundred people into a collective unrealization. . . .

Kean is *recognized* by his audience the way the Venus of Milo is. When they think of him, it is as a real being who is the essential connecting link between the individual realities —which do not themselves possess a common imagination— and the collective Hamlet of unreality. The tickets to see

Kean as Hamlet sell like hot cakes, just as tourists throng to San Pietro in Vincoli to see a block of Carrara marble as Moses. Actors are made by the role as doctors are made by disease. A national theater has a *repertory*, the outcome of the judgment of the objective mind; and the repertory *awaits its men*: the *Hamlet*s pass, Hamlet remains, demanding and summoning new interpreters. The roles consolidate into jobs —the juvenile lead, the star part, third murderers, the watch, and so on—and designate, in the abstract at first, their future holders. Since they are themselves real centers of unrealization (products of a job of work, conserved and constantly reworked from generation to generation, they may be developed but no word may be altered in them and whoever interprets them implants them in himself as categorical imperatives), they mark out their future interpreters *in their reality*; they must have the right voice, figure, and expression. Better still, constituted character comes into play: diffidence, an inability to cope with circumstance together with a nose like the toe of a boot, and you have the comic juvenile lead, forever baffled by the turn of events; aggression coupled with a touch of arrogance marks out candidates for the job of tragedy king or queen. It is in fact chiefly a matter of appearance, and it may be readily supposed that the tragedy monarch recruits his interpreters from those who *play the monarch* in real life. No matter; for—as we shall see better shortly—the role and the man must be suited; and as the role requires the man with the seriousness and intransigency of the practico-inert, that is, a worked-up material, the candidate's appearance, if he is finally accepted, receives a status of *being*. He is chosen as having "the requisite *qualifications*." Thereafter, the successful candidate undergoes a long hard apprenticeship; he works just as hard as a blacksmith or heavy carpenter; he *learns the trade*, the whole set of skills for collective unrealization: how to *produce* illusion and how to *prevent* it from being dispelled. In short, the imaginary no longer means simply abandoning himself spontaneously to appearing, for now it is the end product of a stringent work process; he learns everything—to breathe, walk, speak—all over again. Not *for its own sake*, but so that the gait shall be a *demonstration* and breathing shall modulate another *demonstration*, the voice. It is a long apprenticeship; training an actor involves a social expenditure that can be quantified. The investment will pay off if he wins top honors at the School of Dramatic Art; for a number of years, computed in accordance with the chances of contemporary life, he will contribute to filling the theater and raising the box-office receipts, part of which will be reinvested in that theater; in fact, then, he is *productive*. As a result, he may reach the Comédie-Française and sign a contract with the state under which he will not quit the company before a stipulated date. So here we have him defined in his being: he is a civil servant, a wage earner filling a particular job for a particular period and receiving in return a real power, that of unrealizing seven hundred people on certain nights and in accordance with certain skills and certain directions (prescribed by the role) by making them participate in his own unrealization. So he is *instituted*; the public's acclaim will do the rest, and if he is highly acclaimed, he will be raised to the rank of a *national asset* as the *man of illusion*. It is *in his being* that he will be consecrated, in some countries, as a Hero of Labor or Stakhanovite of illusion, and in others—in France, for instance—he will be decorated or, in England, knighted. Which means that he is recognized as having a *real power* of illusion and is being thanked for using it for the benefit of the community. This is why young people are often rather disappointed, when they meet a famous actor, to find an impeccably dressed man, with a stern countenance, restrained gestures, and a decoration in his buttonhole, a crashing bore in his parade of conservative opinions: but where are the madness of King Lear and the fury of Othello hiding? The answer is that they are not hiding anywhere: they simply are not, that is all. But that night he will once more be consuming his being, though without risk, for the consumption is nicely calculated and strictly confined on every side by iron rules. Let him enjoy his being for the moment, for he *is* an official member of the company of the Comédie-Française, highly appreciated for his abilities and professional conscientiousness; he is this respectable man, a member of the middle class, in receipt of large fees from the films in addition to his regular salary, the more careful of his real being in that unreality as a whole is black and white and he has to combat the bad reputation that certain irresponsible persons are trying to fasten on him. Beyond this, he is of course stark mad; the imaginary is devouring him. The respectable bourgeois you see is his being and his *display window* too; for he displays himself as a man who, except on the boards, abhors self-display. But now it is *his being* that he is putting on display, unrealizing himself into the reality he has won. We may say that he clutches to himself the reality that has come to him from outside. An actor—especially if he is a great one—is first of all a stolen child, without rights, truth, and reality, a prey to some sort of vampires, who has had the luck and the merit to get himself rehabilitated by society as a whole and to be instituted in his being as a solid citizen of unreality. He is an imaginary who exhausted himself playing roles to gain recognition and has finally been recognized as a worker on the assembly line of imagination, for his being has come to him through the socialization of his powerlessness to be.

(Pp. 785–90)

The Comic Actor

Farcical comedy has just as much of a cathartic function as tragedy in that it preserves laughter as dissociative behavior and permanently provides the social individual with an opportunity to dissociate himself from the absurdities or flaws he discovers in his neighbor which implicate him because he does not always have time or is not always able to hold them up to ridicule. A cuckold is of course absolutely ludicrous; but if he is my brother and I know that he is suffering, I am very liable to display a suspect compassion for him. The theater is there to get me out of the difficulty, for the theater is where people laugh at cuckolds, and there I can implicitly mock at my brother because he is lumped in with the rest; the monarch of nature strides majestically to the performance to affirm with a hale and virile gayety his *racial* supremacy over the submen who are impertinent enough to imitate him. A helot will dedicate himself there to exciting a collective laughter of self-satisfaction by wallowing in subhumanity in order to smear his own self with the stains that might tarnish the "human personage" and to display them as the taints of an inferior race vainly trying to approximate to ours. In the darkened halls the "human person," relaxed and unnumbered, guffaws on every seat, asserting its domination by the violence of its mirth. Unlike the magistrate who has the mischance to fall down and *become laughable* by a sudden and spontaneous serialization[1] of the bystanders and suffers, vainly rejecting the status of externality imposed upon him, the professional comic actor knowingly tries to provoke his audience's serialization by demonstrating to it the manifest contradiction between his being-external-to-himself and his subjective illusion. He takes himself seriously[2] so that this seriousness may be instantly denied by a remorseless mechanism—both outside him and within his false internality—which can reduce him to pure appearance; he commits himself to acting only with the intention that his act, baffled, deflected, negated, or retorted against himself by the force of circumstance, shall proclaim itself a ridiculous dream of sovereignty at once revealing that praxis, the privilege of the human race, is forbidden to submen. The cathartic function begins where that of the uncontrolled laughter ends; the laughter starts the derealization of the guilty, and the comic actor completes it: he unrealizes himself into *another*, a fixation abscess of this or that absurdity of ours or of all of them at once; and the public is solemnly forewarned by posters that he never existed. He is as it were an admonition to the public: the object of your uncontrolled laughter will never implicate you, for it does not exist; the drunkard does not exist nor the bewigged justice of the high court who fell flat on his face, for these are the dreams of submen and promptly exposed. Nothing is real which is not serious and nothing is serious which is not real. The comic actor therefore appears as a clown who releases man from himself by an ignominious sacrifice for which no one thanks him. Let him not expect any sympathy from those who laugh at him, for is he not instigating a whole theater to dissociate itself from him and to treat him as *external*? But in the first place, is it conceivable that the serious persons watching his contortions will not view his proclaimed intention to arouse their mirth as suspect and fundamentally *ridiculous*? Laughter safeguards the serious; but how can anyone be serious if his job is to make himself a ridiculous object? How can he help being placed on the same footing as the submen whom the uncontrolled laughter *institutes* as ridiculous, since he is, after all, simply embodying them? And if he is a man like the spectators, how strange his intention to present himself night after night as a subman. Their subhumanity must fascinate him. If so, he is more disquieting and guiltier than a drunkard or a cuckold, for they do not know what they are doing. But he quite knowingly presents himself for punishment by laughter, and so is a traitor to his kind, a "human person" who has sided with the enemies of man. The comic performance is healthy, of course, it reassures and releases and ought to be approved of—though cautiously—as an *institution*; but the social individuals who *present* it must be vile or flawed, for what a man worthy of the name *ipso facto* rejects—actually does not even need to reject—is being exiled by the laughter of the company of his kind; how could he do other than despise wretches who do their utmost to get themselves expelled from it every night? Better still, how could he help dissociating himself from them by laughing *at them*, since they are, after all, those most likely to implicate him?

It is no use arguing that people do not laugh at them, but at the characters they are playing. The public hardly knows the difference. It is not entirely wrong in this, because anyone who harbors the project of presenting a comic character to others must be predestined to it, that is to say must already be ridiculous, which we know means already derealized by the mirth of others. In this sense, the alter ego which the laughers assign to the ridiculous object and the persona displayed to them by the comic actor have this much in common, that both of them are imaginary. Odette Laure, the comic singer, let the cat out of the bag when she said one day in an interview, "If you want to be a comic singer, you must not like yourself much." That is the root of the matter: if the comic actor is to throw himself to the wild beasts every night, knowingly excite their cruelty, refuse all recourse to internality, and publicly reduce himself to external appearance, then he must have been constituted in externality to himself at some decisive period of his life. We laugh at very young children, and they know it and delight to make us laugh at them. But this laughter is kindly; the adult is amused at these submen imitating the man he is; and he laughs at the sight of his own gestures decomposed by these clumsy little bodies as they try to learn them; it is kindly because he knows quite well that these submen are men in embryo. The children exaggerate their clumsiness and seriousness to ingratiate themselves. The stage of putting on an act does not last long, however; it disappears as soon as the child acquires the inner certainty of his singularity and is able to set what he makes of himself within his self-awareness against what he is to and through others. The future comic actor is one who *fixes* himself at the age of the ridiculous. Some accident or the family structure must have constituted him in externality; they must have kept him at a distance, must have refused to consider the inner motivation of his acts and to share in his pleasures and pains, and they must have appraised his behavior by the degree in which it conformed to the imperatives of a pre-established model rather than by its singular meaning. The child will first discover that he is someone in whose place no one ever puts himself; he will find that the sovereign authority of the grown-ups insists on making his externality the truth of his life and regarding his awareness as mere chatter; he will observe, without grasping the reason for it, that the kindly laughter which he delighted to excite is turning sour. What has happened is that for some reason or other, his parents and kin hold that his development has been arrested, that his clumsiness—which they found so charming only a year before—now shows that he will never internalize the "human person" which society proposes to him, and that consequently this reveals the impossibility of his ever being a man—which is the specific definition of subhumanity. The family laughter at once becomes as it were a dissociation, for the parents vow that they cannot recognize themselves in their offspring and do not believe that he is *of their blood*. A good debut for a future comic actor. If the small boy is docile enough to find a growing difficulty in *putting himself in his own place*, still experiencing his feelings but no longer entering into them, and if, anguished by his estrangement, he lives in the clandestinity of the unreflecting and then dissociates himself in the full light of reflection and is willing to see it only as a means of arousing mirth in others out of an agonized desire to be the first to laugh at himself in order to rejoin the adults in their seriality, then a vocation as comic actor has come into being, together with a *ridiculous image,* a furious enslavement of the internal to the flat appearance of the external. Thus you have a monster, unrealized by the uncontrolled laughter of others; a traitor to his own self, he will henceforth do his utmost to feed the image which others have of him. If he later becomes an actor in earnest and acts Sganarelle or Pourceaugnac, what has changed? These are, it is true, *roles*. But what inner certainty does he have to set against them? Far from being able to stand aloof from these characters, he must have been *constituted* a character himself if he is to be capable of embodying them. Within him there is a permanent persona, which is quite simply *the ridiculous,* and other temporary personas, which are images for a night or a season. But we should not go further and believe that he unrealizes himself in the one rather than in the others, for, clearly, the basic unrealization has been constituted and the unfortunate actor has long been doomed to exploit his body and his internality as the *analogon* of the basic *imago*, that of the subman taking himself seriously. It is true that the permanent persona professes to be his own person and passes over its unreality in silence rather than that the characters are impersonations and the public is informed by poster that it will be laughing that evening at Hirsch in *Arturo Ui*. But the role is in fact merely a singular piece of information about the basic persona, namely that it will be worked up, chased, toned down in some places and accentuated at others, but no more. *With what* is the actor to excite laughter but with the only *analogon* available to him, and by what means other than by methodically exploiting his personal experience is he to produce the ridiculous? Tonight Pourceaugnac is on the program; he may have a hundred different faces, but the face he has tonight, on these boards, in the blaze of these footlights, is Fernandel's; it is Fernandel's body and no one else's that lends itself to the squireen from Périgord, it is his buttocks and no one else's that are threatened by the enemas leveled at them by the apothecaries. And if the player is to express the poor provincial's bewilderment, let us not assume that he will be drawing his inspiration from traits of behavior he has studied in others. Observation is useful, of course; he will use it to supervise himself. But he does not reproduce; he invents. And in this specific case we can agree with Wilde that nature imitates art, for there are no perfect idiots except on the stage. In short, he nourishes his character from his own substance. To say that he *acts like an idiot* or that in unreality he becomes the idiot he would be if he were stricken with idiocy is still not going far enough; for in order to produce the *analogon* of the persona he displays he makes himself the fool that he *is*. The actor awakes in himself the cloudy mass of panic, terrorized incomprehension, fear, obstinacy, slyness, and ignorance which is everybody's sign of alienation passing under the name of stupidity, and he churns it up to unrealize himself through it into a magnificent idiot. What, in brief, is he doing except what he has always done, ever since some contact that went amiss constituted him ridiculous? A dialectic is most certainly initiated between the character and the player of the role; the former transforms the latter to exactly the same degree as the latter transforms the former. But these relations are between images. The role, moreover, serves as an alibi, for the actor seeks release from his persona and believes that he can escape into the character. In vain: for within the gay and intoxicating exhilaration of being no more than an alien image, there persist a disquiet and a profound hostility which drives him to debase himself so that others may triumph, because he is in fact conscious that he is choosing this or that disguise *to make people laugh at him*, as he always has.

The public is not fooled, for when rubberneckers recognize a famous comic in the solitary and grave passerby wrapped in meditation, they burst out laughing. Many actors have complained of this: one of them says that he cannot take a train journey without seeing smirking faces flattened against the windows of his compartment at every stop; another is irritated at being unable to enter a restaurant without arousing the diners' mirth; a third has had to give up bathing except in lonely coves because there was a tempest of laughter along the beach whenever he appeared in a bathing suit. We *make people laugh*, all of them say, at certain times, for that is our job; but outside working hours we are no less serious than you are. From one point of view this is perfectly true, for what would we see if we did not know "what they do for a living"? A man just like all men and, more particularly, a bourgeois just like all bourgeois; comfortably and elegantly dressed, they have indecipherable and vacuous faces just like everyone else, an easy courtesy, an engaging manner, reassuring in every respect; special peculiarities— none. And their normal preoccupations are precisely those of all bourgeois—money, the family, the job, an affair perhaps, most certainly the car. There is nothing noticeable about them. But do what they will, the crowd unmasks them; something is bound to happen; the elastic, tranquil stride and the air of relaxation are bound to be shattered, the gent is bound to fall down and his face will mirror the dismay and idiocy that have made him famous; a bird will shit on his head; the universal clumsiness or his own brand of it is sure to disclose his secret ridiculousness—that is to say, what the public takes to be his truth. The only mistake made by these fairly malevolent witnesses is that they confuse ridicule with truth. Strictly speaking, the comic actor has no truth, since he sacrifices concrete existence to the abstract being of appearance; and the seriousness he displays off the stage, though just as "authentic" as that of those who laugh at him, has one feature that distinguishes it from all others: that it is constituted *against* the basically ridiculous; in this sense, it does not much differ from the seriousness he displays on the stage, the function of which is to assert itself against the comic and ultimately to be defeated by the implacable concatenation of disasters and to be proclaimed as a false seriousness. There is only one difference: on the stage the disasters are *certain*, the character is bound to lose his human dignity, whereas off the stage they may be said to be improbable; or in other words, this respectable and slightly intimidating gentleman will cross the street without mishap and soon be out of sight; nothing will befall him. Nevertheless, the passers take his dignity as an invitation to laughter, for it offers itself to *destruction* amidst mirth; and if heaven or hell does not take it at its word, that is their affair, not his, for the actor has done all he should. They are quite right; the worthy character is a role which the actor assumes in his private life; arising as it does from an attempt to mask the ridiculous, it is neither more nor less true than the ridiculous: let us say that it is convenient in certain circumstances and the actor could not live if he were not able to assume respectability at the proper moment. Yet it is true that he scarcely believes in it and that it is a composite role, or rather one which he borrows from his characters—and where else would he get it from if not from them?—and is, so to speak, thesis without antithesis, the moment of sovereignty established for its own sake, severed from self and negative, when the force of circumstance unmasks the imposture of it and reveals that the sovereign is merely a disconnected mechanism running free. In this sense, clearly he himself is summoning the witnesses who recognize the actor by the hilarious expectation of a denial. Or rather, the moment of the contradiction incorporated in the paroxysm of laughter is the moment of recognition: here's a respectable man—but no, it's not, it's Rigadin. The serious is proposed, is decomposed and recomposed, only to be distintegrated once more: being dissolving into appearance. In this case the laughter is aggressive, because it comes from indignation: you tried to dupe us, to get us to take you for a man, but we're not that stupid, we know you are a clown.

(*L'Idiot de la famille,* vol. 1, pp. 825–31)

II

DOCUMENTS
AND INTERVIEWS
ON THE PLAYS

Bariona, or
the Son of Thunder

(*Bariona, ou le Fils du tonnère*)

Sartre wrote *Bariona* in the fall of 1940 for his fellow
prisoners' Christmas in Stalag XII D at Trier, to which
he had been transferred in August. An unpublished letter
to Simone de Beauvoir, dated December 1940, from
which we are giving a large extract here, supplies details
on Sartre's life in the POW camp and in some sort
marks the beginning of his career as a dramatist. The
text of *Bariona* is published in *The Writings of Jean-
Paul Sartre*.

I first landed in a pretty queer place, the camp's aristocracy,
the infirmary. There are also the powerful plutocracy of the
kitchens and the politicians or barracks leaders. I was
ejected from the infirmary by intrigues, and trying to avoid
work on the land, for which, until further notice, I have
little talent, I reached the inoffensive circle of the players,
rather the grasshopper sort, people rather like Racine under
Louis XIV. A lot of bowing and scraping and impeccable
sentiments. They are pretty decent people, actually, the de-
centest I have come across since war broke out. They have a

real little theater in which they play to the fifteen hundred prisoners in the camp on two Sundays each month. In return for which they get paid ten pfennigs a day, may get up late and don't do a damn thing all day. I live with them in a large room, inhabited by guitars, banjos, flutes, and trumpets hung on the walls, with a piano on which some Belgians play swing in the style of the College Inn pianists. I write plays for them which are never acted, and I get paid too. However, my usual companions are priests, especially a young assistant priest and a Jesuit novice, who in fact hate one another and actually come to blows about Marian theology and look to me for a decision. So I make the decision. Yesterday I happened to refute Pope Pius IX about the Immaculate Conception. They can't make up their minds between Pius IX and me. And you should know that I am writing my first serious play and am putting all of me into it (writing, staging, and acting it) and it's about the *Nativity*. Don't worry, I'm not going to become a Ghéon, not having started like him. But please believe that I *most undoubtedly* have talent as a dramatist; I have written a scene about an angel announcing the birth of Christ to the shepherds that took everyone's breath away. Tell Dullin that and that some of them were moved to tears, too. I remember what he was like when he was putting on a play, and I draw my inspiration from him, but am always far more polite, since I don't pay my players. It is to be on December 24, in masks, there will be sixty characters, and it's called *Bariona, or the Son of Thunder*. Last Sunday too I acted in a mask, a comic part in a farce. All this amuses me a good deal, among other even funnier farces. Later on, I shall write plays.

In a letter to Yves Frontier dated October 31, 1962, Sartre gave his permission for the publication of *Bariona* in a limited edition not for sale, and explained:

Though I took my subject from the mythology of Christianity, that does not mean that the trend of my thinking changed even for a moment when I was a prisoner of war. It was simply a matter, agreed on with my fellow-prisoner priests, of finding a subject most likely to appeal to both Christians and unbelievers that Christmas Eve.

Which he stressed again in 1968, when he told Paul-Louis Mignon:

Finding out that I had written a mystery play, some people have gone so far as to suppose I was going through a spiritual crisis. Not at all! I was linked with the priests who were prisoners in the camp by a common rejection of Nazism. The Nativity seemed to me a subject most likely to appeal to both Christians and unbelievers. And it was agreed that I should say what I liked.

What was important to me in this experiment was that as a prisoner I was going to be able to address my fellow prisoners and raise problems we all shared. The script was full of allusions to the circumstances of the moment, which were perfectly clear to each of us. The envoy from Rome to Jerusalem was in our minds the German. Our guards saw him as the Englishman in his colonies!

I acted one of the Three Wise Men. Which of them? I don't remember now.[1] But I was expressing existentialist ideas in refusing Bariona the right to commit suicide and making him decide to fight.

Why did I not take up *Bariona* again later? Because the play was bad. It sacrificed too much to long expository speeches.[2]

(*L'Avant-Scène Théâtre,*
nos. 402–403, May 1–15, 1968)

The Flies

(*Les Mouches*)

Sartre wrote the following jacket copy for the publication of *Les Mouches* in book form (Paris: Gallimard, 1943).

Tragedy is the mirror of Fatality. I did not believe that a tragedy of freedom could not be written, since the ancient Fatum is simply an inverted freedom. Orestes is free as regards crime and beyond crime; I have shown him as a prey to freedom, just as Oedipus is a prey to his destiny. He struggles beneath this iron fist, but he will have to kill in the end, and he will have to shoulder the burden of his murder and carry it to the other shore. For freedom is not some vague abstract ability to soar above the human predicament; it is the most absurd and the most inexorable of commitments. Orestes will go onward, unjustifiable, with no excuse and with no right of appeal, alone. Like a hero. Like all of us.

In an interview with Yvan Novy at the press showing, published by *Comœdia* on April 24, 1943, Sartre explained what he had intended, without alluding directly to the play's political content.

My intention was to consider the tragedy of freedom as contrasted with the tragedy of fate. In other words, what my play is about can be summed up as the question, "How does a man behave toward an act committed by him, for which he takes the full consequences and full responsibility upon himself, even if he is otherwise horrified by his act?"

Obviously the problem raised in these terms cannot be comfortably accommodated with the principle of purely inner freedom, in which some philosophers, including some quite reputable philosophers, even Bergson, have tried to find the source of emancipation from destiny. A freedom of that sort is always merely theoretical and spiritual. It does not stand up to the test of fact. I wished to take the case of someone freely circumstanced who does not simply remain content with imagining himself free, but emancipates himself at the cost of an exceptional act, no matter how atrocious, because only an act of that kind can bring him final liberation from himself.

Notwithstanding the danger of updating classical tragedy, from which I have adapted the structure and taken my characters, I maintain that my hero commits what seems the most heinously inhuman crime. His gesture is that of the justiciar, since he kills a usurper to avenge his father, who was killed by him. But he carries the punishment further and lets it fall on his own mother, the queen, whom he sacrifices too because she was an accomplice in the original crime.

By this gesture, which cannot be isolated from his reactions, he restores the harmony of a rhythm which transcends the notion of good and evil. But his act will remain sterile if it is not total and final, if it must, for example, involve an acceptance of remorse, a sentiment which is simply a reversal, because it is tantamount to a continuing bond with the past.

Free in conscience though he may be, a man who has so far transcended himself will not become circumstantially free unless he restores freedom to others, unless the consequence of his act is the disappearance of an existing state of affairs and the restoration of what ought to be.

The necessary condensation of drama required a dramatic situation of particular intensity. If I had invented my hero, the horror he would have inspired would have inevitably foredoomed him to misconception. That is why I resorted to a character who was already situated dramatically. I had no choice.

After the Liberation, Sartre explained more fully:

Why stage declamatory Greeks . . . unless to disguise what one was thinking under a fascist regime? . . .

The real drama, the drama I should have liked to write, was that of the terrorist who by ambushing Germans becomes the instrument for the execution of fifty hostages.

(*Carrefour*, September 9, 1944)

In one of the pieces in which he pays tribute to Dullin, Sartre recalls how *The Flies* came to be produced.

I have two things for which I have to be grateful to Charles Dullin—apart from the friendship and respect I have felt for him ever since I have known him. He it was, together with Pierre Bost,[1] who saved my first manuscript by a warm recommendation just as it was about to be rejected by Gallimard's readers,[2] and he it was who produced my first play, *The Flies*, at the Théâtre Sarah-Bernhardt in 1943. If *Nausea* had not been published, I would have gone on writing; but if *The Flies* had not been performed, I wonder whether I would have gone on writing plays, since my main concerns kept me so far from the theater in those days. So when I think back to the years from 1938 to 1943, I find the two main forms of my literary activity go back originally to Dullin.

To recommend *Nausea* to Gaston Gallimard, whom he knew pretty well, was a kind and generous thing to do, but

after all it was no great effort. With *The Flies* it was quite
the reverse. Under the Occupation people seldom went out
in the evening; the theater was virtually moribund; no matter
what play he put on, Dullin found it extremely hard to fill
the huge hall of the Sarah-Bernhardt. To produce a play
by an unknown playwright was to risk losing his theater,
especially as the political tone of *The Flies* was not calculated to please the critics, all of whom were collaborating
with the Occupying Power. Dullin was perfectly well aware
of this, and I too was so well aware of it that I sought out and
found a backer, who went to see Dullin and tried to over-
whelm him with a flood of verbiage. Dullin heard him out
in silence, with a wry smile and his traditional peasant
skepticism. In point of fact, one fine day, the day on which
the decision was to be made, my backer jumped into the lake
in the Bois de Boulogne. He was fished out, but I learned
that he hadn't a penny.[3] I went by myself to the meeting place
all three of us had arranged and had to break the news to
Dullin. He listened to me in silence, with a mischievous
gleam in his eye. Not a sign of disappointment. When I had
brought my little speech to an end, I suggested that he should
give me back my play. "Why?" he asked. "I'm putting it
on anyway." I am none too sure that he had much faith in
it. But, despite all the risks, he was set on continuing at the
Sarah-Bernhardt the policy of producing the work of young
writers that he had followed at the Atelier, naturally hoping
for success, but not worrying about it unduly. Well, he took
all the risks—and lost; the play was savaged by the critics
and played for about fifty performances to half-empty
houses.[4] Not for a moment did he hold it against me. He
was the sole master of his ship, and he took his own responsibilities. And I feel my friendship for him come over me
again as intensely as it did at that time, when I remember
how distressed he looked when he told me he was taking
the play off, but only on the very last day before it had become literally impossible to continue.

But after all, in a way neither of us had lost. Dullin's greatness will lie in the fact that it was he who discovered writers who brought him total flops and then went on to success on other stages. Besides, he had in this case done what he had long been wanting to do, to stage a modern tragedy. Is *The Flies* a tragedy? I really don't know, but what I do know is that in his hands it became one. He had a complex idea of Greek tragedy: he believed that it should express savage and unbridled violence, but in strictly classical terms. He did his best to adapt *The Flies* to these two requirements. His intention was to impound and express the Dionysiac forces and express them in a free and close-knit play of Apollonian images; and this he was able to do. He knew that; and his complete success in the production— extracting something from my play which probably was not in it, but which I certainly had hoped to put into it—was ample compensation, as he saw it, for the play's lack of success. I too gained something: the rehearsals taught me everything I know about the craft. I was astounded to watch Dullin meet all my tyro's demands with resources deliberately—and of necessity—kept to a minimum. Nothing was presented, everything suggested. Richness, intangible and born of poverty, violence and blood presented in calm contemplation, and the union of these opposites, patiently contrived, all went to the creation before my eyes of an astonishing *tension* which had been lacking in my play; and this has ever since become—to me, at least—the *essence of drama.* My dialogue was verbose; Dullin conveyed to me, without reproaching me about it or advising me to make cuts at first, but simply by talking to the actors, the realization that a play for performance must be precisely the opposite of an orgy of rhetoric; that is to say, it must be the fewest possible words bound together irreversibly by an irreversible action and unremitting passion. He said, "Don't act the words, act the situation"; and by watching him at work I came to understand the deeper meaning with which he alone invested this commonplace precept. To him situation was the living totality organized in time so that it glided irresistibly from birth to death and had necessarily to create forms of expression which reflected both its indivisible totality and the particular moment embodying it. I adopted his precept for my own practice in the form of "Don't write the words, write the situation." You must compose exactly as he made his players act; in the theater you can't pick up your marbles and start again; for when a word is not one which can be taken back once it has been spoken, you must very carefully withdraw it from the dialogue. This austere poverty, a fascinating mirror of the riches of which it will always give us only the imaginary reflection, this irresistible movement which engenders a play to kill it, was the essence of Dullin's art. And that was what he taught me. After the rehearsals of *The Flies*, I never saw the theater again with the same eyes.

(*Cahiers Charles Dullin*, vol. 2, March 1966)

When the Compagnie des Dix, directed by Claude Martin, staged the play in the French Occupation Zone of Germany in 1947, Sartre wrote:

After our defeat in 1940 all too many Frenchmen gave way to discouragement or yielded to remorse. I wrote *The Flies* and tried to show that *remorse* was not an attitude Frenchmen should choose after our country's military collapse. Our past no longer existed. It had slipped between our fingers before we had had time to grasp it and hold it up to our gaze in order to understand it. But the future—even though an enemy army was occupying France—was new. We had a grasp on it; we were at liberty to make it a future of the defeated or a future of free men who refuse to believe that a defeat is the end of everything which makes a man want to live his life as a man.

The problem is the same for the Germans today. I believe that for the Germans, too, remorse is sterile. I do not mean that the recollection of past faults should be expunged from their memory. No. But I am convinced that complacent remorse is not the way for them to obtain whatever pardon the world may grant them. The better course is a total and genuine commitment to a future of freedom and work, a determination to build that future, the presence among them of the greatest possible number of men of good will. This play is not intended to guide them toward that future, but to encourage them to strive toward it.

(Verger, no. 2, June 1947)

The Flies was performed in German at the Hebbel-Theater in Berlin in 1948 in a production by Jürgen Fehling. Sartre visited Berlin at the time and took part in a debate which was followed by a large and intensely interested audience. The play, with an expressionistic and brutal staging reminiscent of the concentration camps, gave rise to lively discussion and to attacks against Sartre and his philosophy in the Russian-licensed press. The debate, held on February 1, 1948, was published in the magazine *Verger* (no. 5, 1948), under the title "Discussion Around *The Flies*." Besides Sartre the speakers were Monsieur Lusset, the French Cultural Attaché in Berlin, Günther Weisenborn, Monsieur Theunissent, Edouard Roditi, Walter Karsch, W. D. Zimmermann, Jürgen Fehling, and Professor Steiniger. Some long extracts from it are given below.

SARTRE   The whole debate turns on the question of what the meaning of *The Flies* was when the play was performed in Paris in 1943 during the Occupation and what is the significance of its present performance in Berlin. . . .

STEINIGER   In your view, Monsieur Sartre, repentance is not represented in *The Flies* either as pure hypocrisy or as renunciation of self. Another philosopher—Karl Marx, I believe—once said: "When a whole people feels shame at injustices committed, it is already quite close to performing a revolutionary act." Do not deceive yourself, Monsieur Sartre; your play's success is largely due—apart, of course, from its dramatic and literary qualities—to the fact that it bestows a gigantic pardon, a summary general absolution. Hence my first question: Are you conscious of assuming, and how do you assume toward your own country, the responsibility for preventing, by your opposition to repentance, the German people from finding itself through its own efforts, acknowledging its responsibilities, and thereby completely and actively renewing its moral existence?

SARTRE   That is a very interesting question, for it hinges on the problem of repentance and, secondly—indeed, the two things are closely coupled together—on the question how far a play which may have been good in 1943, which was valid at that time, still has the same validity and, in particular, validity in 1948. The play must be accounted for by the circumstances of the time. From 1941 to 1943 many people were extremely anxious for the French to plunge into repentance. The Nazis primarily, and Pétain too,[5] and likewise his press. The French had to be convinced, and had to convince themselves, that we had been madmen, that we had sunk to the lowest depths of degradation, that the Popular Front had lost us the war, that our leaders had been derelict in their duty, and so on and so forth. What was the purpose of this campaign? Certainly not to make Frenchmen better, to make different men of them. No, the aim was to plunge us into such a state of repentance, of shame, that we would be incapable of putting up any resistance. We were to find satisfaction in our repentance, even pleasure in it. All the better for the Nazis.

By writing my play I was trying by my own unaided effort, feeble though it might be, to do what I could to root out this sickness of repentance, this complacence in repentance and shame. What was needed at the time was to revive the French people, to restore their courage. The people who were revolted by the Vichy government, who regarded it as an abject thing, all those in France who wished totally to reject domination by the Nazis, understood the play remarkably well. The *Lettres françaises*, which was being published underground at the time, said so quite clearly.[6]

The second reason is a more personal one. At that time there was the problem of attacks against the Nazis, and not only the Nazis but all members of the Wehrmacht. Those who took part in these attacks obviously did so without losing their peace of mind about it. They certainly never dreamed of making it a matter of conscience. In their view, they were at war, and throwing a grenade at the enemy was an act of war. But a further problem became attached to it —and it was a moral problem—that of the hostages. The Wehrmacht had started executing them at that time. Six or eight hostages were shot for every three Germans; and that had very important moral implications. Not only were these hostages innocent, but, it should especially be borne in mind, they had done nothing against the Wehrmacht, and most of them were not even members of the Resistance. At the start they were mostly Jews, who had not yet had time to think of overt resistance and had no share whatever in the responsibility. The problem of these attacks was, therefore, of prime importance. Anyone who committed an attack like that had to know that, unless he gave himself up, fellow Frenchmen would be shot at random. So he was liable to a second form of repentance: he had to resist the temptation to give himself up. This is how the allegory in my play is to be understood.

That is why people did not consider the play pessimistic at the time it was performed, but quite the reverse—optimistic. In it I was saying to my fellow Frenchmen: You do not have to repent, even those of you who have in a sense become murderers; you must assume your own responsibility for your acts, even if they have caused the deaths of innocent persons. There is the further question how a play which was regarded as optimistic at one time has come to have a quite different meaning in Germany today, how it can seem in another country to be an expression of despair, to be fundamentally pessimistic.

STEINIGER   I can perfectly appreciate that the Nazis wanted to instill remorse into your country. In our country I think they would like to inhibit it, and they are now forging explanations which, beyond good and evil, are preparing the next massacre. (*Applause*) . . . .

SARTRE   If we look at France in 1943 and Germany in 1948, the two situations are, of course, very different, but they do have some things in common. In both cases people are tormenting themselves about a fault which relates to the past. In 1943 they were trying to convince the French that they should look only at their past. Against that we were claiming that true Frenchmen should look to the future. Anyone who wished to work for the future should act in the Resistance, without repentance, without any feeling of remorse. The problem of guilt also arises in contemporary Germany, the guilt of the Nazi regime. But this guilt is simply a matter of the past. As seen today this guilt is bound up with the Nazis' crimes. To think only of that past, to torment oneself day and night even, is a sterile feeling, a purely negative feeling. Not that I hold that all sense of responsibility must be ruled out. On the contrary, I say that a sense of responsibility is necessary, that it is the key to the future. When various different elements are combined in repentance, concepts become confused, and that leads to misconceptions about the content of guilt or the recognition of the feeling of guilt. I am aware of my guilt, and my conscience suffers from it. This induces the feeling that is called repentance. Perhaps I have also felt an inner complacence in my repentance. That is simply passivity, looking backward; I can get nothing out of it. On the other hand, the sense of responsibility can conduce to something else, something positive, that is to say the necessary rehabilitation, action for a fruitful, positive future.

I knew also of Marx's observation about a nation's

shame which may lead it to revolutionary acts. Incidentally, the quotation comes from Marx's youthful writings and he scarcely ever reverted to the subject. But what exactly does Marx mean? He means the shame engendered in a nation by a present, a contemporary situation. His observation cannot possibly apply to a past situation. He means that the feeling of shame applicable to a specific situation, to Germany in 1848, for example, may inspire action if it is not restricted to repentance, desolation, a negative bad conscience. . . .

. . . Orestes' predicament and his decision can be accounted for to some extent. [During the discussion, a clergyman had blamed Orestes for failing to assume the responsibility for his act of liberation, since he leaves Argos and no one knows which way he is going, Marx or Christ.] If you look carefully at the social situation set out in the play, there is no problem, I believe, for in the end Orestes has a choice between freedom and slavery. If I see that someone has a choice, once he chooses freedom there is, as far as I can see, no problem; for the main point is that he did choose freedom. There would be a problem, and a serious one, if he had chosen slavery. Orestes decides in the end for freedom; he wishes to liberate himself by liberating his people, and through this liberation he wishes once more to belong to his people. We do not understand this exactly only because we do not perhaps give enough thought to the situation in Argos. But in the theater, on the stage as in life, this free choice always means a genuine liberation, and the main thing in the end is the will to liberation. Is is the expression of a freedom asserting itself. If we look at it like this, we can reject all interpretations, whether dialectical or psychoanalytical, and not simply reject them, but add them to the interpretations of the oppressed.

I had not thought of comparing Orestes with Christ. In my view, Orestes is not a hero at any point. I do not even know whether he is an exceptionally gifted man. But he is a man who does not wish to be severed from his people. He is the first to take the road to freedom, at the very moment when the masses can and must become conscious of themselves; he is the man who by his act is the first to show them the road. When he has done that, he can return in peace into anonymity and be at rest within his people. . . .

No Exit

(Huis clos)

As far as we know, there is no interview by Sartre on *No Exit* when it was first performed. On the other hand, Sartre produced a preface (which we reproduce in full below) for the recording of the play by the Deutsche Gramophon Gesellschaft (DGG 43902/3), with Michel Vitold, Gaby Sylvia, Christiane Lenier, and R.-J. Chauffard. It clears up a number of misunderstandings about the work's philosophical meaning. Extracts from this oral preface were reproduced in the French press (in particular *L'Express*, October 11–17, 1965) when *Huis clos* was broadcast by the ORTF[1] in a production by Michel Mitrani.

There are always accidental causes and primary concerns involved in the writing of a play. The accidental cause is that when I wrote *No Exit* in 1943 and early 1944, I had three friends and I wanted them to perform a play, a play of mine, without giving any one of them a better part than the others. That meant that I had to have all of them on the stage at the same time and all of them had to remain there.

Because, I thought, if one of them goes off, he will be thinking as he exits that the others have better parts than he has. So I wanted to keep them together. And I asked myself how one could keep three people together and never let one of them go off and how to keep them together to the end, as if for eternity.

Thereupon it occurred to me to put them in hell and make each of them the others' torturer. This was the accidental cause.

I should mention that, as it turned out, my three friends did not perform the play, and as you know, the parts were taken by Vitold, Tania Balachova, and Gaby Sylvia.[2]

But at the time there were also more general concerns; what I wanted to express in the play was something beyond what was simply dictated by the circumstances, and what I wanted to say was that hell is other people. But "hell is other people" has always been misunderstood. It has been thought that what I meant by that was that our relations with other people are always poisoned, that they are invariably hellish relations. But what I really mean is something totally different. I mean that if relations with someone else are twisted, vitiated, then that other person can only be hell. Why? Because other people are basically the most important means we have in ourselves for our own knowledge of ourselves. When we think about ourselves, when we try to know ourselves, basically we use the knowledge of us which other people already have. We judge ourselves with the means other people have and have given us for judging ourselves. Into whatever I say about myself someone else's judgment always enters. Into whatever I feel within myself someone else's judgment enters. Which means that if my relations are bad, I am situating myself in a total dependence on someone else. And then I am indeed in hell. And there are a vast number of people in the world who are in hell because they are too dependent on the judgment of other people. But that does not at all mean that one cannot have relations with other people. It simply brings out the capital importance of all other people for each one of us.

The second point I wanted to make is that these people are not like us. The three persons you will be hearing in *No Exit* do not resemble us, inasmuch as we are alive and they are dead. Naturally, "dead" symbolizes something here. What I was wanting to imply specifically is that many people are encrusted in a set of habits and customs, that they harbor judgments about them which make them suffer, but do not even try to change them. And that such people are to all intents and purposes dead. Dead in the sense that they cannot break out of the frame of their worries, their concerns, and their habits and that they therefore continue in many cases to be the victims of judgments passed on them by other people. From that standpoint they quite obviously *are* cowards or villains. If they were cowards in the first place, nothing can alter the fact that they were cowards. That is why they are dead, that is the reason; it is a way of saying that to be enwrapped in a perpetual care for judgments and actions which you do not want to change is a living death. So that, in point of fact, since we are alive, I wanted to show by means of the absurd the importance of freedom to us, that is to say the importance of changing acts by other acts. No matter what circle of hell we are living in, I think we are free to break out of it. And if people do not break out, again, they are staying there of their own free will. So that of their own free will they put themselves in hell.

So you see that relations with other people, encrustation, and freedom, freedom as the other face of the coin which is barely suggested, are the three themes in the play. I should like you to remember this when you hear that hell is other people.

I should like to add in conclusion that I had a very rare stroke of luck—very rare for dramatists—that at the first performance in '44 the roles were played by the three actors and also by Chauffard, the majordomo of hell, who has invariably acted him ever since, so extremely well that I have never afterwards been able to imagine my own creations save as Vitold, Gaby Sylvia, Tania Balachova, and Chauffard. The play has been revived since then with other actors, and I would like to place on record that I have seen Christiane Lenier act Inez and thought her admirable in the part.

The Victors

(Morts sans sépulture)

All Sartre's statements to journalists when the play was first produced on November 8, 1946, together with *The Respectful Prostitute*, are more or less summed up in the passage below.

This is not a play about the Resistance. What I am interested in are extreme situations and people's reactions to them. I thought at one time of situating my play during the Spanish Civil War. It could equally well take place in China. My characters ask themselves a question which has tormented so many of our generation all over the world: "How would I stand up to torture?" A question which their fathers did not have to ask themselves. As one of them remarks, his father, who was considered a hero because he got killed, might perhaps have given in had he been tortured.

Since I believe that modern drama must be contemporary, I would not write another play like *The Flies* today. I chose an adventure in the French underground as a frame, and I have tried to show the sort of intimacy which finally grows up between the torturer and his victim, and goes beyond the conflict of principles. The Vichy militiaman needs to humiliate the man of the Resistance, to force upon him a cowardice akin to his own: for that gives him the only justification he could have.

(*Combat*, October 30, 1946)

Later Sartre was to pass the following verdict on *The Victors*:

The play was a failure. To put it roughly, I was dealing with a subject in which there was no room to breathe, for the victims' fate was absolutely predetermined, no one could suppose that they would talk, so there was no suspense, as it is now called. I was putting on the stage characters whose destiny was plainly marked out. There are two possibilities in drama, suffering or evasion. The cards were already on the table. It is a very grim play, lacking in surprise. It would have been better to make a novel or a film of it.

(*Les Cahiers libres de la jeunesse*, no. 1, February 15, 1960)

The Respectful Prostitute

(La Putain respectueuse)

The Respectful Prostitute was staged in New York in an adaptation by Eva Wolas on February 9, 1948, and became a hit (over 350 performances). The text retranslated here comes from a translation of the play with an introductory note by Richard Wright, published in *Art and Action*, tenth anniversary issue 1938–1948 (New York: Twice a Year Press, 1948, p. 17). In it Sartre reproduces several comments which he had already used when the play was first produced in November 1946. Cf. *The Writings of Jean-Paul Sartre*, volume 1, notes 46/91 and 48/160.

Preface to the American translation

When this play was produced I was told that I was very ungrateful for the hospitality I had received in America. I was accused of being anti-American. I am not. I do not even know what the word means. I am antiracist, for I do know what racism means. My American friends—all I met and liked very much—are also antiracist. I am sure that

I have not written anything that could distress them or reveal any ingratitude on my part.

I am accused of seeing the mote in my neighbor's eye and failing to see the beam in my own. It is true that we French have colonies and that our treatment of them leaves much to be desired. But with oppression there is neither mote nor beam; it must be denounced wherever it exists.

The writer can do little; he can only say what he has seen. I have attacked anti-Semitism. Today I am attacking racism in this play. Tomorrow I shall be devoting an issue of my magazine to an attack on colonialism. I do not suppose that my writings are of any great importance or will change anything or even bring me many friends. No matter: I am doing my duty as a writer.

So much for the background. I welcome the fact that the readers of *Twice a Year* are to have an opportunity of judging whether I was insulting the United States or simply depicting relations between blacks and whites which are not confined solely to America.

It would be strange if I were accused in New York of anti-Americanism at the very moment when in Moscow *Pravda* is denouncing me as an agent of American propaganda. If that did happen, however, it would show one of two things, either that I am indeed unhandy at my job or that I am on the right track.

Sartre wrote the following in the *Bulletin N.R.F.* for July 1947 by way of introduction to the volume entitled *Théâtre* (*Les Mouches, Huis clos, Morts sans sépulture* and *La Putain respectueuse*), published by Gallimard in 1947.

In any circumstances, in any period, and at any place man is free to choose to be a traitor or a hero, a coward or a conqueror. In choosing slavery or freedom for himself he will thereby choose a world in which man is free or enslaved —and the drama will arise from his efforts to justify this choice. Faced with the gods, faced with death or tyrants, we still have a single certainty, whether triumphant or agonized: that of our freedom.

Referring to these remarks, Sartre stated in an interview with *New Left Review* (November–December 1969), reproduced in *Situations IX*: "It's incredible, I actually believed that." (See Jean-Paul Sartre, *Between Existentialism and Marxism* [New York: Pantheon Books, 1974], pp. 33–34.)

Dirty Hands

(*Les Mains sales*)

Extracts from interviews at the press showing

I hesitated for some time [between two titles, *Crime passionnel* and *Les Mains sales*]. I was rather afraid that *Les Mains sales* might be given a biased interpretation because the play's setting was a leftist party. In the end I kept it because it is not a political play *in any sense*.

Could it be called "peripolitical"?

To be quite accurate, a play *about* politics. If I had to take a quotation for a heading, it would be a remark by Saint-Just, "No one governs innocently." In other words, you cannot be in politics—of any sort—without getting your hands dirty, without being forced to compromise between the ideal and the real.[1]

Why did you choose to situate the play in a party of the extreme left?

Out of sympathy with them; because I knew them better. Because the complex question of the "end" and the "means" does not arise, or at any rate is not such a burning issue, in conservative or reactionary parties.

(Franc-Tireur, March 23, 1948)

You maintain that idealism and purity are in the right?

Certainly not. I do not take sides. A good play should raise problems, not solve them. All the characters in Greek tragedy are in the right and all of them in the wrong: that is why they slaughter each other and why their death achieves a tragic grandeur. Besides, when Hugo gets out of prison, he realizes that those who made him kill Hoederer did so only for tactical reasons and that they are now carrying out the same policy as Hoederer. He realizes that he has killed for nothing, that he has acted against himself, and so he gets himself killed.

The situation you describe happened in almost all the occupied countries. The same problem arose in the workers' parties, whether they were to collaborate with the bourgeois parties within the Resistance.

True. But the problem is an even more general one. Lenin was the first to deal with it, in *Left-Wing Communism: An Infantile Disorder*. It also arose before the war in the Socialist Party when it was brought to power by the Popular Front.

Then there is no allusion to Gaullism in your play?

None whatever. All the action takes place within the proletarian party. The only question I am dealing with is, I repeat, whether a revolutionary may risk jeopardizing his ideals for the sake of efficacy. Has he the right to "dirty his hands"?

(Combat, March 31, 1948)

The theater's job is not demonstration or solution. It thrives on questions and problems.

Who is to decide between Creon and Antigone?

As in Sophocles, none of my characters is in the wrong nor in the right. A remark by Saint-Just, "No one governs innocently," supplied me with the theme of *Dirty Hands*. Taking that as my starting point, I have put on the stage a conflict between a young, idealistic bourgeois and political necessity. This young man has deserted his class for the sake of this ideal, and it is for its sake too that he will kill the leader whom he admired but who was more concerned with the end than with the choice of means. And I go on to show that he will lose this right by exercising it. He in turn will have dirty hands.

Just as Orestes must avenge his father, but when he has killed his mother it is against him that the Furies will turn . . . Is your play irrelevant to contemporary events?

Obviously not. Technically, it is a dramatic play in "ordinary" language and it takes place during the German Occupation. My characters are in a situation roughly similar to that during the Truce of Paris.[2] The Red Army has the enemy on the run, liberation is coming closer. But in the meantime, are three hundred thousand more lives to be sacrificed, or should one treat with the enemy? You will see, therefore, why I went back to the title I first thought of.

Why did you choose actors from the Boulevard theater?

Actors who play the classics have a special technique. The Boulevard remains the school of natural behavior. An actor with that experience is free to twist and turn. Classical actors are always specialists. André Luguet gives the necessary authority to the realistic leader whose part he plays. François Périer has a complexity which well suits his character of a bourgeois who has turned to Marxism. Paula Dehelly and Marie-Olivier[3] bring out the difference between the militant and the woman.

(*Le Figaro*, March 30, 1948)

In *Sartre par lui-meme* (Paris: Éditions du Seuil, 1955, pp. 48–49; new ed., 1967, pp. 44–45), Francis Jeanson reproduced the following statement by Sartre about *Dirty Hands*:

In the first place, I wanted some of the young people of bourgeois origins who were my students or friends and are now twenty-five years old to find something of themselves in Hugo's hesitations. I have never found Hugo a sympathetic character, and I have never thought he was in the right as against Hoederer. But I was trying to present in him the torments of a certain type of youth which, though it is emotionally inclined to a protest of a kind which is very specifically communist, does not go as far as joining the party because of its humanist educational background. I did not want to say whether they were right or wrong; if I had, my play would have been propagandist. I simply tried to describe them. But Hoederer's is the only attitude I think sound.

Conversation with Paolo Caruso about *Dirty Hands* (1964)

With 625 performances in Paris and 300 in the provinces and a great many abroad in translation, *Dirty Hands* remains Sartre's most successful play. Sartre was greatly irritated, however, when his play was used as a cold-war weapon, and in 1952 decided to permit its performance only if the Communist Party in the country where it was to be performed agreed. *Dirty Hands* was banned, therefore, in Vienna (in 1952 and 1954), in Spain, in Greece, in Indochina, and in Antwerp (in 1966). Only after 1962 did Sartre permit new productions of *Dirty Hands* in Yugoslavia, Italy, and Czechoslovakia (1968).

The text of an interview that Sartre gave on March 4, 1964, to Paolo Caruso, the Italian translator of the *Critique de la raison dialectique,* at the time of the performance of an amended version of *Dirty Hands* by the Teatro Stabile in Turin (first night March 24, 1964), is reproduced below. Despite some repetitions, this interview seems essential for a proper understanding of the play. For more detailed information, see *The Writings of Jean-Paul Sartre,* volume 1, notes 48/145–54.

The text of the interview was first published in Jean-Paul Sartre, *Le Mani sporche,* an Italian edition of *Dirty Hands,* translated by Vittorio Sermonti (Turin: Giulio Einaudi editore, 1964, pp. 137–49). That edition also includes a long excerpt dealing with *Dirty Hands* from Simone de Beauvoir's *The Force of Circumstances* (New York: J. P. Putnam's Sons, 1965, pp. 150–52).

PAOLO CARUSO   I wanted to ask you, first, what you thought about *Dirty Hands* just after you had written the play, that is to say, before it was performed in public; secondly, what you thought of it after the public's and critics' reactions; and thirdly, what you think of it now, sixteen years later. In other words, did you "rediscover" the work when it had assumed an objective dimension, a social reality, after its exposure to the public gaze? Do you see it differently now, in changed historical circumstances and in the light of the changes that have occurred in the world and in yourself? Lastly, has your judgment changed in the light of your present ideas, the present stage in your development? A development which is, I think, brought out very well in *The Condemned of Altona,* your most recent dramatic work (though it is more than four years old now), some of the themes of which were already present in *Dirty Hands,* but with quite a different slant.

SARTRE   That is a good question, because a play is far less its author's property than a novel, for instance, and because it can often have unexpected results. Indeed, what happens between audience and author at the dress rehearsal and on the following nights gives a play a certain objective reality which the author very often had neither foreseen nor intended.

CARUSO   You are alluding, if I am not mistaken, to "mediating" factors that exist in the theater but not in a book: the staging of the performance by the director, the actors, and so on.

SARTRE   . . . and the way everything appears. There is also the fact that the audience—especially an audience that is committed and is therefore open to the influence of the moment—goes to see the play for reasons that are precisely the reasons that will prevent it from wholly understanding it.

CARUSO   Inevitably, of course, they are prepared to prejudge or expect things.

SARTRE   And one can't deny, objectively, that at a certain moment, given the circumstances in which it appears, a play assumes an objective meaning which is assigned to it by an audience. There is nothing to be done about it; if the whole of the French bourgeoisie makes *Dirty Hands* a hit and if the Communists attack it, that means that something has really happened. It means that the play has beccome anticommunist *of its own accord*, objectively, and that the author's intentions no longer count. What am I doing, then, at this particular moment? Well, making a test, for we are in a different period; I am questioning the play's objectivity anew. On the whole, I have a subjective certainty, to use Hegel's term, about the play, my point of view, which I tried to re-examine before I accepted the Teatro Stabile's proposal to give it a public performance. My point of view has changed slightly, but in essence it is still the same; I still think, subjectively, that is to say **as far** as what I wrote is concerned, that it is not an anticommunist work but just the opposite, a work by a fellow-traveler. But if at Turin the play actually turns out to be an anticommunist work, and if my agreement with the forces of the left does not prevent the rightist press and the bourgeoisie from saying that it is anticommunist, the question will have been settled once and for all, and *Dirty Hands* will never be performed again. This is why I attach great importance to the performance by the Teatro Stabile. It is, as I said, a test.

CARUSO   But what do you expect? You believed in 1948 that you had not written an anticommunist play. Do you still take the same view as you once did? Or rather, has the objective meaning of the play remained exactly the same?

SARTRE   Definitely not. My point of view has remained substantially the same, except that I now give the drama another meaning, or rather, another practical value. I maintain, if you like, that the main factor in the misunderstanding was that the political assassination in the play was seen as a constant element in the fight within the Communist Party. Someone even went so far as to write, for instance, that if Thorez fell out with a party comrade, he would have to pay someone to murder him. But of course, that is not the meaning of the play at all. In a period of underground armed resistance—take the case of the Algerian FLN, for example—cases occur in which the physical elimination of an opposition is necessary, because the opposition poses a terrible threat. This happened in France during the Resistance, and not only among the Communists, of course. There are things which have to be done which I, personally, consider inevitable. Briefly, it is not possible to conceive of an underground armed struggle against a stronger enemy carried on by the same means as the means used by a democratic party, even a centralized one, which is acting in the full light of day, because they are two totally different things. But it is precisely the political crime which people emphasize to show that the play is "leftist"; despite the fact, too, that Hoederer, the positive hero, says at one point, "I have nothing against political crime; it always happens when circumstances demand it."[4] In other words, political crime has been made out to be a weapon used solely by parties of the left and to be typical of the way they act, whereas it is absolutely certain that these parties customarily have a quite different technique. It is as if one had shown an act of sabotage during a resistance movement and somebody had come and told you, "According to you, it's the Communists who are the saboteurs," whereas in fact everyone knows that the method of sabotage in the factories is rejected by the Communist Party as ineffective.

CARUSO   I should say that the communist parties might be blamed for the opposite fault, for eschewing sabotage even in cases when it appears to be the only possible form of action, but certainly not for being "systematic saboteurs."

SARTRE   No doubt about it. They have always disapproved of sabotage as an erroneous method because it is too individualistic. For similar reasons they have taken a stand against political assassination, even in circumstances where the struggle was difficult enough to require it. Nonetheless, everything changes in the context of a resistance movement; and in this particular case it is no longer a Communist who is compelled to resort to political murder when necessary, but a member of the Resistance. Because in such circumstances there are also some well-known cases of political assassination on the other side.

CARUSO   So this was an initial misunderstanding to be cleared up. But how did it come about? You have explained the phenomenon by which the play became, in the view of the public and the critics, objectively an anticommunist play, tinged in some sort with a reactionary meaning, and this phenomenon has no predetermined cause, but is the result of several factors. Simone de Beauvoir has, however, set out a definitely chronological sequence in *The Force of*

Circumstances: to begin with, the bourgeois press was not sure that it could applaud the play; it waited for the Communists' reaction, and it was only after the Communists had damned it heartily that it started to lavish praise on it.

SARTRE   It is quite true that the misunderstanding first arose among the Communists, and for two reasons, one of them a deep one, the other accidental. The deep reason is Stalinism, that is to say the fact that a *critical* "fellow-traveler" was not tolerated at that time; a wholly assenting fellow-traveler, yes, but a critical fellow traveler was an enemy. Now, you know very well that I have always wanted —and I still want—to be a critical fellow-traveler in relation to the Communists. I believe that an intellectual is in duty bound to combine discipline with criticism; this is a contradiction, but a contradiction for which we have the responsibility, and it is our business to reconcile the two. Criticism without a discipline, without a basic assent, does not work; but assent without criticism does not work either (it may work, but that is not the particular business of the intellectual). An intellectual is precisely a person who, for his own purpose and by an objective method, sees a form of positive reaction define itself before him and has the duty to express it.

CARUSO   And the accidental reason?

SARTRE   It is what I now consider a mistake, though a slight one: the foundation of the Rassemblement Démocratique Révolutionnaire (RDR), that is, a group which I joined *from the left* (the proof is that it was I who led to its breakup, for leftist reasons). Briefly, as soon as we were repulsed by the party, we tried to form a leftist group which would have been independent, but standing alongside the party. There were errors, as I pointed out in my essay on Merleau-Ponty ("Merleau-Ponty vivant"); the first was that even if we had been successful, we would only have been able to attract a paracommunist following, and thus deprive the Communists of potential support.

CARUSO So it is natural enough that the CP should have regarded you as competitors, that is, adversaries.

SARTRE Perfectly natural. Besides, there were persons within the group who tried to take advantage of it for reasons of personal ambition. The group had been formed long before *Dirty Hands* was performed,[5] and it was inevitable that the play should be labeled RDR and so be regarded as anticommunist.

CARUSO You have given me two reasons, both of which are, however, external to the work. To these reasons I would add that the play in itself is so constructed that, by internal necessity, it leads the public, and even you yourself, to identify with Hugo. Not to *sympathize* with him, and even less to feel that he is in the right; Hugo is in the wrong from start to finish. It is Hoederer who must be in the right. But Hugo is in the right *for* Hugo, and naturally, for the public and for the author, insofar as they identify themselves to some extent with Hugo. For as Hugo is the protagonist, one inevitably puts oneself in his shoes, takes part in some sense in his drama, and feels his contradictions personally, even though one may feel an antipathy to the character. Then the last words with which Hugo tries to justify his own suicide—"A man like Hoederer does not die by chance. He dies for his ideas, for his politics; he is responsible for his death"—are a protest against the attempt by the party leaders to falsify the past, a protest whose force the audience cannot but feel. So the audience quite rightly comes in the end to find Hugo in the right and those whom, by an oversimplification, it calls "Communists" in the wrong, because it repudiates the "mystification enforced with idealistic violence" for which you yourself have blamed certain pseudo-Marxists. I think this is the *internal* reason why it has been possible to call *Dirty Hands* anticommunist. And the leftist audience could not disapprove of Hugo's final gesture and accept his comrades' party line. Praxis and political realism have their imperatives—but for the future

rather than the past. No one can approve of someone who falsifies documents and distorts the meaning of past history.
SARTRE   Yes. And this is undoubtedly the reason for the Communists' hostility to *Dirty Hands, at that time.* My play is not intended as an apologia, but rather as a *critical support* of the socialist movement, and it exercises its criticism precisely by attacking the Stalinist methods that were then being used. Falsification of the past was a systematic practice of Stalinism. For example, any trial held under that regime involved the defendant's whole past, even where very well known Communists were concerned. Anybody who is a traitor at a particular point must necessarily always have been a traitor. Today it is not so, but at that time it was. By reason of certain dogmatic principles, for notorious dialectical reasons, a man could not have been a revolutionary and then, at a given moment, no longer be one. Once he is no longer one, he has never been one: that is the Stalinist principle. You go back to the defendant's birth, therefore, and you "come to realize," by falsifying everything, that he has always been a counterrevolutionary. It is precisely against this falsification of the past that Hugo is in the right in his final speeches. He is in the right, but at the same time there is nevertheless an imperative of praxis which ensures that Louis and his comrades can no longer take over Hoederer's policy and declare that he was a swine. At most they can say that, basically, there was an error concerning the moment when the new tactics should have been adopted.
CARUSO   Certainly, according to Stalinist logic. But it's perhaps rather too obvious to add that they might have acknowledged their own errors, as indeed they have in some cases . . .
SARTRE   Yes, but when an error leads to murder . . .
CARUSO   They could always say that they were in good faith, convinced they were serving the purpose of the revolution, even present it as an unavoidable error. To go back to

our subject, it looks to me as if Simone de Beauvoir's version, with which, I think, you agree pretty well, made far too little of this side of the question, that is, the psychological mechanism, which, in my view, did a great deal to put the anticommunist label on *Dirty Hands*. I repeat, Hugo is in the wrong. Like any committed intellectual, or any intellectual who is thinking of committing himself to a revolutionary path with the pretext and half-formed wish to preserve his bourgeois "nature," he is in a situation almost as ambiguous as that of the worker priests . . . He is in the wrong right up to the end of the play. But as far as the audience is concerned, the way that the final speeches give the whole of the rest of the play a meaning that justifies Hugo and condemns the revolutionary party is dramatically very effective indeed. Hugo's gesture is taken seriously and it cannot be understood, as Simone de Beauvoir claims, as a sort of whim or a gratuitous obstinacy in taking upon himself a murder he has committed without even knowing why, without even having decided who—Louis or Hoederer— was in the right, and almost to show others and himself that he was capable of committing it. That is there, of course, but what the audience tends to follow is something else. Hugo has been placed in Hoederer's entourage to kill him; he was to be the instrument for a murder, and his intentions, his hesitations, and the meaning he gave the crime are irrelevant on this level, for Hugo was simply the weapon for the crime; what is more relevant is the meaning given it by the leaders, those who took over the leadership after Hoederer. This meaning cannot thereafter be dissociated from Hoederer's death. To change it is a falsification, and the audience does not condemn Hugo, who wants to prevent this, but the others who want to perpetrate it.

SARTRE   But wait a moment. Hoederer himself agreed that the murder should not appear as a political assassination. As he dies, he says, "I was sleeping with the girl," which is not true but enables him to save both Hugo and party unity. He too wants to prevent splits within the party, that is, to prevent some condemning the murder and others approving of it as the elimination of a dangerous traitor.

CARUSO   Certainly. But perhaps this element seemed less important to the audience.

SARTRE   But it was important to me.

CARUSO   I'm sure of that. But I am not discussing the play's meaning just now; I am simply trying to understand how it could have been regarded in that way. How did one meaning come to prevail over others? Why that meaning rather than another? I don't think the only reason was the two "external" causes you have mentioned. Indeed, I think that another and no less important reason is that the audience does, as I have said, identify more with Hugo than with Hoederer. Hoederer is almost an embodied ideal, *the* revolutionary for whom the audience feels a great admiration. He has the positive role. But the human drama, from the first act to the last, is Hugo's. What the audience is chiefly interested in is what happens to Hugo, and it sees the world of the play through his eyes.

SARTRE   That's true. But even if that is stipulated, the play's meaning does not coincide with Hugo's fate. I wanted to do two things. First, to examine dialectically the problems of the imperatives of praxis at the time. You know that in France there was a case similar to Hoederer's, the case of Doriot, even though it did not end in murder; Doriot wanted close relations between the French Communist Party and the Social Democrats of the SFIO,[6] and he was expelled from the party for that reason. A year later, to prevent the situation in France from degenerating into fascism and on specific Soviet instructions, the CP took the road which Doriot had advocated, but without ever admitting that he had been right; and it laid the foundations for the Popular Front. That is what interests me, the dialectic necessity within a praxis.

There is also another point I must make clear: I can

entirely appreciate Hugo's attitude, but you are wrong in thinking that he is an embodiment of myself. Hoederer's role is myself. Ideally, of course; don't think that I claim to be Hoederer, but in a sense, I feel much more fulfilled when I think of him. Hoederer is the person I should like to be if I were a revolutionary, so I am Hoederer, if only on a symbolic level.

CARUSO   But in another sense you are also Hugo.

SARTRE   No. Hugo is my students, or rather my former students; they are the young men who found it extremely hard between 1945 and 1948 to join the Communists because, with their petty-bourgeois background, they were faced, not with a party that could help them, but with a party that in its dogmatism either made use of their defects and turned them into radicals, extremists, and the like or repulsed them, thus putting them in a quite intolerable position. In the circumstances, I wanted to show the contradiction between an intellectual youth (with all the defects of an intellectual youth, but a youth which can always be helped to overcome the phase it is passing through— because revolutionary intellectuals can, after all, exist) and a moment in the objective development of the revolutionary dialectic which held out no prospects for them at all at that time. Hugo has my sympathy because I can say that Hoederer might have made someone of him. And it is clear that without the incident—the contingency—which I purposely introduced with the scene between Jessica and Hoederer, Hugo would have given up the venture, would not have killed Hoederer, and, if Hoederer had won, would have gone on being his secretary, would have been trained by him, and would have become somehow or other a true revolutionary. But Hugo went into the party attracted by Louis and people like Louis, which basically means that Louis's dogmatism, which is not a dogmatism of the far left, was translated into "leftism" by Hugo.

CARUSO   A dogmatism, in short, which better suited Hugo's idealism.

SARTRE   Of course. To come back to the reasons why *Dirty Hands* could be interpreted in this way, I think there is yet another reason, one even more objective than the rest. If a young man—of the Musset type—in a dramatic situation is dealing with mature people and struggling with great difficulties, the audience is tempted to identify with that young man.

CARUSO   In the present case, however, without meaning to. Because Hugo is presented as a negative element, some-one weak-willed.

SARTRE   A right-wing critic, Jean-Jacques Gautier, has called him a sort of Hamlet.[7] Not entirely wrongly, I think. For when we watch *Hamlet,* we sympathize with the pro-tagonist because he is young, because he is engulfed in difficulties, and so on. Yet he is in the wrong, since the play ultimately puts him in the wrong; he should have made up his mind to kill the usurper without so much fuss and so many complications. I do not recall ever hearing anyone say that Hamlet's hesitations bored him, that Hamlet is too simple, or anything of that sort; we take him as he is; he is no positive hero, but we identify with him. Well, from this point of view, I think that this is how the bourgeois have always seen *Dirty Hands.* And it should not be forgotten that Hugo is someone from their world. And what happens? Coming as he does from their world, despairing of the left, he can no longer escape, he has to die. That is the "bour-geois propaganda" which can be found in *Dirty Hands.* The bourgeois have seen virtually what father says to son: "I too was a revolutionary in my time, but I got over it later." Something of this sort must have happened. They saw the performance and asked each other, "What is this young fellow doing with people of that sort?"

CARUSO   Nevertheless, for the bourgeoisie it's a rather

dangerous kind of propaganda, because basically the reasons why Hugo abandoned his class are the most genuine thing about him, as the play brings out very effectively. I can well see, therefore, why the right-wing press failed to welcome it at once and of its own accord and why it waited to see what the Communists' verdict would be. Thereafter it made the play a hit by way of appropriating it for the bourgeoisie, by way of giving the public a lead and ensuring that it found a morality of a certain sort—its own—in it.

SARTRE   I would like to tell you an anecdote in this connection which will show you how far the case of this young radical threw dust in the bourgeois's eyes and prevented them from seeing the play's real meaning. Camus attended one of the final rehearsals with me—he had not yet read the text—and as we were going home together after it, he said to me, "It's very good, but there's one detail I don't like. Why does Hugo declare, 'I do not love men for what they are, but for what they ought to be,'[8] and why does Hoederer reply, 'And I, I love them for what they are'? As I see it, it should have been just the other way round." In other words, he really thought that Hugo loved men for what they are, because he would not lie to them, whereas he saw Hoederer as a dogmatic communist, someone who had regard for men for what they ought to be and deceived them for the sake of an ideal. Precisely the opposite of what I meant.

CARUSO   It is almost incredible that someone like Camus, who was very far from being stupid and knew you well, you, your ideas, and your writings, and had discussed things with you a hundred times, could have made a mistake like that.

SARTRE   And yet he did, and you can see how it could have come about. The refusal to lie is a radical fact in Hugo. Personally, I think that there should be as little lying as possible *within the limits imposed by the imperatives of praxis*. Lying should not be condemned nor, of course, approved *a priori* (by making a Machiavellian technique of it, for instance), but there is nothing abnormal about its happening when circumstances require it. When Hoederer says, "It is not I who invented the lie and I shall use it if it is necessary,"[9] I think he is quite right. There has never been a political situation in which lying, by omission at any rate, does not become absolutely essential. I maintain that we must fight to free ourselves from lies *even more fiercely than for anything else*; we must fight against lies by fighting for the establishment of a classless society, but I do not think one can absolutely deny the need for lies in certain circumstances. When Hugo says that one does not lie to one's comrades, this very assertion arouses the bourgeois spectator's contempt. Because the bourgeois, with his idealist morality, lies constantly, even while he *declares* that one must not lie; whereas Hugo is a character who believes in what he says. To him lying to men means humiliating them in every way. Hoederer tries to speak the truth as far as possible; lying is not in his nature, except that he does not recoil either from lying or from political murder when they are the necessities of praxis. Incidentally, this is the thesis which I shall be expounding in philosophical terms at the Istituto Gramsci in Rome in May at a symposium on the topic of "morality and praxis."[10] I shall try to explain in what sense morality does not exist apart from praxis. Morality is nothing but a self-control exercised by praxis over itself, but always on an objective level; consequently, it is based on values which are constantly becoming outdated because they are posited by previous praxis. This is precisely what Hoederer means. But the bourgeois of course say, "This boy is right, one must not lie, and the Stalinists do nothing but lie."

CARUSO   I think that nowadays, however, many "right-wing" members of the audience will inevitably feel some sympathy for Hoederer; and one criticism that could be made of *Dirty Hands* is precisely this: a certain amount of idealization of the character of Hoederer and, concomitantly, a certain amount of idealization of the class struggle. It is grotesque that the opposite should have been believed. Everything in the play is in a larger dimension than reality: hands become far dirtier than in actual politics, the conflicts are often on a much lower level, the situations are even more ambiguous and corrupting.

SARTRE   But do you know that some Trotskyists have attacked me precisely on this point? They say I have idealized the revolutionary struggle in the Stalinist period.

CARUSO   That seems a more intelligent criticism, at any rate.

SARTRE   And others, applying some of the ideas expressed in *The Condemned of Altona* to the socialist countries, have explained to me that the latter is basically, with its black tragedy, much *truer* than *Dirty Hands*. Franz can in fact be interpreted as a young militant who wakes up on the day after the Twentieth Congress with bloodstained hands and reacts in his own way to the revelation. I think you too started out by pointing to a similarity of theme on a deeper level between *The Condemned of Altona* and *Dirty Hands*.

CARUSO   Yes, I did. And I also made some allusion in very general terms to the conflict between the individual and history.

SARTRE   But in reply to the Trotskyists' criticism I say that the text of a play should be a myth. Consequently, if there are any sordid little facts in the day-to-day struggle, they do not *directly* concern me when I am writing the text of a play.

CARUSO   No doubt about that. There is one more point, however, on which I do not agree with your statement that you don't identify yourself in any way with Hugo. I would contend that Hugo and Hoederer do in fact represent the two poles of your development, even if simply in time sequence. Because you started out from Hugo's position: you too felt drawn to the proletariat in a rather irrational way when you were young. You have said so many times in your writings.

SARTRE   Yes, but never at such a level of idealism.

CARUSO   No, certainly not. But, for example, in an un-published note going as far back as just after the German-Soviet pact quoted by Simone de Beauvoir in *The Force of Circumstances* you say, roughly, "Now I am cured of an infantile malady, an irrational support of the CP."[11]

SARTRE   I can't say you're wrong. Anyway, my real in-clination is to be, as I have said, a critical "fellow-traveler." And I think that it should now be possible to be one, even within the party.

The Devil and the Good Lord

(Le Diable et le Bon Dieu)

Samedi-Soir, a mass-circulation weekly, published (June 2, 1951) an interview with Sartre, headed "There is no difference between the Devil and the Lord—personally, I choose man." The principal passages from it are reproduced below.

To tell you the truth, I must admit that the tale is based on a play by Cervantes[1] which Jean-Louis Barrault once related to me. A bandit who has wearied of doing evil decides one day to throw dice to determine what his behavior shall be in future. Clap of thunder, threatening growl in the heavens, flash of lightning . . . The bandit loses and devotes himself to doing good. Later we find him as a monk of sorts at a prostitute's deathbed, resolving to take upon himself all her sins in the form of a species of gangrene.

And God sends the gangrene, and it's what is called a miracle?

Exactly. There's nothing of that sort in my play, of course. True, Goetz, my hero, does evil at the start, and then, on the cast of a die, decides to devote himself just as resolutely to good. But he has in fact cheated: it was not God, but he himself, who made the choice. Similarly, at the end, when he calls down on himself a sort of gangrene in order to save a woman, he cheats for the second time. The whole play is, in fact, the story of a miracle that never happens.

Because Goetz cheats . . .

Goetz cheats because the problem is unreal. Events will show him that. Regardless whether he does good or evil, the results are the same and the same disasters befall him. Why? Because in both cases his acts are determined by relations with God rather than relations with men. First he commits acts of violence to defy God, and the peasants suffer from his plundering. Later he gives it up in order to obey God, but he still dooms them to misery by refusing to organize their revolt. And as far as he personally is concerned, he merely methodically destroys the human part of himself by obeying the divine laws. Man is a very poor thing when he believes in God; he must destroy him if he is to rise again from the ruins of himself. Because he chose the good, Goetz simply manages to ruin himself to the point of senile decay.

Senile decay? A depressing conclusion . . .

But only as far as decay. For there is a final scene. We have twice come to a dead end and have found that God destroys man no less surely than the Devil does. Then Goetz is offered a more radical choice: he decides that God does not exist. That is Goetz's conversion, the conversion to man. Breaking away from the morality of absolutes, he discovers a historical morality, human and particular. He had cherished violence formerly in order to defy God, and had then abandoned it in order to please God. He now knows it is necessary at some times to engage in violence and to behave peaceably at others. So he leagues himself with his fellow men and joins the peasant revolt. Between the Devil and the Lord, he chooses man.

So you are presenting us with a solution for the first time. Is this a foretaste of your essay "Morality," which was to be published eight years ago,[2] or the concluding part of The Roads to Freedom? *And there is the problem of action, which is raised but not solved in* Dirty Hands . . .

Contrary to what has generally been supposed, my sympathies in *Dirty Hands* are with Hoederer, the militant, rather than with Hugo. Hugo is a young bourgeois idealist who does not understand the imperatives of concrete action. Goetz is a Hugo who is converted.

Then your characters are intended to express the various possible attitudes toward social realities?

Certainly. But these attitudes are confused from our point of view, it must be noted, because of the special conditions in the sixteenth century, which I tried faithfully to reproduce. In particular, all the characters have their being within a religious atmosphere. The road that Goetz follows is a road to freedom, for it leads from belief in God to atheism, from an abstract morality divorced from space and time to concrete commitment. Beside him another character, Nasti, would be the revolutionary, but because he is living in the sixteenth century, he has a religious dimension. He therefore calls himself a prophet; in another age, he would have founded a political party.

What struck me when I was studying the Reformation was that there is no heresy to which some form of social unrest is not, basically, the key, but it is expressed in an ideology appropriate to the times. The Cathars, the Anabaptists, the Lutherans, and the rest are invariably some oppressed group seeking to express itself, but doing so in a religious form, because the age would have it so.

Then the clash between Goetz and Nasti would be the clash between adventurer and militant if it were transposed to our time?

Goetz is an adventurer who will never be converted into a militant by his failure, but an adventurer who will ally himself to the death with the militant. Goetz and Nasti are finally reconciled by a dual defeat, for the militant comes to understand the meaning of risk and to see that he may be mistaken, while the adventurer realizes that all he is really doing is preserving the old order. Goetz's failure is something like that of the kind of anarchism propounded by its classical teachers. For example, he decides to distribute his lands to the peasants, but this fails because his act, being a purely individual act, has no connection with the concrete situation as a whole. The only solution is a total solution.

And besides the Goetz-Nasti duo . . .

Besides them there is chiefly Heinrich, the priest. Whereas the play is on the whole optimistic with Goetz, the darker side appears in Heinrich. Our fathers were prone to believe that one could stay pure regardless of circumstances. Nowadays we know there are some situations that corrupt an individual right into his inmost being. One of these I have taken here. Heinrich is a poor parish priest in the sixteenth century, raised by the Church, admitted to the priesthood, placing all his faith and his whole loyalty in the Church. But because of the situation of the Church in sixteenth-century Worms, he falls into a dilemma: if he sides with the poor, he betrays the Church, but if he sides with the Church, he betrays the poor. It is not sufficient to say that there is a conflict in him: he himself is the conflict. His problem is absolutely insoluble, for he is mystified to the marrow of his bones. Out of this horror of himself he chooses to be evil. Some situations can be desperate.

It has been said that you were thinking of Genet when you created this character.

Not in the slightest. Genet is far more like Goetz in his first period. What has struck me most about Genet is the strict morality of evil he imposes upon himself. Goetz is the same.

There are also the women, of course.

Two of them, who define Goetz's configuration more precisely, first in evil and then in good. The second of them, Hilda, tries to reach a human relationship with him, but she fails because he kills the human in him since the only relationship he has is with God. He says the same thing to the woman as Claudel does: "If you love me, torture me."

> Another interview (with Louis-Martin Chauffier, Marcel Haedrich, Georges Sinclair, Roger Grenier, and Pierre Berger) published in *Paris-Presse–L'Intransigeant* on June 7, 1954, includes some interesting further explanations. The opening passage was reproduced as jacket copy on the back cover of the white Gallimard edition.

This play may be regarded as a supplement or sequel to *Dirty Hands* although the action takes place four hundred years earlier. I want to show a character as alien to the spirit of his age as Hugo, the young bourgeois in *Dirty Hands*, and equally rent by contradictions. Here the statement is couched in rather broader terms. My hero, Goetz, played by Pierre Brasseur, is rent by contradictions because, as a bastard of noble and peasant parentage, he is repelled by both sides alike. The problem is how he is to abandon his rightist anarchism to take part in the peasant war. I wanted to show that my protagonist, Goetz, who is a sort of freebooter and anarchist of evil, destroys nothing when he thinks he is a great destroyer. He destroys human lives but fails to destroy either society or the bases of society. Everything he does ultimately benefits the prince; and this irritates him profoundly. When, in the second part, he tries to do absolutely pure good, it has no meaning either. He gives lands to the peasants, but these lands are recovered as a result of a general war, which in fact breaks out in consequence of his gift. Thus, by trying to do absolute good or evil he merely manages to destroy human lives. The whole play is about man's relations with God, or if you prefer it, man's relations with the absolute.

If you were a Catholic writer, might you have written the same play about the sin of pride?

Yes, with the sole difference that to me pride is God. Goetz holds that the judgment of God is focused on him and takes from him his nature as man. Your relations with God may be good or bad, but in any case they isolate you from other men, even if your principle is the love of men.

Can you define your morality in relation to Christian morals?

Not in a couple of words. This is one of the things I am concerned with in the next volume of *The Roads to Freedom*. Roughly, I would like to say this. In the first place, all love is against God. As soon as two people love one another, they love against God. "All love is against the absolute because it is the absolute itself." Then: "If God exists, man does not exist, and if man exists, God does not exist." An essential line in the play is, "You do not love at all, if you do not love everything."[3] I was thinking of a Latin text which runs: "Lord, give me the eyes of a lynx that I may see what is hidden in the nostrils and the ear holes of a woman. . . . I who would shudder to touch dung with my finger tips, how can I desire to hold in my arms the sack of excrements itself?"[4]

From an interview with Claudine Chonez published by *L'Observateur*, May 31, 1951:

. . . Goetz perceives the total indifference of God, who lets him act without ever showing himself. So when Heinrich, who has lost his faith, reminds him of this, he is forced to the conclusion that the divinity does not exist. Then he understands, and turns toward men. Morality hitched onto God can only end in antihumanism. But in the last scene Goetz accepts the relative and limited morality which befits the human destiny; he replaces the absolute with history.

> Some time after the first night (June 7, 1951), Sartre gave an interview to Jean Duché in order to reply to some of the arguments against the play put forward by some critics. When it published this interview, *Le Figaro littéraire* (June 30, 1951) noted that Sartre had made these statements before François Mauriac's editorial "Jean-Paul Sartre, the Providential Atheist" had appeared in *Le Figaro* on June 26.

It has been said that I wanted to demonstrate that God does not exist, and that I failed. But like all writers, I am versatile, to prove the nonexistence of God I have the essay.

People think you are a philosopher who writes novels and plays.

They're quite wrong.

And Goetz's development is very much like a reasoning which reaches its conclusion with the assertion that man is alone.

I was not trying to prove anything. There was a cheap and vulgar bronze in *No Exit*. I put it there simply because I thought that the only object a man would be able to contemplate in hell would be something ugly. Well, people have asked me about the philosophical meaning of that bronze! No, I was not trying to prove anything. I wanted to deal with the problem of man without God, which is important, not because I have any kind of nostalgia for God, but because it is hard to visualize the man of our time between the U.S.S.R. and the United States and in what ought to be some kind of socialism. It is the pressing problem, but in the twentieth century people are only vaguely aware of it, without thinking it through. In the sixteenth century you find similar problems, embodied in men who thought of God. What I wanted to do was to transpose this problem into a personal adventure. *The Devil and the Good Lord* is the story of an individual.

The fact remains that everybody, critics and audiences alike, considers your play an engine of war against God.

The mistake has arisen, I think, from the fact that there are very few critics who are real atheists. All of them were outraged, except two kinds—the anarchists of the right and the communist extreme left. As for the middle-class critics—and "middle-class" embraces far more than just the Catholics—my play itself fails to involve them because they are obsessed by the row stirred up by the play. There is nothing wrong with being shocked, but it should be after the performance, not during it, because being shocked hinders the dramatic illusion. The general public is more receptive.

Don't you think they will follow the critics?

I don't know at all yet. In any event, it will not be for lack of warning. The critics arrogate to themselves a right of sovereignty; they feel obliged to raise the alert—Daniel-Rops, for instance, asked if he could come and see the play four days before the opening, and we let him come. On the following Saturday he published his article, which was intended to set the tone. I must say that certain standard reactions tend to become established in audiences. A speech by François Périer in *Dirty Hands* sometimes got a chilly reception and sometimes was greeted with applause during the first two weeks. After that it was always applauded.

How is the audience at the Théâtre Antoine behaving now, after two weeks' performance?

Well, there's one example of an unexpected reaction that recurs every night. Before he massacres the inhabitants of

Worms, Goetz says to the Archbishop's envoy, "I will kill them according to my office, and the Archbishop will forgive them, according to his own." That seemed to me to be a piece of black humor, the Archbishop blessing massacres. But they do not hear this line, because they are already laughing. And why are they laughing? Because Goetz has just said, "I am a soldier, and therefore I kill." That is a sentence which comes perfectly naturally from a sixteenth-century mercenary, and I never had the slightest intention of hitting out at contemporary soldiers, in Korea or anywhere else; my ideas about them are not that naive.

May an audience not come with preconceived ideas?

Certainly it may. On the first night, which was the critics' preview, the audience was scared. When Goetz apostrophized Christ on the cross in the scene about the stigmata, the audience wondered whether he was going to strike the crucifix. They did not know "how far I was going to go too far," as Cocteau puts it. The real audience is still to come. At present there are a great many foreigners, hangers-on of Paris fashionable society, sensation seekers, and students. What has become standard is the silence during the scenes: no coughs, no handkerchiefs. Which means that people are paying attention; they come with the idea that there are some ingenious points to be grasped. I am not too sure that I welcome this attention, because the audience is not at ease. But at any rate, they are not like the critics, thinking about the author, having to answer the question what sort of play it is, and coming up with the answer that it is a piece of "Hegelizing Nietzscheanism." The kind of spectator I like is the woman who said as she left, "If Goetz had managed to be good, would he have gone on?" I should like the audience to feel that it is simply faced with the enigma of a man, and that the only question it asks should be, "What is going to happen?"

In the first act the question is, Will he do evil? In the second and third, Will he do good? In point of fact, the first is a prelude. The first three scenes in the second act (scenes four, five, and six) are a further exposition; I gave them a slow tempo, so that the audience can listen with half an ear. The action is gathered together in scene seven and reaches its climax in scene ten between Brasseur and Vilar.[5] I should like the audience to keep the full force of its attention for scenes eight to eleven.

It has also been said that you wanted to write the anti-Soulier de satin.

Writing anti-things is not good literary practice. But since you mention it, *Le Soulier de satin* is far more of an affront to an atheist, to the radical socialist of the period, whom Claudel was getting at, than *The Devil and the Good Lord* to a Catholic. But the Radical Socialists did not raise a howl. The Catholics did.

Because the Catholic says, "No salvation outside the Church." He is totalitarian.

Yes. What an extraordinary privilege is granted to people who are of the tradition as against those who are not! His belief in God does not make Monsieur Daniel-Rops shed blood or tears. But so far as I am concerned, he is sure that I am expressing some sort of repression; if I say that God does not exist, I must have suffered blood and tears; my play would not contain these blasphemies, these insults to God unless I believed in Him. He forgets that I am representing the speech of people in the sixteenth century. In the twentieth century we discuss such things sedately. But these violences are not my own. "The Church is a harlot," Nasti says. It is a remark of Savonarola's. "You are a bastard." —"Yes," Goetz replies, "like Jesus Christ."[6] I took that from Clement VII. If you read the book of the play, you will find a pretty unorthodox soliloquy, which was cut in the acting version: it is by Saint John of the Cross.[7] And Goetz's outburst to Hilda, isn't that horribly "existentialist"? "Give me the eyes of the Boeotian lynx so that my gaze may penetrate this skin! Show me what is hidden in your nostrils and inside your ear holes. I who would shudder to touch dung with my finger tips, how can I desire to hold in my arms this bag of excrement?" It is a quotation from Odo of Cluny, a monk of the Cluniac reformation, which I copied out of Huizinga's *The Waning of the Middle Ages*.[8]

I have some other objections. Goetz's reversal at the end of the first act, setting Good and Evil on a throw of the dice, seems arbitrary. Is it historical?

No, I was not intending to write a life of Goetz von Berlichingen. I took the episode from Cervantes' *El rufián dichoso*, as related to me by Jean-Louis Barrault. Only, I made him cheat.

So that he himself, in fact, suddenly chooses the road to Good. It seems to me—and this is the basic criticism I have to make—that the experiment was foredoomed to failure, because it was artificial and founded in pride, that is, it was against God.

My answer is that Goetz's pride is God. He really thinks far too highly of himself when he sets himself against God (think of it, to incur the wrath of an infinite being!), and too highly of himself again when he prostrates himself before God. Jean Genet is quite right in saying that the worst pride is humility. Goetz will learn modesty.

Are you sure that God does not exist?

I am convinced of it.

Convinced or certain?

Certain. I was born into a family that was half Catholic and half Protestant. What with all the arguments one way and the other, I reached a conviction at the age of eleven. This was supplemented by my own reflections, which finally made me absolutely certain about it. . . .

I could prove it to you, but that is a matter of philosophical reasoning, which would take us too far.

. . . Goetz will learn that his relations are not with God but with the peasant or the poor village squire. Here you have the problem.

And here, too, there may be an ambiguity for which you yourself are responsible. The drama is played out between Good and Evil rather than between the Devil and the Lord.

True. The problem is the same, whether God exists or not. In any case, the point is not to find a basis for a morality in order to find favor in his sight, but to base it on oneself; and if God existed, man would find favor in his sight by being himself, by accepting himself and accepting other people in their finiteness. The sentence from Odo of Cluny repeated by Goetz means that his love of God prevents him from loving woman in her finiteness. Hilda answers him: "You love not at all if you do not love everything." Goetz does not love men. Jouhandeau's remark is very apposite, that he could not love men if he did not love them against God. And Malraux has Kyo say in *Man's Fate*: "Men are not my kind, they are those who look at me and judge me; my kind are those who love me and do not look at me, who love me in spite of everything, degradation, baseness, treason, *me*, not what I have done or shall do—who would love me as long as I would love myself."[9] That is what Goetz finally understands. So that it is absurd to say that Goetz goes back to Evil. In reality, he finds the way to a human truth.

There is a criticism by Catholics which seems to me to have more truth in it, that the reign of Godless man begins in violence. I am well aware of that. But history shows pretty well that the reign of God too is accompanied by violence.

Kean

Sartre wrote this note entitled "About Kean" (dated November 8, 1953) for the program for his adaptation of Alexandre Dumas's *Kean, ou Désordre et génie,* which opened at the Théâtre Sarah-Bernhardt on November 14, 1953.

When Kean, the famous actor, temporarily in Paris, was performing Shakespeare in English at the Odéon, Frédérick Lemaître took him around the cabarets. Kean drank and told all about his life; Lemaître drank and listened to him, thinking, "There are only two actors in the world, he and I." Kean went back to England and died shortly after. Frédérick Lemaître thought, "Now there's only one actor in the world"; and to convince the public that this was so, he conceived the wild idea of identifying himself with the deceased. Monsieur de Courcy, the renowned hack, was therefore commissioned to concoct a play about Kean, with the lead for Lemaître. But what about Alexandre Dumas? How does he come into it? I don't suppose anyone will ever know exactly. The only thing we can be sure of is that he put his name to it and got paid. The play is now among his collected works, with him as sole author. Its success went to Lemaître's head, and he ended up by completely merging his identity with Kean's. Toward the end of his life he was distressed to learn that *Kean* was being revived—at the Odéon, I believe—but with an Italian in the part. He was so enraged that he plastered up posters all over Paris saying, "The real Kean is me." Much later, the part attracted other actors, notably Lucien Guitry. After the First World War Ivan Mozhukhin played Kean in a film.[1] The reason for this abiding success is that the play is always contemporary; a famous actor can update it every twenty-five years. Lemaître, Guitry, and Mozhukhin, one after the other, have told the audience about their art, their private life, their hardships, and their misfortunes—discreetly, modestly, but according to the rules of their trade, that is, by sliding into someone else's skin. All the great actors who played the part successively enriched it with memories of them. By now Kean, with his chaos, his genius, and his misfortunes, is no longer a historical character; he has been elevated to the rank of a myth, the patron saint of actors. If Pierre Brasseur tonight has all the luck I wish him, the miracle that has attended the play for a hundred years will occur once again. You will not be able to tell whether you are seeing Brasseur acting Kean or Kean acting Brasseur. The adapter had little to do, except scale some rust and air out some mustiness, just clean up a little so that the audience's full attention will be brought to bear on the extraordinary sight of an actor whose role is to play himself.

Extracts from interviews

I am very fond of *Hernani*. But an audience laughed a performance of *Hernani* off the stage some six months ago. Whose fault is it? Neither the audience's nor Victor Hugo's, but the gap of a century, which means that we no longer react in the same way as an audience in the Romantic period. There's the problem that engaged my interest, and that is certainly the reason why I adapted Alexandre Dumas's *Kean*. . . . I have tried to solve a problem rather than merely evade it. I have tried to bring the melodrama up to date without in any way intending a parody. This has led me to reflect on the personality of what is called an actor.

Are you going to write an essay on it?

No, I don't think so. If an essay is needed, you have my adaptation. The actor is the reverse of the player, who becomes a person like anyone else when he has finished work, whereas the actor "plays himself" every second of his life. It is both a marvelous gift and a curse; he is his own victim, never knowing who he really is or whether he is acting or not.

(*Combat,* November 5, 1953)

On the posters for Kean *it says that you have adapted Alexandre Dumas's play, and when we are in our seats, we keep wondering whom we are applauding—you or the creator of* Monte Cristo.

Well, the truth is that Brasseur had the idea first. He spoke to me about it. Personally, I am very fond of Dumas; I think he is an excellent novelist and wrote some very good plays. The idea tempted me. But some things had to be adapted to the change in the public's taste. I don't, of course, compare Dumas to Sophocles, but I rewrote *Kean* rather as Cocteau "tightened up" the *Antigone*. I have, indeed, completely altered the part of the girl, Anna, who in Dumas's play was wasting away with some secret sickness. The notion of the consumptive heroine is not credible nowadays, and the idea that a cure by theater was more effective than any medical treatment would have looked ridiculous. I have made Elena more of a coquette and have touched up the character of the Prince of Wales. Beside the king the prince was simply a figurehead. But please note that I am merely drawing a modern conclusion from an idea which Dumas could not carry to its conclusion because, though he was a liberal and a progressive, he was rather inclined to be carried away by the pomp of royalty. . . . Another change comes in the second act. Originally, Kean recounted to Anna the splendors and miseries of the actor. However much of a novelty that was in the nineteenth century, it would naturally have been boring now, after fifty plays on the same theme, including Guitry's. . . . The whole of the work has been fun. Actually, I have only changed what has rather dated, and the line that is most applauded every night—you know, "Go and plough through your Shakespeare!"—is Dumas's own.

Among all the tributes to Kean, *only the last act has not escaped criticism. It seems to be by Dumas, however, and absolutely necessary to the plot.*

Certainly. Could there be any other ending? Dumas tied up the loose ends. I have kept all the scenes in the last act. I like the optimistic ending. That's too bad for anybody who would prefer to have it left hanging and the whole play pessimistic. Molière ended *Tartuffe* on an optimistic note, though the play might appear to be pessimistic. Why blame Dumas for doing the same?

According to some critics, Kean *gave you an opportunity to reassert some of your philosophical ideas through the character acted by Pierre Brasseur. Was that your intention?*

Dumas the Existentialist? That's a joke. I got the idea of the actor sometimes putting on an act to deceive himself from conversations with some good actors, notably Brasseur himself. To them it is a problem. But one should absolutely not conclude that everyone is putting on an act, and especially not derive a theory from it. The character Elena also puts on an act, because she belongs to the world of the idle. There is no philosophical theme of any sort in the play.

(Anonymous interview from an unidentified paper)

In an interview with Renée Saurel published in *Les Lettres françaises*, November 12, 1953, Sartre gives the following personal details about Kean:

. . . The interesting person is the "real" Kean, a bastard— that is to say, guilty in puritanical England, humiliated, Kean as clown, an acrobat, born and bred into the profession. He played minor parts at Drury Lane, but he really only started on his career with Shylock, standing in as an understudy. He made a sensational debut, playing the part in an entirely new way. In Garrick's time Shylock was played as the conventional ghetto Jew. Kean played him as wealthy, well-dressed, around forty, somber and sinister. He put his own character as a bastard into Shylock's part. Indeed, that is the essence of his contribution to the stage: he played a composite role *lyrically*. For the first time in the traditional English theater someone was acting out his own nature and his own personality. From that point of view, of course, he was a bad actor, or rather truly an actor, not just a player. The opposite of someone like Fresnay, for example, who is always just as good from the beginning to the end of a play, because he works hard at his part. Kean's successes were, as a matter of fact, always very much disputed. Sometimes he was terrible for half a play—and he knew it—and then, when it came to "his" scene, he was sensational. . . .

He died of tuberculosis at the age of forty-six after a performance of *Othello*. He usually played Iago. On that particular night, as an exception, he had consented to take Othello to let his son—who had an undistinguished career —make his debut as Iago. He died about a week later, worn out by the rowdy and debauched life he had led. The end of his life, too, was sensational. From Shylock onward, he always played his parts as himself. He was the Myth of the Actor incarnate. The actor who never ceases acting; he acts out his life itself, is no longer able to recognize himself, no longer knows who he is. And finally is no one. All the characters in *Kean* are more or less like that: great in that they grapple with shadows, which are their own character. In the play there is really only one character that is nearly genuine: Anna Damby, the pure and anemic girl whom Kean finally—in the play—marries. But to come back to Kean's life. His last years were pretty hectic. He was married and unfaithful to his wife. He even got a divorce, which caused quite a scandal. He was a bully, got blind drunk, assaulted people with deadly weapons simply for the fun of it. Friends of his urged him on by founding the Wolves' Club, which got him talked about. But that was the age when respectable England drove out Byron. Kean was also exiled.

To America?

Yes; and I'd like to tell you a little about his American adventures, which throw light on certain constants in the American character. Kean had already been to America before his exile. The tour he made on his first visit was to end in Boston, where the theater had been booked for fifteen performances. Very few people turned up. Half a house, a third of a house. At the fourth performance even fewer. He refused to go on, and went back to the friends with whom he was staying. Meanwhile, the Bostonians were at last coming to the theater. The house gradually filled. The Boston public, which considered itself the most enlightened in America, was furious. Quite rightly, indeed. Kean was attacked in the newspapers. He replied haughtily. And now he was back, a miserable exile, among the Americans. He was asked, "You want to go on? All right, but the tryout will be at Boston." He consented to the publication of a letter expressing his regret for the earlier incident. And he reap-

peared on the same stage in *Richard III*, which he had refused to play. But the house had been "stacked"; it was
crowded with hired toughs. Howls, whistles, baked potatoes.
They climbed on the stage, beat up the actors. The Bostonians even tried to set fire to the theater, but were dissuaded
when somebody reminded them that it was *their* theater.
They hunted Kean through the town, searched the houses,
as if it had been a lynching party. Kean was hiding under a
bed at a friend's house. And on that bed his friend's wife
was just giving birth to a child! He managed to leave Boston and reach New York, arriving there sick and exhausted.
He then tried a tour of the South. The slaveowners gave
him a far better reception, and he was able to play his
whole repertory. Then he returned to London. The scandal
of his private life had been pretty well forgotten. But so had
he. He had to start all over again. He did so, courageously,
and succeeded in making his mark again in three or four
years. . . . He recovered the audience with which he had
had such excellent relations, the public which had once
shouted, "You swine, you wife-leaver!" when he came on
stage. Dumas and Lemaître saw the romantic side of the
story.

He died shortly after his return?

Yes, after helping his son's debut, as I told you. In fact,
his last words were "Did he go over?"

Dumas's play was produced shortly after Kean's death?

In 1836, three years after it. At the Variétés. The play, in
fact, has a story of its own. Lemaître had said to himself,
"Kean is myself." Himself on a more international scale.
Himself if he had acted Shakespeare. Apparently Lemaître
told one de Courcy, who is supposed—whether rightly or
wrongly I don't know—to have been the founder of *Le
Figaro*, to write the play. I got a letter from Madame Mas-
son de Tourbet, whose maiden name was de Courcy, with

a photocopy of a document which does in fact seem to show that de Courcy, with the assistance of someone called Théaulon, worked on the play, which was perhaps "supervised" by Dumas, who put his signature to it. You know that Dumas very often used ghost-writers. . . .

What have you done with the play? Have you kept close to the plot and the characters?

As close as I could. I have only dropped a couple of scenes which were rather too improbable. As it stands, I find the play interesting, not for the plot itself, but because it is, as it were, a unique opportunity for an actor, an "actor trap." I've kept as close as I could to Dumas's text—or, if you prefer it, the text by Dumas, de Courcy, and Théaulon. Nowadays people are more lucid, more aware of problems. They are as divided, as contradictory, but not so much "acted upon" as they were in Kean's time, when there was little general awareness of what was involved. I have tried to bring that out.

Is there any other interest, a social interest, for instance, besides the interest in the hero?

Le Figaro has recently criticized me for playing down the social side of the play, of all things! Its progressive aspect! There simply is none in Dumas's play, I can assure you of that. Dumas was, as a matter of fact, rather snubbed by the aristocracy, but, as you will see, the Prince of Wales behaves very decently in *Kean*, in fact he appeals personally to the king to induce him to moderate the ill-treatment of Kean after a particularly outrageous scandal.

Kean shouting at the Prince of Wales in the box with his mistress Madame de Koefeld?

Yes. Kean vehemently insulting the prince in public. I have completely respected the spirit of the play in rewriting it. I have not parodied it in the least, because I find parody a feeble mode, good only for cabaret. And I am wholly in sympathy with Kean, who was an extraordinary fellow, far in advance of his time, astounding contemporary critics and indulging in attitudes which would have been acceptable, say, fifty years later. . . .

I felt that Kean's story might be truly moving, the story of a man who became an actor in order to find an escape from his resentment against society and brought to it a sort of revolutionary force. There is a touch of *Hernani* in *Kean*, and I am very fond of *Hernani*.

Nekrassov

Extracts from an interview at the press showing

What I have tried to do in *Nekrassov* is to write a satirical play. First, because it is the only form in which one can express one's ideas about contemporary society, and secondly, because there is a sort of latent censorship which stifles this particular kind of play. There is Marcel Pagnol's *Topaze*,[1] of course, and very good it is; but what I am talking about is satirizing the structure of society itself. A kind of satirical function existed in ancient Greece, but it no longer exists today; and after the initial reactions to the rehearsals of *Nekrassov*, I can well see that the satirical play will find it hard to make its way.

It has been said that your play is an attack on the press?

No, not on the press, but on a certain kind of press and its methods of putting out anticommunist propaganda. . . . It has been claimed that my target is Pierre Lazareff. But that is not true, because I do not think the evening papers are anticommunist as a matter of policy. The reasons for this misconception are (1) that I chose an evening paper simply for convenience of staging, and (2) that Louis de Funès, the actor who was originally to take the part, is short and so is Pierre Lazareff. Actually, even though I think that real names may be used in satire, I did not intend to attack any definite persons. . . .

You mentioned satire, Topaze *in particular, but isn't there also Marcel Aymé's* La Tête des autres?[2]

Indeed there is, but the essential difference is that *La Tête des autres* attacked an institution reputed for its dignity, which refrained from reacting, whereas *Nekrassov* is directed against a section of society which is sacrosanct. If you want evidence of this, you can see that a certain sort of press is already crying out before it even knows what my play is about and before it has been hurt! The way the reactions are going, I am not at all sure that my play will get an audience.

(*Combat,* June 7, 1955)

With the headline "By denouncing the methods of the anticommunist press in my new play, I wish to make a writer's contribution to the fight for peace," *L'Humanité* (which, like the rest of the communist press, was to support the play wholeheartedly) published an interview with Sartre on the day of the first night (June 8, 1955), in which he said:

In point of fact [*Nekrassov*] should be called a satirical farce, because what I meant was a satire. In a society like ours the spoken form, the dramatic form, is what best suits satire. Unfortunately, satire has become unfashionable. I am thinking of ancient Greece, where it served as a regulator. It has degenerated into the revue, which is usually reactionary anyway. The satire was a fairly loose form. It was the allusions to contemporary events that enlivened it; look at Aristophanes. What I have tried to do is to revive the tradition of satire by adapting it to our taste for the well-made play. . . . You know what *Nekrassov* is about, a confidence man who passes himself off as a Soviet minister who defects and makes sensational revelations to the mass-circulation press just before a by-election. . . . It is a truth exaggerated; I mean by that *typical*. Nekrassov recalls Matusow, the notorious (anticommunist) witness for the prosecution in the American courts. Matusow would make a splendid farcical character—if it were not that he actually sends people to jail. Of course, this sort of play is liable to run into adverse criticism. . . . "Right-wing" satire is invariably tolerated; we shall see whether "left-wing" satire will be. . . .

This one has made a stir even before it has been produced, has it not? Isn't it true that some people are hoping there will be trouble?

Le Figaro has published an article which amounts to provocation. It said that the play is "crypto-communist." They have forgotten their Greek at *Le Figaro*. *Crypto-* means "concealed." But I am not concealing my intentions in any way; in *Nekrassov* I want to show what harm an anticommunist press campaign can do. To incite a demonstration against my play without even knowing what it is, simply on the basis of gossip, is outrageous.

In this case it is not "truth exaggerated," but truth distorted, yet the method is typical all the same, typical, that is, of Le Figaro. *Your purpose, therefore, is . . . ?*

I wish to make a writer's contribution to the fight for peace. We undertook obligations in Vienna; we must fulfill them.[3] At a time when *détente* is growing, when the Four-Power Conference is about to be held, one of the most powerful brakes on our hopes, on what we are trying to do, is what this sort of press is doing to poison the atmosphere. I wanted to set down its methods in black and white, to open the eyes of men of good will among its own readers. . . . It's rather a negative way of doing things, but here and now the theater is likely to be more useful through its negative side, that is to say through satire.

It is in fact a very positive sort of "negative." Probably you would not repudiate the term "demystification"?

Absolutely not. It is most certainly a demystification. The play shows that I want to treat social reality without myths. In *The Devil and the Good Lord* I approached this reality, but through myths. I want to be quite clear. But it must be admitted that there is a cleavage between the subjects I want to deal with and the present audiences in the Paris theater. Basically, to stage a play like this in such circumstances is a paradox. . . .

> *L'Humanité-Dimanche* (June 19, 1955), some ten days after the first night, carried the following remarks, in which Sartre considered the reactions to which his play had given rise.

I have found that some of the audience were disappointed because they felt that the play was not malicious enough. But I definitely did not want my characters to be wholly black. Sibilot is not just a mercenary journalist; he is also mystified, a victim of the ideology pushed by his paper. Palotin has an enthusiasm for his trade, newspaper work. Nekrassov, the individualistic crook, amuses himself, pulls the strings, but he too is merely a cog in the system and, like all the others, has abjectly to surrender all his principles. All of them simply express a certain state of affairs. It is institutions, structures, that determine men's actions. I have shown my characters as victims of a situation rather than their nature. In a different context they might have been different. This is why a leftist satire must be a satire of institutions rather than individuals.

Isn't Marcel Aymé's La Tête des autres *an example of that?*

It is. It was a fairly virulent satire, but it did not arouse general indignation because it was aimed only at individuals or a group of individuals. It was dealing with judges subject to an occupational disease, warped by it, but it was not an attack on justice as a whole, a class justice. There would have been an outcry if the play had shown judges no worse than others driven to commit infamous acts by necessity, compelled by the logic of the system and of the class employing them. It is quite true that there are the beginnings of social criticism in Marcel Aymé, but it was not carried to its conclusion. Find better judges and justice will be better, was all it said. The situation in *Nekrassov* is the reverse. My journalists are not bad men. It is the cause which they are serving that is bad.

Some critics have accused you of "blackening" Demidov, however.

But he is not wholly unlikable either. He is just another victim. He has committed a fault: he has written a few dishonest articles and has been fairly well paid for them, and now he is left in the lurch, without a penny, doomed to die of hunger, a wreck of the cold war. I wanted to depict in him the downward slide into a more and more helpless situation, with no future whatever.

Conversely, some critics found scene 7 "edifying," discovering in the progressive woman journalist some sort of a Joan of Arc, a kind of girl scout.

That was the thing that surprised me most. In fact, the audience is told very little about her and she does nothing very heroic or dangerous! . . .

The theater today belongs wholly to the bourgeoisie. I once gave a lecture on the theater at a workers' university and I asked my audience what they thought of the play they had seen most recently. Well, they had not seen one, because they never went to the theater! Paris is exactly like the class struggle. The bourgeoisie has set up house in the center after driving the workers to the outskirts. The theaters are far away and they are expensive. The TNP has done a splendid job, but it is still curbed by its contracts with the government. In the hands of the bourgeoisie the theater can now deal only with restricted, tolerated subjects, light, harmless plays which do not criticize anything. At the end of the nineteenth century there was a realist bourgeois drama, fairly daring at times. At that period the bourgeoisie did not yet feel itself threatened directly. There are no longer even plays about true love; the implications would cut too deep.

Love is trifled with, it is not talked about in depth. Pirandello did produce some fresh topics in his time, with a certain amount of virulence to them. There's nothing like that today. Hence a crisis in the theater, because a gifted author, tempted by the prospect of success, has to cast his material into molds that will fit the demand.

Sartre was later to judge *Nekrassov* with a severity rather excessive in relation to the play's quality.

It is a part failure. It should have been focused on the paper rather than the con man, who is of no great interest in himself. It would have been better to have shown him enmeshed in the paper's machinery. But that was not the only reason why the critics disliked the play. I attacked the press, and the press counterattacked.

(*Les Cahiers libres de la jeunesse*, no. 1, February 15, 1960)

The Condemned of Altona

(Les Séquestrés d'Altona)

Sartre has given more interviews on *The Condemned of Altona* than on any other of his plays. The most interesting is with Bernard Dort, author of studies of Brecht, for the magazine *Théâtre populaire* (no. 36, 4th quarter 1959). As it is dated January 4, 1960, it took place some months after the opening (September 23, 1959). We have thought it important enough to give in full, before a number of extracts from earlier interviews.

DORT After *Nekrassov* in 1955 you told us, "As far as I am concerned, I have nothing more to say to the bourgeois,"[1] and that you did not intend to write anything more for the theater under the conditions prevailing in it at that time. Yet the conditions under which *The Condemned of Altona* is now being performed differ very little from those under which your previous plays were performed. Have you changed your mind, or do you think that there has been some change in the world or in the theater?

SARTRE   It's not I that have changed, but the situation. At
the time when *Nekrassov* was produced, physical violence
was not yet widespread in France as it is today; it had not yet
been promoted to an official style of maintaining law and
order. There was, of course, some machinery for law and
order, but it was the traditional, or what I may venture to call
the normal, machinery.

What I felt was really serious was that new machinery
for imposing law and order had been set up in Algeria and
even in France itself, machinery which no one can claim was
really necessitated by the situation; for there was no necessary connection between furthering the capitalist system and
the practice of torture in Algeria. Indeed, it might well be
argued that the reverse was true. In fact, torture harms the
capitalist cause, and the more clear-sighted among the
bourgeois know it.

That is why I felt that the problem set by it needed to
be ventilated—to be raised in terms of theater, the best
method for reaching the greatest possible number of people,
including the bourgeois.

When one wants to question the basic interests of the
bourgeoisie, it's no use talking to the bourgeois. The mystifications bound up with capitalism become increasingly apparent; the bourgeois are familiar with them and take them
for granted. If by way of exception they permit them to be
demonstrated, they promptly depreciate the fact that one
demonstrates them. Marx noted in his time that the bourgeoisie had become class-conscious and hence aware of itself as a class. Nowadays it is perfectly lucid and cynical
about its historical development.

But if one simply takes some phenomenon which occurs as it were on the margin of this historical development,
one can do it for a bourgeois public. This applies, I think,
to French colonialism, which has traditionally been marginal. (Our colonies have always cost more than they
brought in.)

I do not mean to say, however, that I wrote *The Condemned of Altona* solely for a bourgeois audience. I believe that these marginal phenomena should be demonstrated to our people as a whole—all the more so since racism is not the prerogative of the bourgeois class in France, but a reaction common to sectors of the people which are basically opposed to each other and engaged in a struggle against each other in defense of conflicting interests. So why not try to arouse a contrary reaction in those sectors of society?

So I think that *The Condemned of Altona* could be performed before a people's audience just as much as a bourgeois audience, for I have tried in the play to demystify heroism—that is, military heroism—by showing its link with irresponsible violence. That is a matter of concern to everybody.

DORT   Then why did you situate your play in Germany, if it is just as specifically French?

SARTRE   Primarily because I wanted a fairly wide audience, and that wouldn't have been possible if I had directly tackled the problem of violence as it occurs in French society today. I don't go so far as to say that my play would have been a flop or that its performance would have been banned, but the self-censorship would have come into play before it came to that, and I wouldn't have been able to find anyone to stage it; there wouldn't even have been any commotion, it would simply have been stifled.

But that's not the only reason. For though we are not Germans, though our problems are different from theirs under Nazism, there are very special relations between the Germans and us. We were once in exactly the same position with respect to them as the Algerians are with respect to us today.

If my play is really what I intended it to be, I should hope that the audience's first reaction would be to condemn the people shown, the same sort of people who once worked out of the rue des Saussaies.[2] And secondly, that the audi-

ence should gradually become more and more uneasy until
it finally recognized that these Germans are ourselves. One
might say that the theatrical mirage should fade until it gives
place to the truth behind the mirage.

This satisfies what I conceive to be an aesthetic requirement of theater, the need for distancing the object to some
extent by displacing it in time or space. First, the passions
on the stage should be damped down sufficiently to prevent
their standing in the way of conscious realization, and
second, there should occur what I would term the disappearance of the theatrical mirage, what Corneille meant by
the *illusion comique*. The spectator should be like an ethnog-
rapher settling among the peasants of a backward society;
at the start, he treats them almost as objects, and then, little
by little, as his study progresses, his point of view is modified
and he finally discovers that in studying these peasants it is
himself that he is studying and discovering.

DORT   Aren't you afraid that this rather oversubtle mechanism may fail to work in the reality of the Paris theater?
And that the reverse may happen, that the spectators may
leave *The Condemned* reassured, self-justified, and convinced that they are different from Franz? Would it not have
been better to present an ordinary soldier, with whom they
would identify themselves at first and who would then
progressively become, logically and normally, a cold-blooded
killer? Or perhaps a German soldier serving again in Algeria
and engaging in his former "trade" all over again there?

SARTRE   No, the second alternative you mentioned would
tend to show just the reverse of what I want to show: it
would imply that if you are going to be a torturer in Algeria,
you must have been a torturer before that. What I maintain
in *The Condemned* is that no one in a historical society that
is changing into a society of law and order is exempt from
being a potential torturer.

This is something that I believe the spectators of *The
Condemned* have really seen; none of them has taken the

Germany I show literally, none of them has thought that I was really talking about what happens to a German ex-soldier in 1959. Behind this Germany all of them have seen a substitute for Algeria—all of them, even the critics.

DORT But haven't you taken situations that are at once too exceptional and too specific? What I mean is that by taking the Gerlachs, who are kings or princes of industry, haven't you invested your heroes with a sort of romantic halo which hardly makes for what you called the disappearance of the mirage? And on the other hand, by specifically situating your play in Hamburg and in a capitalist society in which the age of managers is taking over from the age of owners, have you not made it almost impossible for the audience to make the necessary transposition?

SARTRE I took the von Gerlachs, a great industrial family, seminoble or ennobled under the Second Reich, purposely. For what I wished to emphasize was that these people were not Nazis; they merely used the Nazi label, but in fact despised the Nazis, who were, in their eyes, as guilty as communists or socialists might have been of "bringing the plebs to power." Such families really existed. What interested me, too, was that I could quite credibly endow them with an almost pure Protestant pride.

If I had taken some non-Nazi petty bourgeois, everything would have been out of focus; the problem of their collaboration with the Nazis would not arise. The fact of their not being Nazis would have been purely a matter of chance or a psychological fact. Anyway, the Nazis had very potent means for making them become, or seem to become, Nazis. We would have relapsed into a theater of special cases, of personal reasons.

With characters like the Gerlachs I had at once a basic contradiction to work with, the contradiction between these people's industrial power, title of nobility, past, and culture and their collaboration with the Nazis whom they despise. They think against and act for. In this way I could bring out clearly the problem of *collusion,* which is essential for the understanding of men.

I think Brecht was not successful with *Terror and Misery of the Third Reich* because he failed to show this collusion. He evoked the fear very strikingly in some passages, but no more. That's not sufficient.

I venture to think that the petty bourgeois can understand each other through theatrical characters so different from them as these Gerlachs better than through petty bourgeois like themselves, for they hasten to dissociate themselves from the other petty bourgeois they are shown and refuse to understand them. Here again you find the need for distancing—

DORT   Would it not have been better, then, to deal with the Gerlachs comically? Actually, that is one of Brecht's cherished notions: he thought that comedy was more suitable than tragedy for presenting the contemporary world on the stage; he even maintained that it, rather than tragedy, "treats human suffering with contempt."

SARTRE   Yes, Adamov also thinks that the bourgeois can only be comic on the stage. And Lacan says that man is comic, whereas woman is not. That's arguable . . . Only, don't forget that there are no bourgeois without workers, any more than there are colonialists without colonized or exploiters without exploited, and though the one may be comic, the others can hardly be.

I had, therefore, to stick to the letter of my play. Millions of Jews dead in the camps and the gas ovens, that was Nazism. It was impossible to show things with such associations comically.

I once tried to treat a serious subject—serious because it was a lynching—comically, in *The Respectful Prostitute.* But even in that play the comic, a species of black humor, was not self-evident. In Paris *The Prostitute* was played as burlesque. In London too, thanks to Peter Brook. But everywhere else they made it into a drama, and what was a farce turned into a ridiculous melodrama. Besides, what you can do in one act cannot be done in a longer play.

Adamov's *Paolo Paoli*[3] is comic, and I am wholly in favor of the savage tone of the play, which in fact shows serious matters, the exploitation of man by man (the men being, first, Chinese convicts, then becoming men closer to us, characters in the play, Marpeaux, for instance). But the period he chose, the turn of the century, was appropriate. Adamov is now writing a play on the Commune,[4] and I can't conceive that he will make something comic out of that.

We should analyze this more closely; obviously, you can obtain distancing through the comic. But does that distancing achieve the disappearance of theatrical illusion of which I was speaking? I fear not; for in the characters of comedy the spectator does not recognize himself, but his neighbor.

Distancing should not destroy the *Einfühlung*[5] cherished by the Expressionists. The two should go together. If you want to make an audience understand what returning from a war and remembering that one has committed atrocities in it means, you have to make the audience identify with your hero. It must take *him* as an incentive to *its own self-hatred*.

Suppose I had taken as my subject the story of an NCO who has committed unspeakable atrocities in Algeria returning home on leave and finding himself in a comic environment. . . . No one would be prepared to identify with, or even be assimilated to, such a character. Theatrically, too, it would be no good: a comic Feldwebel is an insect; you can only see him from outside; as a man he is impervious. Impervious men are no use in theater. Particularly when you want to tackle the problem of collusion I mentioned just now, the problem of the perversion of a whole generation of young people.

My subject is a young man returning from Algeria who

has seen certain things out there, has perhaps had a share in them, and keeps his mouth shut. It is impossible to despise him, impossible to distance him from us by the comic —impossible theatrically and even politically. For we have to admit that the political situation in France makes it imperative to recover such people for society despite the dirty brutalities they may have perpetrated.

I am not interested in brutes. Anyway, you get brutes in all wars; there were plenty in the 1914 war; but what there was not—and that is what I want to talk about and that is our problem today—was a youth demoralized by the complicity forced upon it.

DORT   Then why didn't you show the progress of this demoralization over a period of time, the collusion itself rather than the results of collusion?

SARTRE   It rather depends on *where* you show what you want to show. I don't think that it's possible to show collusion like this in theatrical terms. In a novel, yes, provided that it does not take up more than a chapter or a part of the novel. To show collusion on the stage would be to make it an artificial structure, something cursorily contrived and overfamiliar.

Anyway, there's no point in taking a defeat as the starting point of a work—whether a novel or a play—and then merely showing the deterioration of what existed to start with. Generally one tries, therefore, to counterbalance it by finding some compensation, and so one invents positive heroes. You can see what oversimplification that leads to.

It's pointless to devote a play to showing a soldier first refusing to bury those who have been shot, then consenting to, and then, under pressure from his unit or propaganda, finally attending interrogations and even taking a hand in torture.

What you have to show, on the contrary, is people *afterwards*. They have been torturers and killers and assented to it. How are they going to live with it or be unable to live with it? To me the ideal subject would have been one that showed not only the return of the man who has made himself what he is, but also his family around him, around his silence. He acts as a ferment generating a multiplicity of contradictions, and he himself is nothing but contradictions . . . Starting from that, one could flesh out a whole social study in theatrical terms.

In *The Condemned* I have inflated this subject into a myth.

DORT   We come back to the same question: Does not the myth draw a veil over the reality of the subject you were wishing to deal with—the reality of the war in Algeria, precisely since one of its characteristics is the way it seems to fit into our society without causing any visible disturbance?

SARTRE   You have to make things visible in the theater; you have to give them a general application. I have done that in order to treat the question of violence and its links with military heroism.

You think my characters are far too exceptional. But that's an optical illusion; in the theater all characters are, or seem to be, exceptional, Mother Courage just as much as Galileo.

Coming back to transposition. Obviously, if I had situated my play in France at the present time, I could have taken a petty-bourgeois family. Unlike the German petty bourgeois under the Nazis, they are not yet being subjected to any very heavy pressure. If they are against the Algerian war, they can say so. In Germany, only a few big industrialists were in that position. Since the position of the Gerlachs was very similar to that of the French Duponts or Durands today, the Gerlachs refer the French petty-bourgeois spectator back to his own position and so to himself.

In any case, this is only a preliminary question. Once we have situated the attitude of these people who think against and act for, the play can begin.

DORT   But isn't one essential relationship, that of the characters' social and economic conditioning, nevertheless distorted? Aren't the Gerlachs basically freer than the French petty bourgeois?

SARTRE   Let us not define economic conditioning solely in terms of scarcity—or of abundance versus scarcity. Economic imperatives affect these industrialists just as much as they affect the French petty bourgeois; the Gerlachs are conditioned by the necessities of production and raising productivity, which take the controls out of their hands, just as much as proletarians are conditioned by poverty.

Viewed in this perspective, Franz's case is no longer to be regarded simply as psychological; it is the case of a man doomed to impotence by his father's power. His father has "taken care of" all Franz's youthful extravagances. Even if he had not, they would have been "taken care of" in any event—because Franz is a Gerlach, the son of one of the biggest industrialists in the world. So Franz cannot evade the objective contradiction arising from the fact that he is at once a future leader and irresponsible.

Further, the developments in German society compel the father to realize that his real powers are passing out of his control. The managers are replacing the owners. He does, of course, still keep a definite influence on the operation of his firm, but he no longer makes the decisions; it is others who calculate, plan, and make the choices. Here too we have an objective development.

DORT   Wouldn't it have been possible to show this development visibly? In *The Condemned* you merely suggest it.

SARTRE   Show it visibly? But how? By including a scene in which a technician shows old Gerlach that what he wants is no longer feasible? That would have been hard on the ear, tedious. Or find a symbolic way of showing it, for instance by suggesting that the Gerlachs' subordinates are no longer as servile as they used to be? That would be very elementary—and worse, it is not true; the external relations of subordination have not changed; what has changed is the content of those relations.

Some things simply cannot be shown on the stage; they can only be stated. I can think of three: genius, scientific research, and work. True, geniuses have often enough been shown on the stage, but the results have always been lamentable. At best, people have managed to depict a picturesque romantic silhouette, but they have never been able to give an idea of work, of genius at work. This is equally true of scientific research; Brecht himself is hardly convincing when he tries to show us Galileo at work. And work—which after all encompasses the other two—has never been shown as such. You can only grasp it from outside, as a spectacular activity, or show its repercussions on a group of people, such as a family.

I'm afraid our young followers of Brecht are not sufficiently alert to these impossibilities.

DORT No doubt. But don't you think that the director can, if not show, at least suggest what the writer, the playwright, cannot manage to show when writing his play, when working out dialogue (and accompanying it with a whole lot of stage directions)? We feel that you have not so far given directors sufficient credit, you have not given the staging and final performance of your plays all the importance they deserve. A dramatic work can "inflate" on the stage. Between things and characters there can be created—and that is the director's job—a species of dialectic——

SARTRE I must pull you up at that term "dialectic." There can be no such thing as a dialectic between things—stage properties, which are objects—and characters. In the theater the action of man upon things differs fundamentally from the action of things upon man; one is subordinated to the other; they are not connected dialectically.

DORT Then let's say a dialectic between the significations of things and the significations of characters, as we find in the performances of the Berliner Ensemble, for instance——

SARTRE   But that's nothing new, indeed it is very ancient, even . . . And besides, I think it applies mainly to the film, much less so to the theater.

Too much attention should not be drawn in the theater to things insofar as they are an objective reality; the spectator is quite conscious that they do not exist, that they are false. In film, however, things are at once more real and more unreal; they are presented to us through a whole play of illusions; once we have entered this play, we can take them as real. Let's take as an example the scene of the theft of the typewriter in *The Four Hundred Blows*,[6] which I found excellent: the lad entering that ultra-modern building, the way everything seems strange to him, the way he gets hold of the typewriter, appropriates it when everything around him is utterly strange to him—that's something you can't do in theater.

In theater the actor's gestures are of more account than objects. Or to put it more accurately, objects are brought into being by gesture. Jean-Louis Barrault was quite right that to mime going up stairs bring the stairs into existence. He was exaggerating about it in practice, of course—but look at Chinese theater. The object is not needed in theater. It is superfluous. The gesture engenders it simply by being gesture, by using the object.

DORT   Still, wouldn't it have been possible to make your characters' environment more specific in order to show their objective contradictions more plainly through this environment itself?

SARTRE   That's true. We had thought of having the third act of *The Condemned* take place in a room in the same style as the first act, but with the furniture changed to modern, with objects in the Scandinavian style, a bar, glass-topped tables, and so on. It is Werner's and Johanna's apartment, the apartment of a different generation who do not belong there. We gave it up for financial reasons only.

Clues of this sort by means of decor or objects are, I

believe, necessary. But should they be taken any further? Should they supply a basis for the outline of a theatrical aesthetic, as you are inclined to do with the example of Brecht and his work with the Berliner Ensemble? I don't believe so. It takes a great deal of tact to make decor or objects counterpoise theatrical action, besides a good deal of reflection, especially on the philosophy behind any such aesthetic.

That Brecht was able to give physical expression to war and the duration of war in his production of *Mother Courage* is beyond question. But would that method suit every case?

DORT   You may be raising a question broader than the question simply of decor and properties. Isn't it, basically, the question of the choice between what Brecht called dramatic theater, that is, a theater of conflicts, and epic theater, that is, a theater showing contradictions over a time span and describing a society from outside?

SARTRE   Can one describe a society, one's own society, from outside? I don't think so. One can do it only from inside. The description of society by theater is therefore always a pseudo-description, since the describer is within the object he is describing.

Objective and subjective must necessarily be blended, as they are in *The Condemned of Altona*, in which there is, I grant you, a large subjective element.

Shakespeare himself, indeed Shakespeare especially, does not describe from outside; his characters are intimately bound up with the audience. That is why his plays are the greatest example there is of people's theater; in this theater the public found and still finds its own problems and re-experiences them.

Don't forget that the spectator's relation to what is presented to him is comparable to the relation between a man and his image in a mirror. The face that appears in the mirror has nothing in common with what the man regarding himself is objectively to another person. The man is not seeing himself in it, therefore, and cannot make any judgment about himself.

As to the need for what you, following Brecht, call epic theater, I am inclined to agree, for I believe that theater should represent man as he is changed by the world and the world as it is changed by man; but I don't believe that this can be raised to the status of a general law. As I said a moment ago, the prerequisite for any form of playwright's work is a philosophy.

It is perfectly possible to conceive of writing two fundamentally different epic plays on one and the same subject—the conquest of Algeria, for example. One would represent very sympathetically the courage and cruelties of the poor whites who colonized Algeria; the other would be a testimony to their individual toughness and collective greed. Yes, I can see that even rightist epic plays could be possible (if only right-wing writers were more intelligent than they are). I would go further and say that some epic plays by leftist writers seem to me to "veer" to the right even against the author's intention. Take that play by Michel Vinaver, *Les Coréens*,[7] which I find interesting in more than one respect. It glorifies a tranquil and virtually spontaneous humanism, in which war enters only as a temporary disturbance. The village in the backwoods of Korea, divided between North and South, has no notion of the savage oppression of the peasants and proletarians in South Korea by the Syngman Rhee regime. If you transposed the play to the context of the Algerian war, it would become totally meaningless.

DORT   We have never wished to make epic theater a formal aesthetic category. Brecht himself flatly rejected that notion. His epic theater is based upon an analysis of the contradictions of capitalist society, and he conceived of the *Verfremdungseffekt* [distancing effect] as the means for bringing out and throwing light on those contradictions, to show what he calls the "social gestus" of an act.

SARTRE   Yes, but here we are getting back to the preli-

minary question of the philosophy, the system of values, behind the play. Brecht was, of course, a Marxist, but to say
that is not quite sufficient. At the bottom of his work there
lies a certain sort of Marxist ideology, which died with
Brecht. Today this ideology needs recasting; I mean that we
have to cast it in some other form, close to but necessarily
different—times have changed—from Brecht's.

As to the analysis of the contradictions of our society,
well, of course, all theater has to deal with them. The theater
is a place where our contradictions become apparent. Hegel
was the first to note this, but the fact goes back to antiquity.
Since then there has been only one single change: in the
ancient theater the various different terms of the contradictions were each represented by a different character, whereas
in modern theater these contradictions have been internalized
and can coexist in a single character.

Brecht stressed anew the need to show our contradictions plain. Here he seems to me to come close to the Greeks
and to the French classical writers—much closer to them
than to Shakespeare, to whom he is now customarily compared.

These problems, however, range so widely that we can
merely mention them here in passing. In this area of aesthetic
reflections, or should we say reflections on the modes of
expression proper to one or another art form, the confusion
currently prevailing stands in the way of examining these
problems in depth. Perhaps we shall have to revert to them
one day.

Extracts from interviews

This play was far harder to do than *No Exit*. In *No Exit*
there were three people to be developed—here there are five
—and there were no incidents; everything was produced
from the impetus that the persons acquired by acting upon
each other. Here there is something similar, but there are
five persons to be developed instead of three, five persons

who are interrelated and mutually interdependent. The difficulties have increased commensurately. For example, the father and the son communicate from a distance without seeing one another. The movement—it may differ from play to play, sinusoidal or helicoid—I see here as a spiral. It was not easily brought off. And in addition, I wanted to introduce into *The Condemned* a dimension that was not present in *No Exit*: the past. There was talk of the past in *No Exit*, but it was not a factor in changing the present. Here the characters are dominated, gripped by the past throughout, just as they are by each other. It is because of the past, their past, everyone's past, that they act in a certain way. As in real life.

What particular emotion do you wish to convey in The Condemned?

The feeling of the ambiguity of our age. Morals, politics—nothing is simple any more. There are some acts, however, which are unacceptable.

(*L'Express*, September 10, 1959)

The play is about a family of German big industrialists ennobled under Wilhelm II, with very large shipping interests inherited at a time when the owner and the managing director of a firm were the same person. When the Nazis were ruling, von Gerlach, a tough and cynical character, held that the plebs had come to power. But objectively the Nazis needed foreign markets. Despite his reservations about them, Gerlach made a deal with them. How? By a contradiction which is the very core of Gerlach's soul. He cannot stomach the concentration camps, his upbringing forbids; but he reasons, "I cannot stand the Nazis' atrocities, but it's not I that build the camps; I only sell them the land on which they are built."

His fortune is immense; he is a captain of industry. He

is the product of his environment, which is changing; and even while he is collaborating with the Nazis, it causes him to hold them morally in horror. An impotent horror, though. Lutheranism has some part in this, besides the tragic spectacle—wholly internal—of his inability to exercise power, in every sense of the word, as he once did.

After the war, when all the crimes had been consummated and accepted, the same deep contradiction between his psychological background and German reality is once again imposed upon him. Plans for rebuilding the merchant fleet in Western Germany are part of American cold-war policy in Europe. Gerlach collaborates with the American capitalists. Once again his firm eludes his control, because there are other participants in it and other phenomena which weave the complex web of the contemporary life of capitalism, wholly committed as it is to technocracy. The functions of ownership and management are separated, and personal power—or rather the components of power—disappears.

This is the dramatic environment in which Gerlach struggles. He has a son. He had him thirty-five years earlier—that is, at a time when he was still the unchallenged master of his shipyards. He has brought him up to be the future master. He has handed down to him a role and a concept of responsibility at a time when he can no longer exercise them, neither he nor his son. It is his fate to cope, at his stage of education, with a command which is slipping from his grasp. Raised as a great capitalist in the fashion of the Florentine dream of a dominant and artistic Italian merchant prince, Franz, the son, tries to preserve his Protestant puritanism by attempting to save an escaping prisoner hunted by the Nazis. The victim is killed before his eyes, and he is required to rehabilitate himself by volunteering for the Wehrmacht at the age of nineteen. War breaks out. At the Russian front, cut off from his rear guard, Franz has absolute power of life and death over the local inhabitants. An intoxicating but precarious power. He is present at crimes which horrify him, his unit is wiped out. He returns home, crossing war-devastated Russia, Poland, and Germany. He thinks about what should be done to prevent such ruin from ever happening again. Above all, he thinks of his future, and beyond that, Germany's future. If Germany recovers and changes, he himself is nothing but a war criminal. So for thirteen years he shuts himself up, puts himself under restraint, to avoid seeing this resurrection, because it completely liquidates what he was and what he is in his own eyes. He refuses to see his father, who loves him deeply and is not unaware that it is his own image that is reflected in his son's personality. Should he be confronted with reality? That means risking his destruction. The father's feelings about him are ambivalent. You can see that the drama is played out beforehand. Gerlach meets his son and tells him the truth, with the intention that both shall decide to commit suicide. They drive along the Elbe embankment and kill themselves.

. . . It is my belief that the world makes man and man makes the world. I have not wished merely to put characters on the stage, but also to suggest that objective circumstances condition the make-up and behavior of a particular person at a particular moment. I had thought of giving my play a different title, "Loser Wins,"[8] for example; but that would have meant that it lacked the reverse side of the coin, which seems equally important: "Winner Loses." . . . I have tried to describe a situation which really exists, to draw up a world's death certificate. . . . I have set in motion men through whom capitalism expresses itself, as Marx put it. . . . When I speak of the ambiguity of our time, I mean that man has never been so prepared to win his freedom as he is today, and at the same time he is engaged in the most serious conflicts. . . . I had previously written plays with heroes and conclusions which, in one way or another, muffled the contradictions—*The Devil and the Good Lord,* for example. But in the bourgeois society in which we live it is very hard for an author like me to write anything but critical realism. If a hero is reconciled with himself in the end, the audience watching him—in the play—may also reconcile themselves with their questions, the unsolved questions.

(*France nouvelle*, September 17, 1959)

I do not think we can make an exact comparison between our present situation and that of our German neighbors. The situations differ radically. There remains, then, a general problem, that of the responsibility of a soldier compelled by circumstances to go too far, a case of conscience which will exist at all times and in all places. To situate and date it in the France of today meant running too many risks. Not the least of them being falling into socialist realism, the very negation of theater. It is not a political play, please note, but a contemporary subject from which I have been careful to keep my distance in order to transcend it and so retain in it its part of myth. In *Nekrassov*, the only one of my plays in which the action takes place in France and in our own time, this detachment was achieved, I believe, by the comic or grotesque element in the situation. All my other plays, with the sole exception of *The Victors*, testify to the same wish to achieve distancing.

(*Le Monde*, September 17, 1959)

I wished only to show the negative aspect. These people cannot renew themselves. They have gone bankrupt: "the twilight of the gods."

(*Les Lettres françaises*, September 17, 1959)

I should like to ask your opinion of the roles of Leni and Johanna; they each strike me as a species of vampire.

I quite agree. Leni and Johanna kill Franz: one of them little by little, keeping him alive, doubtless, but slowly killing him nonetheless; the other killing him off, since she is at the heart of the truth, and the truth will kill Franz. For Franz is a man who can bear neither the lie, because that would mean madness, nor the truth, because that would mean death. So I do indeed regard these two women as a species of vampire, but I don't, of course, mean by that that I am expressing a general opinion about what woman may be.

Take Kafka, for example: some of the women in *The Trial* were certainly pretty odd; they probably did represent more or less his personal opinion of the ties between man and woman.

There is nothing of that sort here. Leni and Johanna are in fact both creations of Franz himself, since he demands to be lied to; and when Johanna goes up to see him, determined to tell him the truth, it is Franz who finally creates a fascination that compels her to lie by coaxing her and trying to reveal his own lie. From that moment on, it is the circumstances which impose this species of *folie à deux* upon them, because anything else is unbearable. The two women cannot, therefore, be anything but vampires. At bottom, Franz's only human relationship is that with his father. The whole story is simply the summing up of a fifteen-year relationship; and Franz will use his sister Leni against their father.

But what in fact are these women?

Each of them is looking to her own interest, not, strictly speaking, Franz's. Leni's monstrous passion—I wanted the incest in the play for many reasons, one of them being to show that she was not and could not be—for that would have been incomprehensible—simply a woman who is devoted to Franz but has a misconception of his interests. A selfish element, which might or might not be blindly selfish, was needed.

Leni's point of view does not extend to the ethical problem at all. She thinks about Franz: "You did it, you tortured, all you need do now is take it upon yourself. Very well, you simply say, 'I have tortured', and that's all there is to it, it's done with." Leni does not realize that it is precisely here that the problem arises. Can horror be accepted just like that when one is Franz? And Leni proudly accepts her incest, accepts it fully, saying, "Yes, I accept it; why don't you too?" She is wholly incapable of seeing that it is absolutely not the same thing to proclaim her incest in a family which is pretty far gone on the way to disintegration anyway, and at a time when morality is pretty lax, as calmly to proclaim that one has tortured people to death. Leni will lie, then, so long as Franz is incapable of saying, "Yes, I did it and I take it upon myself." And at the same time, Leni knows perfectly well that Franz will never say that. So we are perpetually in a sort of provisional state, in which Leni is at once dominant and dominated. For Franz is, of course, also using his sister.

Johanna is a somewhat different case. With no special sympathy for Franz, though her mind is to some extent dominated by the image of him conveyed to her in the first act, at first she genuinely intends to say to him, "Listen, these are the facts; now give us back our freedom." But the flaw in her is that she is of the same kind as he is. He has been struck to the heart, for he aspired to become great and became a torturer. It may well be that an ordinary man might find it easier to say to himself, "I was led to it," and possibly it may be easier to rehabilitate someone who has done that sort of thing and confesses, "Yes, it was vile, but I couldn't help it," than to rehabilitate someone who had staked his all on greatness and had even at one moment believed that greatness required him to go that far, and who all of a sudden discovers that his action was completely meaningless and that this greatness was false in any case and even utterly void. Johanna finds the equivalent of greatness in beauty. This is merely another form of void, for where Johanna places herself, at the level of a film star, beauty requires recognition, recognition by the public, and without that her beauty does not exist; she is merely a pretty woman, attractive to many men, but not a beauty. A beauty is the film star about whom people say, for instance, the beautiful Ava Gardner. Johanna had her recognition for a brief instant and then, as often happens, ceased to have it. Whether it was because she was not quite beautiful enough, or because she did not act quite well enough, or because the public's taste had turned to girls of seventeen whereas it had previously liked young women of twenty-five, we do not know. In short, Johanna has lost her status, and thereafter there is nothing for her—the void. Beauty had seemed to her a justification, like greatness. This is obviously a case of what is called "alienation." You cannot alienate a merely pretty woman from her prettiness; that means nothing. She may, indeed, be rather too affected, but that's not alienation. But if a woman is told about her beauty in a certain way, then alienation applies; and if the notion of beauty changes, there is nothing left but a void, and it is in fact a void because it is the opinion of other people. Johanna has never seen herself as beautiful; she knew that others found her beautiful and then she knew that they found her less beautiful. But she always saw herself in the same way in the mirror, that is, neither beautiful nor not beautiful, but simply a piece of material to be worked up.

Just like Franz, who is neither guilty nor not guilty, but a consciousness that has to be enlightened.

But that's not the ground on which they meet. Franz forces Johanna to share in a bout of *folie à deux*: if she will tell him that Germany is dead and thus serve Franz's greatness, then he will tell her that she is beautiful. And since a rather exceptional person is telling her so, Johanna will serve

Franz. She will believe him. In other words, Johanna believes that someone like him (in the published book I had
stressed the prophetic aspect of Franz very strongly, but in
performance we had to make some cuts) can convince her.
This generates the bout of madness, but it can't last; and it
is the collapse of this bout that will make Johanna become
a vampire once more. I have been taken to task about
Johanna's character. For when his sister becomes jealous
and says, "Franz is a torturer," Johanna, instead of replying,
"All right, he was a torturer, but after all, that's how it
was," promptly leaves him. She might have tried to go further or ask for explanations or help Franz. But no, she at
once leaves him in the lurch. The explanation, as I see it, is
that the scene amounts to the following: as soon as Leni
speaks out about torture, Franz no longer wishes to convince anyone; the thing is said, it's finished, he abdicates.
The fact is known, several people know it, so he is at peace.
Now he must meet his father. Actually, Franz rejects all
help. He contrives to make himself abhorrent; he does not
say, "Well, I'll tell the whole story." Johanna can therefore
be forgiven for leaving him; Franz wants no more of her.

Resignation from the women's world.

That's it. Absolutely. Immediately. Because the fact has
become public knowledge. Leni knew, but never told.
Johanna did not know. Now it has been told, and Franz
thinks only of his father, prepares to face his father.

Which, in a way, he had always wished to do.

Yes, fundamentally.

On another level, I have felt that in The Condemned of
Altona *there was a hint of something which we might call,
rather awkwardly, an impression of "up above." In* No Exit
*you were talking about below. Now you speak of crabs, but
they are above, and so we have a species of elevation, of a*

vertical sort of relation. Do you think that we can see in The Condemned *some sign of a seeking for the divine? All your characters are strict Protestants.*

They are. I wanted them to be totally so. It is a Protestant story. It would not be the same with Catholics. For one thing, even if Catholics' beliefs are no longer those of the Church hierarchies, they still find a need for intermediaries between themselves and their faults. Things are quite different here. Here there are the crabs or God, no matter what. Or nothing. So it is indeed entirely Protestant; that's what I meant it to be. I know something about Protestants from personal experience, and what has always struck me about them is the rigid yet lordly side of them, which makes them feel at ease wherever they are. But when they commit a fault, they can absolutely not compromise, because they are directly accountable, without anyone to intercede for them. They lack the ancient institution of the director of conscience, the confessor and the like, who are, so to speak, liaison agents in the world of belief. Even nonbelievers of Catholic origin still find a whole crowd of intercessions; they harbor the notion that there may be persons wiser or more clear-sighted than they. Whereas in my play they have nothing of the sort. So you are quite right that they are Protestants. And the appeal to the above for them conceals an appeal to the God in whom they no longer believe. There's no doubt about that. For them, but not for me. That makes all the difference. I wanted them to be perpetually thinking of a God they no longer have, by way of situating them as both Protestants and contemporaries of ours. They have no defense against an absolute fault. I wanted that, but there was another point, too, that I wanted to stress, a totally different point of view, our own point of view, that of those whom I call "us" because they are unbelievers as I am: I mean the point of view toward History. Not because I regard History as the only master, but simply because we

have a sense of history nowadays. All of us. We know that
we look at the people of the past and judge them. We know
what we have to think, for instance, of the French bourgeoisie at the time of the Commune or of the reactions of the
Versaillese and so on, and this being so, we cannot help
knowing that we shall be judged, and judged by people who
are still very much of an enigma to us. That is why I call
them crabs. What will they be like? At all events, they will
have principles of judgment which we would not understand or would not accept because we have not pursued all
the ways by which they have reached them. We shall be
judged, therefore, by beings whom we cannot understand
and on the basis of principles that are not entirely our own;
yet we shall also be judged, no doubt, as we judge, on the
basis of the principles we have. So this feeling that we are
indeed exposed to a species of a vertical temporal relation
is one which quite a lot of people share nowadays, I believe.

*So the pillar of history weighing on Franz might well be an
equivalent of the God he does not have?*

Yes, but in both cases there is no appeal. To the Protestant
God, none, no intercession. Nothing. He judges. Nor is
there any appeal to the History we are making, which yet
eludes our grasp even as we make it; we simply do not know
what future generations will say. They will be on a different
level, have different perspectives. Thus, when the father says,
"God does not exist, it can even be a great nuisance sometimes" (this remark has led some people to suppose that I
was "nagged" by something "up above"), it is simply a
statement of fact by a Protestant who has the lack of belief
I mentioned just now, and at the same time it is a definition
of contemporary atheism. For indeed it is a "nuisance" to
unbelievers that God does not exist, in the sense that certain
consolations, certain certainties have vanished, along with
a certain number of ideas which they had found mistaken;
after all, an absolute and absolutely good Being can judge.

He has vanished, and nothing is left but disorder. I wanted to show, therefore, not that people should begin again to believe in God, but that our contemporary atheism—as I have written in a number of places—is not a satisfied atheism. It is an atheism which, as a matter of fact, is not far distant from the time when Nietzsche said "God is dead." We are still survivors.

Do you think, then, that Protestant man is closer to being a conscious man than a Catholic is? Do you think that this situation of being, so to speak, "directly connected" makes his consciousness more alert, more aware of things, or helps to do so?

I think he has a better understanding of things. But I also think that Protestantism stopped short somewhere. For example, the noble statement that "all men are prophets." It is very probably an egalitarian concept. Only, it was made far too soon, for the state of social progress had not reached the stage at which a principle of that sort could really be applied—it would have led just at that time to socialist views—and in consequence Protestant egalitarianism remains very much a matter purely of form. As I see it, the best democrats are still to be found among the Protestants. There were fascists among them too, but that is not the point. When a Protestant is a democrat, he really is one. But democracy—I mean bourgeois democracy—is an abstract democracy. In the sense that we treat our neighbor as a prophet, that's to say that he is entitled to drop his vote into the ballot box, but that he may also die of hunger, since after all prophets can die of hunger. So the problem remains intact. There is nevertheless a very deeply ingrained trend within the Protestant revolution toward assuming full responsibility, and sole responsibility, to God. This may lead to a social responsibility, a sole responsibility to a society, without the inevitable intermediaries.

It is perfectly true that, generally speaking, I have got

on rather better in literary life with Protestants or Protestant readers than with Catholic readers. These Protestants, though with all the reservations you can imagine, since they were believers, were far more prepared to accept ideas such as the idea of man's solitude and loss of contact. We found that we were wholly in agreement about the solitude of man. . . .

I do not think—without going into it more specifically —that the theater is a "vehicle for philosophy," to use your expression. I do not think that a philosophy can be expressed as a whole or in detail in theatrical form—no more than in a novel or a film, for that matter. When you come down to it, it can only be expressed in a philosophical treatise. But certainly every literary form can present, say, a philosophical feeling, or be highly charged with it. The novel has its own way of dealing with questions.

As I see it, what eludes philosophy is always the particular case as such, that is to say what happens to an individual. Even if a philosophy is taken as far as possible, it is obliged at a given moment to embrace—if you are taking it in the specific sense of carrying the investigation as far as it will go—the sort of investigation which is likely to end up as a novel. . . .

It seems to me that drama should not depend on the philosophy expressed in it. It should express a philosophy, but the question of the value of the philosophy expressed in a play should not be raised within the play itself. A play should present a total view of a moment or a thing, but it is equally necessary that what it reveals should be revealed wholly in theatrical terms. If we do not in one way or another believe in Marxism—and I must say that I personally wholly believe in the Brechtian form of Marxism— if we do not believe in Marxism as the constituent element, so to speak, of the Brechtian "display window," then we may say, "That's not the way things happen." A myth, for instance, should, I think, be insinuated far more imperceptibly, and it should be introduced in such a manner that it is not even perceived to be a philosophy. . . .

What I call a philosophical myth is something else. It is a way of presenting in a drama a moment of social and personal reality as a single whole. But it must be so thoroughly integrated with the story, the dramatic aspect and the development of the story, that the play cannot be said to be valid by virtue of certain principles nor that one piece of it can be accepted and another rejected.

So theater must be viewed globally, and only globally?

Most certainly. The problem of the individual case seems to me to be material for the novel. I don't think that there are individuals in theater. Hamlet is an individual, of course, but he is primarily a myth, the myth of the individual at a particular moment. But the playwright cannot undertake an investigation in depth that would produce such a very complex character as one of Proust's heroes, for example. One type of theater did try that, but it lost something of its dramatic force and gained very little in return. After all, if you want to create individuals, you need a lengthy exposition and an appropriate dose of associations. Besides, it is far from certain that the public for the novel and the public for the theater are the same. Especially the public one would wish to have for theater, that is to say, a public as all-embracing, in other words a popular audience. Popular does not mean simply composed of people with very little money, but composed of all sorts of different people. Well, with a public like that for audience it is not at all certain that one can examine the reactions of an individual as an individual in front of it. We may well find people who take no interest at all in that sort of thing for one reason or another. On the other hand, to a certain type of person who is more mythically than psychologically inclined, so to speak, the myth containing, if you like, the myth of a psychology may mean a great deal.

In other words, you cannot have philosophical theater that is likely to be good in all cases, but you can have mythical theater. To take an example: because the character of Mother Courage is a striking character, it is in fact on the level of myth, since what it represents is not the misadventures of a woman in the Thirty Year's War—the interest of which would be merely historical—but something with far deeper implications, the contradictions experienced by almost all of us when confronted with war.

Then you must have characters in theater?

Yes, necessarily. And the characters will be neither typical nor individual in the strict sense. They will not be the Duchesse de Guermantes nor Albertine, nor completely abstract beings such as you get in the eighteenth-century theater that represent an exaggeration of a single trait of character. This is not, of course, the origin of Molière's *Miser*, that's not what I mean, but rather the corruption of the classical equilibrium in the eighteenth century. Characters containing in themselves the myth of the particular case, the myth of psychology, but not in fact on the psychological level, psychology—or objective knowledge, if you prefer—having only to serve myth. What you have to find instead is a character containing in relatively compact form the problems with which we are confronted at a given moment. And these problems must not, of course, be particular problems, or very particular problems, but problems of concern to a society at a given moment.

Then is theater, do you think, "the" means for probing into the individual? A more searching means than the novel or poetry or the philosophical treatise? Do you think that the spectator watching the performance of a dramatic work is more susceptible to influence, more struck than someone sitting alone in private reading a book? In other words, does the "existential" element probe deeper in the theater than elsewhere?

The way to probe deepest into the individual as such is still the film, all the same, I cannot conceive of a valid play that would give you the effect that *Citizen Kane*[9] does. After all, Citizen Kane is not solely a character that is confined to totalizing all that Orson Welles could see in the Great American Publisher; he is a very individualized character to whom very particular things could happen and he has very particular traits. I don't know whether that would suit the theater. In theater you have less place for subtleties. As soon as you get into shadings the critics tell you—and with some reason—"This is more of a thing for the novel." In theater the character has to be individualized by the drama. I don't say the plot, but the drama, nothing more. Someone is placed in a certain situation with his conflicts and, as a result, he is an individual. But individuals are actually far more complex than that, and their situation comes from their past, their contradictions, and the various pressures upon them. This can be rendered by the novel, but it is too complicated to be rendered in two and a half hours in the theater. On the other hand, what you present is immediate individuation; but if you do, it is through immediate action, that is to say drama. A person is defined as such or such because he is in such or such a conflict, a narrowly defined conflict.

Take Antigone. She is individualized solely by her specific drama. We know absolutely nothing about her tastes or her childhood memories. We may certainly assume that she has memories, but everything has been swallowed up in the single problem of burying her brother. Similarly with Creon. Creon too has a life of his own, but how Creon becomes an individualized character arises from the problem of the city. We shall find psychological traits in him, but these traits will have to be inferred from the way he has to accept compromises in order to be the leader of the city, to make concessions, to conceive a special type of morality.

We shall, then, find traits of the political man in him, but only when it comes to that moment and precisely because of the problems he confronts.

If a play is well done, a character nowhere, in no other form of fiction, has a greater effect on the public. Nowhere. Including the film. Nevertheless, this effect is of a very special kind. I repeat, theater always treats things on the level of myth. And quite obviously it is better to go and see *Phèdre* performed than a musical comedy, because love as Phèdre's passion is mythical. It's not, as is often taught in class, the psychological analysis that is the interesting thing, but the myth. Even if there had been an advanced psychology at the time, even if Racine had not taken a special interest in the novelty of a rationalist psychology of the passions, even so the fact remains that Phèdre is love, or a certain mythical form of love. Beyond that, the psychology is merely a species of internal description of the myth.

Would that imply that the audience must "think" the characters? Brecht required an additional effort from the audience. Do you think that it is better to present a fully finished work, or should the audience be left a margin for infiltrating a whole dimension of its own?

I think the audience should be left a margin. But I would go in the opposite direction from Brechtian theater. Not that I don't regard that theater as the essential modern development and fully in tune with our times, but simply because I believe there is room for various different sorts of relations with an audience. Not because I disagree with epic theater, but because I believe it is by establishing communications between audience and characters that we shall manage to entrap the audience in the characters' contradictions. But I have a notion that it is not admiration of a character that counts, but participation in it.

In *The Condemned of Altona*, for instance, I don't think it occurs to anyone to admire Franz, who is a victim inasmuch as one is willing to excuse him and a criminal inasmuch as one is willing to condemn him. I simply want Franz's scruples of conscience and inner contradictions carried to the limit, to myth, in order to furnish the audience for a moment with a means of participating in Franz, of being him. (It is for this rather than strictly dramatic reasons that I hold back until the fourth act the revelation that Franz has been a torturer. It is because I want Franz to be the character in whom the audience participates at a moment when things are about to go bad and he is about to become fully involved in his contradictions. At that moment the audience will feel within itself the contradiction presented to it, and will feel it in such a way that it will become its own.) Naturally, the spectator has not been a torturer, but that's not the point; like all of us, he has been an accomplice in one thing or another, you know all the objective complications we all have; and consequently, if the spectator is affected, he is affected through this kind of compelled, objective—or however you like to describe it—complicity. But he is thus affected because he has been given to begin with the possibility of identifying himself with the character. If you present a Nazi brute who is known from the start to be repugnant and to have acted out of sadism or total brutality, no one will be interested in him. He will simply be an insect. We can be affected, affected not in the sense of being merely moved, but truly affected, by a character if we think, "He is perhaps someone like us," even if he presents us with an enduring potentiality of debasement—no one can be wholly innocent—to which any of us is always liable simply because a society exists around us and we know nothing about it. You can see, therefore, what I mean by saying that an audience should be left some freedom. It should not be crushed under multiple and unduly pure characters.

You entirely discard the notion of "heroes."

There are no heroes. Especially nowadays. But the problem is sometimes posited in terms of heroes. For example, the contradiction in the *Antigone* arises from what might be called a cold war between the old families and the city. At that period the city had only just been established and consequently had only just broken away from the old families. The problem was a real one, therefore, and it was natural that someone, Antigone, should represent the patriarchal family and someone else, Creon, the city. Sophocles was probably on the side of the old families, more of an aristocrat than a democrat at the time, to judge by this play at any rate. So it is natural enough that there should be two heroes. The contradiction is external. But in our age, since the contradictions are internal as well as external, we no longer need two characters, for the contradictions exist within a single character. There are no longer heroes in the sense of characters representing a strict, rigorous, and single point of view carried right through to the end, to death or victory. On the contrary, there are contradictions which have to be elevated in one way or another to the level of myth. And the audience's freedom will come precisely from watching the disquiet of a character who attracts rather than overwhelms it. This will cause the audience to feel a similar disquiet about itself right to the end.

(Interview with Alain Koehler,
Présence du théâtre,
no. 3, March 1960, and no. 4, April 1960)

The conversation reproduced below, entitled "Wir alle sind Luthers Opfer" ("All of us are victims of Luther"), was held in 1960 when the German version of *The Condemned of Altona* (*Die Eingeschlossenen*) was produced at fifteen theaters in Germany. The text published by *Der Spiegel* (May 11, 1960) is almost certainly a word-for-word German translation of the shorthand record. It was retranslated into French by Michel Contat, keeping the conversational style.

Monsieur Sartre, your play, The Condemned of Altona, *is situated in Germany, but its subject, or one of its subjects at least, is the problem of Algeria.*

As a matter of fact, the play is neither about Nazi or German guilt nor about the faults committed during the war in Algeria, though there is some allusion to both themes. What I am trying to do is something different: primarily, to show how contemporary man lives and copes with his situation. During the period we have lived through, an age of blood and violence, any adult today, even if he is only thirty of thirty-five, has necessarily been a witness or an accomplice and must assume his responsibilities, regardless whether he is one of those who in France were unable to protest against the atrocities committed during the Algerian war, or one of those who were involved to a greater or lesser degree in committing them, or one of those who condoned or took an active part in atrocities during the 1939 war, or even someone who is neither French nor German. For active or passive complicities of this sort exist in nearly every country. It is a fact that we are living in an age of blood and violence and that we have, so to speak, interiorized this violence and injustice. The problem is, therefore, how to present what we are today.

The problem is universal, but the scene is German. If we understand you correctly, Germany serves as a mythological background, as it were, for a representation of the general problem of guilt and collusion.

I chose this German subject for two reasons. The first was a practical one, to achieve distance in dealing with the problems. Quite obviously, if I had taken political events in recent French history as my subject, I should have stirred up the audience's passions. The stage would therefore have ceased to be a stage and would have become a political platform, and the drama would have overstepped the limits of its function, which is to demonstrate, to represent, and perhaps to secure participation as well, but certainly not to furnish a political platform. There is, too, the absolute need for transposition. Why choose the theatrical form if you wish directly to arouse political passions, since that rules out the opportunity for reflection?

Did you expect an intervention by Trissotin?

Who?

Trissotin.[10]

Oh, yes, Trissotin. I don't know. But at all events an intervention by the public, by people who have not yet recovered their calm. It's the old classical problem of detachment or distancing. That is to say, if you prefer, if I take a French fact, universality at once vanishes, and the result is to set Frenchmen at odds with each other.

So you wanted a universal theme and you had a choice of scene.

I had a choice of scene; and, of course, there is also the particular intention, in that the general theme becomes a particular case. The aim was to talk about Frenchmen to Frenchmen. But we are not the only people who are relevant; I might just as well have taken Cyprus, where a whole lot of things have happened which were not exactly commendable; or I might have taken any other similar facts which can be found everywhere, in the West just as much as in the East.

Do you mean by that the treatment of prisoners, interrogation, torture?

The hero of the play is, in a word, a torturer. For me the whole point was to show that torture is a practice which has become generalized during the last thirty years—that's a fact which I consider of decisive importance—whereas in the nineteenth century torture was regarded as at least despicable.

You said you had two reasons for choosing Germany as your theme?

The second reason is that if you want to hold an audience, you have to take extreme situations. Well, it seems to me that after the National Socialist regime and the '40–'45 war the situation of a forty-year-old German who has been through the war and can consequently question himself internally about all the motives that led him to behave in the way he did and about his complicity as well, the situation of such a German is far more drastic than other people's. The situation is less drastic with Cyprus, for example, or even to some degree with Algeria; there you can simply evade the problem.

And there's de Gaulle.

Yes, there is indeed de Gaulle. But that isn't so much the problem, that's not so relevant. In any case, one can evade responsibility, and many people do. It seems to me that the problem of having to pass judgment on the recent historical past and to assume responsibility for it is far more acute and far clearer for Germans. We French will probably have to deal with the same problem a few years hence.

Monsieur Sartre, a playwright is entitled to represent a general situation, an ordinary situation by means of an extraordinary situation. But Franz von Gerlach gives the impression of being half mad. Is he truly a symbol, an embodiment, a personification of the situation of a contemporary who feels himself responsible for his epoch?

The situation we have here I should be inclined to call extreme, but not extraordinary. It might well be compared to the situation of many young soldiers who have taken part in a war or military operations of which they disapproved within themselves, but during which they became accomplices in certain atrocities. Returning home, these young soldiers have shut themselves up in a sort of silence; they have withdrawn from the political groups in which they had formerly been at home and have gone to earth inside their family or trade. This resembles the beginnings of a voluntary self-confinement to some extent and an evasion, so to speak. At the same time this evasion, of course, amounts to a condemnation which they will neither admit to themselves nor try to express. The situation, therefore, exists. And another form of it which also exists is that frequently found, in which communities of young people who have lived through similar experiences try to win back these young men and bring them back into society by saying, for example, "What you did was very well done and should be done again, if it had to be," or else, "As a matter of fact, yes, it was all very bad, but your share in it was only accidental, it was probably impossible or, at any rate, extremely hard to avoid taking part in such things, and so there's nothing to prevent you now from becoming politically active again, and no questions asked."

Your protagonist, Franz von Gerlach, who tortured prisoners as a German lieutenant at Smolensk, demands a judge. But a butcher of Smolensk usually does not seek out his judge, but tries to evade him.

Yes, but it is precisely his evasion that is his suffering and his sentence, so to speak. The sense of the play is that the father, who loves his son, prefers his son's death to this evasion. Because evasion is the direct sentence, isn't it? Forever to evade, to flee, to lie to oneself, to be a fugitive . . . Evasion is degrading, and that is why the father wants to convert it into suicide.

Yes, but the father has accepted the postwar situation, prosperity and the fact that there has been no punishment.

The father has accepted it. The father is not a scrupulous, not an overmoral man.

He represents the general behavior.

Yes, he represents bourgeois morality. But he has abundantly compromised himself. He too might question himself about the problem of his complicity. For example, he was obviously compelled—as a captain of industry—to convert his industrial firm into an armaments firm. He too is therefore responsible. But he is not in good faith; he is banal and even in bad faith inasmuch as he refuses to put the problem to himself. The only thing the father is concerned with is his son's moral conscience. It is this moral conscience that puts the problem to him, the father. That is, the father would never have indulged in the luxury of an easy conscience if his son had been killed in the war or if his son's conscience were easy. It is through the son that a moral uneasiness invades the house and ultimately penetrates the father.

You say that the son is an extreme case, but does he not also clearly represent certain kinds of Germans whom you wanted to describe?

To tell you the truth, I was not wanting to describe any kind of Germans. The Germans—and please note that I am not saying this simply because I am being questioned by a German magazine—interested me here only insofar as they relate to a problem with which we too have been concerned for some time and, as I said, precisely as an extreme case. Besides, the Germans in whom I am interested are the Germans of 1945, not the Germans of 1960.

Half a generation later.

Yes, I had meant to mention that there is a generation problem. I find that in France the very young are some of those least likely to understand my play. The young in the audiences do not take sides at all; they are neither for Franz—

even if they accept some things about him—nor against him. Or if they are against him, they have no strong feelings about it. To those who are now eighteen he presents just one more problem like any other. They themselves cannot yet consider themselves responsible for anything whatever—they have not yet done their military service and have not yet come into contact with the reality of Algeria.

The action in The Condemned of Altona *is not taken from reality—*

—because the play is not written in the realistic mode. If I had conceived the play realistically—it has been brought to my notice that I have located Altona in the wrong place, for example—

In your play the Elbchaussee runs from Altona to Hamburg and passes over the Teufelsbrücke, whereas it actually starts from Hamburg and Hamburg-Altona and runs in the direction of Blankensee, passing near a place called Teufelsbrück. But that's of no great importance.

I would say that if I had really intended to write a realistic play, the mistake would have been a very serious one; but it is not serious in the kind of play I have written—I imagine the translator will correct the topography. I am more concerned with German problems than with Germans. I remember, for instance, that when I was in Berlin, it was in '47 or '48—

In 1948.

I remember speaking with Germans in 1948 who interested me very much for a specific reason. The discussions I had there at the time have always remained vivid in my memory.[11] In connection with my play *The Flies* I was confronted by two sorts of Germans. Some of them blamed me severely for saying that repentance has no ethical function, that a judgment on the past is of course inevitable and that a change in relation to the past is equally inevitable, but that repentance is not strictly an ethical category. They re-proached me for that because these were Germans who wanted repentance to become, so to speak, a part of Ger-man daily life. Others, however, who interested me far more, were people with divided selves, full of problems. They were not people like Franz—so far as I could see, at any rate—and they said, "We were against the Nazis, we fought the war because our country had to win it, and we refuse to feel remorse." These people interested me far more precisely because they were people who were struggling with prob-lems. For they were also judging themselves, and they were therefore in a very complicated situation. I found this at-titude very much one with which I could sympathize, the attitude of people with divided selves who said to themselves, "So what? I went to war as a soldier, what can I be blamed for?"

Franz, for example—

Yes, there is something of that in Franz.

At the beginning he is a puritan, but at a certain moment he begins to slip.

One minute! I think he begins slipping right from the start. In his first discussion with his father, in act one, in which the discussion takes place when he is quite young and has discovered the prison camp, the concentration camp. He has started to slip the moment he is filled with horror by the prisoners in the camp, the moment he condemns not only the system of concentration camps in the name of the dig-nity of man—which was very fine from the moral stand-point—but the prisoners too, emotionally, as it were by instinct, when he says, "They are no longer men."[12] From that moment he has slipped. His father laughs at him—for he is not exactly indulgent with people, the father isn't—saying, "You do not love men, you only love principles, puritanism."[13]

In the course of the play Franz declares that he wishes to take upon himself the guilt of all the Germans, of his whole century, as the representative of his generation. The course of his moral development runs counter to his father's to some extent. His father, the image of God the Father, if you like——

I reject that notion of God the Father. Catholic critics have advanced it several times, but I simply fail to see what God has to do with it. In point of fact, the father is simply a portrait of a certain type of captain of industry, a type which is, as a matter of fact, obsolete by the time the story begins.

Because representatives of the works council also sit on the board of directors.

Obsolete as a type. But Franz develops like this: he is imbued with an aristocratic puritanism because of the pride he has inherited from his father and his anxiety to deserve by his moral conduct the exalted position of chairman of the board of directors which his father will give him. That is, basically he wishes to merit his possessions by his acts. It is not a direct relation with men, therefore, that led him to condemn the concentration camps and torture, but a direct relation with Protestant morality, or, if you like, an immediate practical humanism in puritan form. What he will always lack is—

A contact—

—a human contact which will be strong enough, when he is tempted to become a torturer himself, to render him incapable of carrying it out because he is dealing with a human being. There is a large component of the abstract in Franz's pride.

Is Franz's representative of a certain German frame of mind, a proclivity to abstract humanism, for instance, abstract rather than practical?

I am inclined to think that Franz is representative rather of a certain Protestant morality. I don't mean to say that all Protestants are like that, but they are prone to abstract notions such as "the dignity of man" and consistency with principle.

You say somewhere in the play, "All of us are victims of Luther."[14]

Yes.

That is a surprising interpretation—at any rate to Protestants.

Yes, you see, French Protestant unbelievers—I say "unbelievers" because many of our Protestants have lost their religious belief but preserve the moral bond very strictly—many of these Protestants, I believe, think or are victims of the notion that the egalitarian revolution was accomplished as soon as Luther said that any man might be the representative of his religious community. These Protestants have a formal concept of equality which often makes them inflexible when it comes to seeing that equality must be all-embracing. They believe, therefore—I know many who do—that every idea represents universal man and they at once pass universal judgments, judgments so rigorously and abstractly universal that the concrete reality of a situation often escapes them—and this consequently leads to the emergence of a kind of aristocratic lawmaker. Or to put it differently, the Protestant becomes an aristocrat of the universal by dint of believing in the egalitarian revolution. I don't know whether you accept this explanation, but that is at all events the sort of man I was trying to depict.

Is Rousseau the French Luther?

Yes, indeed. Traces of Lutheran and Calvinist influence are also to be found in our French Protestants. However that may be, the fact that the Revolution of 1789 happened is very important in France. It produced what might be called a form of lay Protestantism.

According to the evangelical churches, Luther dwelt on a sort of direct responsibility between man and God, whereas the Catholic Church continues to be a delegated institution intermediary between God and the faithful. This direct responsibility should therefore imply consequences that lead in some sort to your philosophy of existential responsibility.

That is true. I believe that the existence of a Catholic hierarchy imposed upon the individual, especially in the confessional, leads to humility—which is not a virtue; modesty is a virtue, but humility is not—and this leads to a certain evasion of responsibility. On the other hand, I believe that this total responsibility to God assumed by man is something truly admirable in the Protestant religion—provided that it is really practiced. Consequently, Protestantism—if we are speaking of religion really practiced—seems to me wholly superior in this respect. But lukewarm religion or unbelief or pride in a Protestant upbringing makes it likely that the real problems and real people may be shirked. For when one lives—if one has had a Catholic upbringing— with the sensation of the huge burdens weighing upon one, the modesty proper to us all, and the difficulty of lawmaking, then one sees the true place of man. I believe, too, that there is a Protestant pride which has a great deal of weight when, as in the case of my hero, it is combined with a human and worldly pride.

About Franz von Gerlach: in the incident of the Polish fugitive, your protagonist was anxious not so much to save the man's life as to preserve his own moral integrity. He wants to continue to feel that he is a moral man—which is also a form of pride. Nevertheless, at that particular moment he was absolutely powerless to save the man.

He was powerless to save him. But he is very intelligent all
the same, and what distresses him most and most disturbs
him is not the fact that he was incapable of saving the man,
but that he was unable to pay the price for his act. He is a
courageous and proud young man and he was unable to
save the Pole; the Pole was recaptured and killed on the
spot. But Franz too had to expect to be killed: he had set
himself up against a power, he knew what he was doing,
he was risking his life and should also have been killed. But
his father was powerful enough to prevent him from being
executed by the SS.

*Franz could do no more himself; but something was done
for him.*

Yes, that's where his real impotence shows up. It's precisely
like when the son of an influential father has an affair and
gets into trouble and his father comes and buys him out.
What Franz did has no more importance than if he had had
some scandalous little affair which had to be hushed up.
He was virtually of no account, and this is what really brings
his impotence home to him.

*Johanna, the wife of his brother Werner, is prepared to for-
give Franz for some of the things he did before he confined
himself, but not others.*

Johanna cannot forgive him for being a torturer; she cannot
or will not, because he does not wish her to forgive him.
Normally, a woman who is falling in love with a man who
has committed a very grave fault, even an atrocious one,
would at least ask him questions to find out whether he has
an excuse and would make some attempt to understand him.
She dares not; but she does not dare because he does not
wish her to. She ought to give him a faith, inspire him with
self-confidence. She tries at one moment to say, "Let's fight
it together," "Tell me it's not true," "Tell me you were in the
hands of your own men and it was others who—"[15]

Both of them are "voluntarily self-confined."

Both of them are "voluntarily self-confined."

In his confinement Franz von Gerlach argues against the notion of collective guilt and says—

It is the father, not Franz, who argues against collective guilt at the beginning. He says, "You must take the seven or eight hundred who are really guilty," and Franz replies, "If you kill the leaders whom the people obeyed and also say 'But the people are not responsible because they were led astray,' that amounts to condemning the people."[16] That is his personal opinion. What he means is, "I was carrying out orders and that is why my responsibility is directly bound up with the orders I was given and my free decision to obey them. If I say I am guilty, they condemn me. But if I am told, 'You carried out your orders, but you are in no way responsible, the leaders are responsible and we have executed them,' I am worse off than if I were condemned. For in that case I am considered totally irresponsible. I was a lieutenant at the front, I obeyed certain orders, I committed certain acts—if they condemn my superior officers but not me, then they make no account of my torments of conscience, my own decisions to go so far and no farther," and so on. Hence he finds that it is too easy a way out to get rid of the leaders and refuse to consider the problem of collective guilt.

Are Franz's speeches to the "crabs" not some sort of plea for the defense against the notion of collective guilt?

Yes, because collective guilt exists insofar as it represents a kind of indifference or a deliberate semi-evasion or toleration in each individual. You can see this in France every day, and in other countries too, if you read the newspapers. We are somewhat reluctant about the need to know, we are rather reluctant to learn the truth, and the result is that, strictly speaking, we are moving toward collective guilt.

Karl Jaspers also wrote something of that sort.[17]

Yes, and as a matter of fact I drew on some of his ideas on some particular points relating to collective guilt itself. Only, Franz, with his pride, obviously cannot give consideration to the problem of collective guilt. It is of no interest to him. It is of no interest because he is one of the upright who would free his fellow countrymen morally from repentance and because he is too proud to believe that his faults differ in no way from those of mere enlisted men. To him the problem is that of his own responsibility, and for this reason his relations to the collective problem are always to some degree false or falsified whenever he speaks of it.

That is his problem. For us, however, the problem is that there are societies in whose name crimes are committed and the society accepts or tolerates them, but refuses to acknowledge them. In the exemplary case that we see in your play, those who have been guilty of those crimes, the proud Franz von Gerlach, for instance, commit suicide. But a society cannot count on the guilty committing suicide.

Yes, that's true, that's quite true. There is indeed a contradiction here; but what you also have to see is, not the problem of responsibility in its immediate form, but the problem of the single man who experiences his responsibility individually even though it is in fact bound up with the collective structure of a society. You see what I mean, don't you? For example, you have soldiers, French soldiers, who have been led into committing atrocities, and when they return home, some of them appear indifferent to politics, as I have already mentioned; they don't quite say, "It's nothing to do with me," but something close to that. What interests me—in the play—is what people like them feel, what they think of the way they themselves are dependent; whether they are conscious of what they did and whether they are aware that this consciousness always has an element of the lie in it. In showing Franz's crime I have also tried to show that it was almost inevitable. There was a brief instant of freedom, but in fact everything combined to drive Franz to his act. He was, of course, free to choose otherwise, even though only for a very brief moment. But basically Franz is so much molded by his family and so much molded by the horrible experience of his powerlessness and so little conditioned to love man, so little used to human ties, that he almost necessarily had to do what he finally did. But he was not obliged to do it, of course. It is certainly here that the problem of freedom is posited, a problem we have not discussed together here. When Franz accuses himself in front of his father, he does not yet know what price he will have to pay for his pride. What his father will explain to him is that, at bottom, he could have done nothing but what he did, and that consequently he was as powerless to do evil as to do good. After that, Franz has no choice but death.

The "court of crabs" of which you speak is an allegory. What does it symbolize?

Franz's pride, which has been humiliated because he has not succeeded in anything, demands overcompensation, as the analysts call it. Hence his compulsion to make himself the prophet of his nation and his century to the centuries to come. This he does—and at even greater length in the published text, which has had to be cut in performance. I wanted to show—and this is the only element in his case which can be called really pathological—that Franz in his pride really does take himself for a witness for his century. In fact, he is a sort of secularized Luther bearing witness to the eternity of the centuries rather than to God, and this is his way of finding God. This, then, is the primary sense, but it is also, of course, an evasion, for Franz displaces the problem. For him the problem is not whether the "crabs" or God or anything you please exists, nor is it a question of spontaneously testifying for his people. His primary purpose is to rid himself of the burden of what he has done by means of his testifying.

But he does not come before this imaginary court as the accused, but invariably and expressly as a witness.

It is his way of cutting himself off from society, his attempt to claim, "I am the advocate for the defense of this Germany," and so on; but at the same time, he dissociates himself from it to some extent. This is the touch of the pathological—this evasion and this pride. But what I was seeking to throw light on and trying to do—I don't know whether I have succeeded or not—was to impress the audience with the idea that the centuries pass judgment on us just as our century passes judgment on the nineteenth or the eighteenth century, and I wanted the audience to feel somehow that it was being subjected to such a judgment. In other words, the whole play is at once directed to the present and removed into the past in relation to something watching us, about whose judgment we know nothing.

Then the "crabs" mean the judgment of history?

They obviously represent the judgment of history, the judgment——

The last judgment?

Between ourselves, there is no such thing as an objective or final judgment.

There are no "crabs"?

There are no "crabs." All the same, there is a judgment, a relative but perpetual judgment. For example, Captain Dreyfus was innocent; that is not a judgment, but it is absolutely certain fifty years later that judgment has been passed on that affair.

You said just now that Franz von Gerlach only had freedom for a very brief moment and that at bottom what he did was inevitable for him. Does that apply, as you see it, to the situation of the Germans or of people in general in those years?

Yes. Yes. I also think——

There are only brief moments when an alternative exists?

Well, let's see—well, yes, I do think so, I do indeed take that view. I think what some psychoanalysts say is to a large extent right, that a murderer's responsibility does not begin at the moment he kills, but at the moment he decides to enter into a system of relations with the victim which leads him more or less irrevocably to murder. I wholly concur in this. The moment of freedom is the moment when the murderer is still capable of changing the relations. The following example is given by a psychoanalyst: a young man has an Oedipus complex—in brief, feelings of jealousy, hate, and love for his mother—and he is quite aware that this may drive him to acts of violence against her. Still, he does not go away, but stays with her. People know of his problems and make him a proposal, telling him that they are prepared to find him a job in a provincial town far away from his mother. The moment at which he becomes responsible is the moment when he rejects this proposal and commits himself to leading a life with her that brings him to murder. It is precisely the same in politics: there are moments that are "crucial," and in our present situation there are also such decisive moments——

In France?

And everywhere else in the world.

We have in Germany——

We have different problems, but so does the rest of the world——

We have in Germany a definition of the theater as a moral institution—by Schiller.

Yes.

In ancient tragedy the hero has no alternative, because he is guilty by the decision or the whim of the gods. The theater conceived as a moral institution should, strictly speaking, give the hero an alternative. But Franz von Gerlach has no alternative.

No, he has no alternative—in 1959. He did have one in 1944.

Franz is therefore already dead, in a way; he is a dead man who has survived.

In a way, yes. The true problem is nevertheless an alternative, but that leads— The true problem is this: Is Franz going to continue living in a state of moral decay until his death, which may not happen till he is seventy, or will he one day confront the situation as it is? That is to say, will he draw the conclusion from his acts and his impotence?

He himself says that death has no meaning for him, and the fact that, in the play, he dies has no meaning either.

I have been adversely criticized for letting him die. I have been asked why he does not go on living and redeem himself. But the objection is rather absurd. When a peasant, a married man and father of three children, becomes a soldier and commits atrocities in a war, and later returns home and has again to deal with the needs of his position in life because he has to earn a living for his family, he can gradually regain a situation, which is in fact a new situation. In doing this he has no need to redeem himself—redemption is a question of religion, as I see it. But what is special about Franz's case is that he cannot just do nothing; he is as impotent before as after—simply because he was raised solely to become a captain of industry and the position for which he was ordained no longer exists. Franz was to have been the authoritarian head of a family firm at a time when the owner of a firm was truly its head. But now he is confronted with a giant complex in which he will have only a subordinate part to play.

He has only to sign the letters others have written for him. He still retains the ownership, of course, but he no longer has the vast power that his father had had twenty years earlier and has lost since. Franz has so much pride, too, and such great difficulties with other people—what I think you call *Kontaktschwäche*—and so little feeling for community, no matter whether the community is socialist or anything else, that he is no longer any use for anything. He commits suicide, not because he has killed or tortured, but because he has discovered that he can no longer do anything. It is his impotence that kills him. Indeed, his father asks him, "Are you any use for anything any more?"[18] And he cannot be.

Does the audience have any alternative?

In the play? Well, that's something else again.

Is it given any incentive to make a choice, a moral choice, any sort of choice, when it is confronted with people who are no longer doing anything and can no longer change anything?

I don't think the play is exactly the sort of play in which there is a moral choice; it does not call for a moral choice, or at any rate, far less than my previous plays did. In *The Respectful Prostitute,* for instance, the character has to choose between lying and telling the truth——

Except No Exit, *in which no one has a choice any more.*

There is no alternative in *No Exit.* That is why I have compared my new play to *No Exit*—it's more of a descriptive play.

The protagonists are dead.

Yes, in both of them they are dead and in both of them what is represented is the "dead part" of us, so to speak.

Franz can no longer do anything. But can the spectators? Can the audience redeem itself?

As I've told you, I don't attach much meaning to the redemption of a fault because I do not believe in repentance. But normally a soldier returning from Algeria can certainly come to terms with his conscience and then join a movement, a party demanding peace in Algeria, for example. He can say what he thinks, he can testify—testify for himself and others; he can act. And this in turn depends on just how people regard peace, how they behave toward the soldiers—if they say, "Yes, agreed, that won't do, there's got to be an end of it; you have done such or such, omitted to do this or that, but that's no reason to withdraw from life."

Old Gerlach in your play has a second son, Werner, Johanna's husband, the heir to the firm. He is not a very likable character, but he is not one of those who say "That's no reason to withdraw from life."

What I have primarily tried to do—by using a rather complicated construction—is to describe the relations between people placed in a certain situation so as to show how each person within the group is the fate of all the rest. It was different in *No Exit*; there the situation was hell, and each was the torturer of the other two; but that was a very exceptional situation. What I meant has, as a matter of fact, been very badly misconstrued, for what has mainly stuck in people's memories is "Hell is other people"—which they thought meant that we should spend our time each torturing others. But that was not what I meant at all.

"Hell is other people"—but the sentence has not, on the contrary, been construed as an exhortation to make life a hell for other people either.

I wished to show in a closed situation how the weakest link in the chain is in fact as important as every other link. In this story I wished to show how Franz's fate depends on that of each of the others, including decisions by the weakest, Werner. If Werner had not decided out of pride and jealousy—toward the end of the third act—to stay within the family, then there would have been no fourth act. Perhaps Werner would have left and Franz would have gone on living—but Werner's jealousy forces his wife to go up and visit Franz, and so it goes. Thereafter, the father appeals to Leni; and you know the rest. What I wanted to show theatrically was a sort of circular movement of the action. It is not a three-character action like *No Exit*, where the diagram is a triangle, but a five-character action which moves in a circle and shows the shift in each character's fate. Each is the fate of each.

So the family represents society, in a sense.

The family does in fact represent society here.

But after all, Werner, the weakest of the five, seems to be the only one who has freedom of choice.

Yes, that's right. If I had had time, however—but the play would have become too long—I should have liked to develop Werner's character further. For as he appears in the play, he is the weakest and consequently the most mediocre. But that is not what he actually is. If I had had the time, I would have treated him differently; I should have liked him to be a truly human person when he is living as a lawyer in Hamburg. I should have liked him to represent the possibility of a choice right up to the end, a real choice,

that between family and freedom—but when it comes to
the point, he hesitates, and indeed he hesitates right to the
end. His liberation by the deaths of his father and his
brother offers him a possibility for rethinking his life, even
life with Johanna. That is what Werner's personality would
have been if I had been given five hours for the performance. But obviously I couldn't be.

Thank you, Monsieur Sartre.

The following is from an interview with Oreste P.
Pucciani, which was published in the *Tulane Drama
Review*, March 1961.

*I have frequently heard your play criticized as a "bour-
geois drama." That seems wrong. As I see it, the first,
third, and fifth acts are deliberately "bourgeois": the reality of "downstairs," the street floor. But the reality of
"upstairs" is quite different; it is avant-garde. There are
two levels: the physical and the metaphysical.*

Yes. Exactly. That's exactly it. Perhaps not "metaphysical,"
but that's the idea. We must start with the bourgeois world;
there is nowhere else to start from. In this sense, existentialism is a bourgeois ideology, certainly. But it is the only
place to start from. In a different world the theater itself
would be different. So would philosophy. But we have not
yet reached that stage. In a society of permanent revolution,
theater, literature would be a permanent criticism, a permanent challenging. We have not yet got that far by any means.
But it is entirely wrong to call my play a bourgeois drama.
Bourgeois drama exists only to eliminate the problem it is
dealing with. This is not so with *The Condemned*. The
double suicide contains a true liberation. There is no
mystery revealed. There is a dialectic.

*Would you like to tell me why you chose that title for the
play? I mean more or less by way of etymology.*

Well, you know what it means. In France we call someone who voluntarily confines himself or who is confined a *séquestré*. I don't know whether you know André Gide's *Souvenirs de la Cour d'Assises*. Perhaps you recall *La Séquestrée de Poitiers?*[19]

Yes, I was wondering whether there was an echo of that.

Undoubtedly.

Sartre wrote the following piece, entitled "The Question," for the program of the revival of *The Condemned of Altona* at the Théâtre de L'Athénée in 1965.

I wrote *The Condemned of Altona* during the Algerian war. Unpardonable acts of violence were being perpetrated in the name of France at that time and French opinion, though uneasy, was ill-informed and indifferent. I therefore felt it my urgent duty to present torture unmasked and in public. Argument was not needed; I thought it had only to be shown naked and unadorned to be condemned.

Five years have since elapsed, peace has been restored in Algeria, and the play has lost its immediacy. Yet I welcome the revival by the Théâtre-Vivant. I am writing these few lines to explain why I do so. In 1959 I did not want to raise what Alleg has called "The Question,"[20] as it concerned mere executants, most of whom were passively obeying orders out of fear or an insufficient awareness of what they were doing. Those to be accused were those who were actually responsible, who gave the orders. To avoid unleashing passions which would have clouded the audience's judgment, however, and to secure the "distancing" essential in theater, I situated the action in postwar Germany. My protagonist is a former German officer to whom I attributed many good qualities (such as courage, sensitivity, culture, and a puritan morality), who claims that he went so far as to commit crimes in order to save his country from mortal danger. His actions are all the more to be condemned; explanations for him can be found, but not a single excuse. Moreover, his voluntary self-confinement, his eagerness to lie to himself, and his alleged madness—which is nothing but a futile attempt to cloud his own mind—show that he has long since become aware of his crime and is wearing himself out defending himself to invisible judges simply to conceal from himself the death sentence he has already passed on himself. Because of the change in place and Franz's ambiguity and monstrous blend of bad faith and clear sight, my play took on, even while I was writing it, a meaning rather different from what I had originally intended. Now that the war is over, it is this half-deliberate and more general significance that I should like to see brought out. None of us has been a torturer, but all of us have been in one way or another accomplices in some policy which we should disavow today. We too evade ourselves and incessantly turn back to ask ourselves what part we have played—however small it may have been—in the History which is ours, which we are making, and which disrupts and distorts actions we must yet acknowledge as our own. We too balance between a state of mendacious indifference and a disquiet which incessantly asks, Who are we? What did we mean to do and what did we really do? How will the invisible judges—our grandchildren—judge us? Thus Franz, the extreme case, the fugitive implacably questioning himself about his historical responsibilities, should, if I am lucky, fascinate and horrify us insofar as we resemble him. Yesterday, *The Condemned of Altona* denounced an intolerable practice. Today, with the restoration of peace, this practice has disappeared in France. If the play is being revived today, if any aspect of it is, as I hope, still topical, it is—apart from any condemnation and any conclusion—simply because it raised, almost despite myself, and still raises for an audience the cardinal question, What have you done with your life?

The Trojan Women

(Les Troyennes)

The most recent of Sartre's works for the theater is his adaptation of Euripides' *Trojan Women*. The play was written in Rome in the summer of 1964 and was first performed on the large stage at the Palais de Chaillot by the Théâtre National Populaire in a production by Michael Cacoyannis. Bernard Pingaud published some comments on it by Sartre in the TNP magazine *Bref*, February 1965. They were later reproduced as an introduction in the Gallimard edition of the book of the play. They are given here in full.

Why The Trojan Women? *Greek tragedy is a splendid ruin, to be visited respectfully with an erudite guide, but it would never occur to anyone to live in it. Enthusiasts for the ancient drama try to revive the tragedies of Aeschylus, Sophocles, or Euripides from time to time as the Athenians might have watched them. But pastiche, no matter how reverently done, is not very credible. Ancient drama is remote from us because it is based on a religious outlook that is wholly alien to us. Its language may attract, but it fails to convince. No doubt this may be a purely personal reaction, much of it due possibly to having taken too many liberties with Greek texts. But since Jean-Paul Sartre has chosen to adapt an ancient tragedy for the TNP, and the most static and least "theatrical" of them all, at that—the very tragedy, indeed, which the Athenians themselves received somewhat dubiously at first—I thought I should ask him why he had chosen it. He explains his choice as follows:*

Contrary to what many people think, Greek tragedy is not orgiastic. We imagine actors in a prophetic trance leaping, yelling, and flinging themselves about the stage. But in fact the actors spoke through holes in a mask and moved about on cothurni. The tragic performance, with its wholly artificial and extremely strict rules, is primarily a *ceremony*, whose purpose is certainly to impress the spectator, but not to engage his sympathies. Horror becomes majestic, cruelty ceremonious. This is certainly so in Aeschylus, who was writing for an audience which still believed in the heroic legends and the mysterious power of the gods. But it is even more so in Euripides, who comes at the end of the tragic cycle and represents the transition to a different type of play, the "everyday" comedy of Menander. For in the period when Euripides was writing *The Trojan Women* beliefs had become rather dubious myths. While the critical spirit in Athens was not yet able to overthrow the ancient idols, it was already beginning to question their validity. The staging had kept its status as ritual, but the public was more interested in how things were said than in what was said; and while it had a connoisseur's appreciation of the traditional set pieces, it saw them in a new light. Tragedy therefore became a sort of allusive commentary on the conventional stereotypes. Euripides uses language that is much the same as that of his predecessors—in appearance. But it has a different resonance, it says something different, because his audience no longer believes in it, or at any rate has less belief in it. With Beckett or Ionesco, for instance, much the same happens: the technique is to use the conventional stereotype in such a way as to destroy it from within; and of course the more obvious and the more striking the stereotype, the more effective the demonstration will be. The Athenian audience "got" *The Trojan Women* just as the bourgeois audience nowadays "gets" *Godot* or *The Bald Soprano*—delighted to listen to platitudes, but realizing that it is watching them being broken down.

This creates a real difficulty for the translator. If I follow the text literally and have to say "white-winged dawn" or speak of Athens "shining like oil," it will look as if I were adopting the language of the eighteenth century. I use the conventional stereotypes, but a French audience in 1965 will be quite incapable of grasping what they mean—because the religious and cultural context is no longer familiar —and will take them literally. That is the trouble with the otherwise excellent Budé translation into French:[1] the conventional stereotype becomes set more firmly instead of destroying itself. Four or five centuries from now, players trying to perform Beckett or Ionesco will have to tackle a similar problem: how to delimit the distance between audience and play.

There is an implicit relation between Euripides' tragedy and fifth-century Athenian society which we today can see only from outside. If I wish to express the sense of this relation, I cannot simply translate the play; I must adapt it.

A purely literal translation was ruled out; so was merely transposing it into modern spoken French, for the language too has to delimit its own distance from us. I therefore took a poetic speech which keeps the ceremonious character and rhetorical values of the original, but alters the emphasis. Since Euripides uses hints and allusions when he is speaking to an audience that is in complicity with him, and even if it no longer believes in the legends still likes to be told them, he can indulge in flashes of humor or tricks of style.

I found that to get something of the same effect I must use a less destructive tone: first let the audience take the legends seriously, and then you can show that they do not work. We accept Euripides' sly humor in Talthybios, because Talthybios is someone like "the Good Soldier Schweik," the average man helpless to cope with what is in store for him. Or Helen's ways, because we are familiar with Offenbach. Everywhere else there would be a danger of destroying the whole play, not merely the stereotypes. I could bring it off, therefore, only by a distancing, by compelling the audience to withdraw some way away from the drama.

But the language was not the only problem; there was also the difference in cultural background. Euripides' text contained a great many allusions that were immediately intelligible to an Athenian audience but are now meaningless because we have forgotten the legends. I have omitted some of them and expanded others. For instance, there was no need for Cassandra to go into a lengthy account of what happened to Hecuba in the end. The Greeks all knew that she would climb up the mast of the ship that took her away from Troy, be turned into a dog, and fall into the water. But when we see Hecuba going off with her women companions at the end of the play, we may well suppose that she will follow them to Greece. The real dénouement is far more powerful. It means that all Cassandra's prophesies will be fulfilled: Ulysses will take ten years to reach home, the Greek fleet will be wrecked and destroyed, Hecuba will never leave the plains of Troy. That is why I added Poseidon's final monologue.

Similarly, the Athenian audience knew that Menelaus would be overpersuaded by Helen after he had rejected her and would take her back on his own ship. In Euripides' play the Chorus does in fact allude to this discreetly, but there is nothing to lead a French audience, which has heard Menelaus' vows, to expect him to change his mind. Hence it has to be shown it, and that is the reason for the Chorus's indignant complaint as it watches the ship leave with the reconciled couple aboard.

Other changes are due to the general style of the play. It is not a tragedy, like the *Antigone*; it is really an *oratorio*. I have tried to "dramatize" it by bringing out conflicts that are only latent in Euripides: the conflict between Andromache and Hecuba's two modes of behavior, at times abandoning herself to her grief, at times calling for justice; the change in attitude of Andromache, a "petty bourgeoise" who first appears in the guise of wife and then in the guise of mother; and Cassandra's erotic fascination, which leads her to fling herself into Agamemnon's bed even though she knows she will perish with him.

All this, you will say, is no reason for choosing the play. So I must say a word about its subject. Euripides' *Trojan Women* was performed during the Algerian war in a very literal translation by Jacqueline Moattir.[2] I was greatly struck by its success with an audience that was in favor of negotiation with the FLN. It was this, of course, that first aroused my interest. You certainly know that the play had a specifically political meaning even in Euripides' own time. It was a denunciation of war in general and colonial expeditions in particular.

Nowadays we are all too well aware of what war means; neither victors nor vanquished would survive an atomic war. That is precisely what the whole play is about: the Greeks destroyed Troy, but their victory will bring them no benefit whatever, because the vengeance of the gods will destroy them too. That "any sane man must avoid war," as Cassandra asserts, was self-evident, for the fate of both sides abundantly demonstrated it. I preferred to leave Poseidon the last word: "All of you will perish."

As to colonial wars, this is the only point where I have ventured to point up the original a little. I refer to "Europe" several times—a modern idea, but it corresponds to the ancient contrast between Greeks and barbarians, between

314 SARTRE ON THEATER

Magna Graecia, which was spreading its civilization through-out the Mediterranean, and the settlements in Asia Minor, where Athenian colonial imperialism was being carried through with a savagery that Euripedes bluntly denounces. And if the phrase "sale guerre" has a very specific meaning for the French, look at the Greek text: you will find it there, or something very like it.

That leaves us with the gods—the other interesting side of the drama. Here I believe I have followed Euripides very closely. But again I had to get distance to make intel-ligible the criticism of a religion that has become totally alien to us. As they appear in *The Trojan Women* the gods are at once potent and ridiculous. In one respect they rule the world; the Trojan War was their work. But viewed close up, they are seen to behave in the same way as humans and, like them, are subject to petty vanities and petty spites. "The gods' backs are broad," Hecuba says when Helen throws the responsibility for her misconduct upon Athena. But the prologue shows that the goddess is capable of be-traying her allies if she is offended. Why wouldn't she have sold her sanctuary to win a beauty prize? Since he is using stereotypes simply to destroy them, Euripides exploits the legend to bring out the difficulties of a polytheism in which his audience has ceased to believe, but without unduly stress-ing the point, simply by contrasting some myths with others. Is monotheism excepted from this denunciation? Hecuba's moving prayer to Zeus, which astonishes Menelaus—and is a foretaste of a sort of religiosity of Renan's type, a religion in which History would in the last analysis be consistent with a Higher Reason—may look like it for a moment. But Zeus is no better than his wife or his daughter. He will do nothing to save the Trojans from an unjust fate, and by a strange paradox, it is the unreason of all the gods combined that will avenge the Trojans.

The play, therefore, ends in total nihilism. What the Greeks apprehended as a subtle contradiction—the contradiction of the world in which they had to live—we who are seeing the drama from outside recognize as a negation, an abdication. I have tried to bring out this reversal: Hecuba's final despair, which I have emphasized, matches Poseidon's terrible prediction. The gods will perish with the humans; and this common death is the lesson of the tragedy.

In the Mesh

(L'Engrenage)

In The Mesh is not, strictly speaking, one of Sartre's works for the theater. It is a film scenario, written in 1946, which has never been shot. Published by Nagel in 1948, this scenario was adapted for the stage and produced by Jean Mercure at the Théâtre de la Ville (formerly Sarah-Bernhardt) in February 1969. Before that, it had been adapted for the stage several times abroad. Sartre made the following observations on it to Bernard Pingaud. They were published in the *Théâtre de la Ville* magazine, November 1968.

The scenario for *In the Mesh* was written in 1946.[1] What attracted me at first was transposing to the screen a technique frequently used by British and American writers before the war, the plurality of viewpoints. The idea was in the air. Remember *Citizen Kane* and *Rashomon*:[2] it was an attempt to break up the traditional continuity of the narrative, loosen up the flashback, and describe an event from several different angles. In the film I was thinking of, not only was the chronology upset, but the same character, Hélène, was shown looking entirely different, her appearance depending on the point of view of whoever was talking about her.

It was in 1946, too, that we began to discover the havoc caused by Stalinism, though we did not yet know the exact truth about the camps. The scenario was to have been called *Dirty Hands*, like the play I wrote two years later. One question worried me, and that was what, in a period of collectivization, is forcible and what is not? Which is the governing force—necessity or a man? As a matter of fact, Stalinism itself was not the issue. I simply started from a widely current assertion, false to a large extent, in my opinion, that Stalin could not have done other than what he did. I thought of a country in which it was really "impossible to do anything else." A small oil-rich country, for instance, which was wholly dependent on foreign countries for its livelihood. And I imagined the case of a man who came to power with revolutionary intentions and was truly resolved to carry them out, yet who finally resigned himself to a policy precisely the reverse because of the demands of a powerful neighbor.

Most of Latin America was in this sort of situation in 1946. Since then, Castro has been able to break out of the circle. Castro understood that the problem was not to seize power but to create, first by guerrilla warfare and then by a people's war, the conditions in which he could really exercise power. So when Jean Mercure suggested adapting *In the Mesh*, my first inclination was to alter the dénouement. I did not touch the scene in which François, falling into the same trap, takes over and continues the policy of the dictator he has just overthrown. But I was counting on the character Darieu to present the other solution, which neither Jean nor François had thought of: guerrilla warfare. Thus the "mesh" would have been broken through by starting a Castro-type policy.

At that moment the events which have become notorious occurred in Eastern Europe. Czechoslovakia has no oil, and Soviet imperialism obeys other laws than American imperialism. But the situation is similar, where a large country claims the right to impose its law on smaller states within its sphere of influence.[3] The Czechs could not, of course, use guerrilla tactics against the Soviet tanks. With extraordinary ingenuity they turned to a different form of struggle: passive resistance. So it seemed to me that I would be weakening the play if I placed the emphasis on questions of method. In the present circumstances, the important point is to draw attention to the permanent and outrageous character of a policy of force practiced in the socialist and capitalist camps alike. This is why I refrained from altering my story.

It must be quite clear that Jean Aguerra, whose trial goes on all through the drama, is not a traitor nor has he sold out. The Americans dominated Cuba before Castro by corruption. A politician who came to power with fairly generous intentions resisted it for a fairly long time, and finally succumbed to it only because he realized that the combination of hostile social forces and the army with foreign pressure made any genuine reform impossible. By choosing a perfectly honest and sincere character who really believes in socialism, I wanted to show that it was not a question of an individual or of character; it is power itself that is corrupt in a country where the foreigner reigns through an intermediary, and those who hold power become, like Jean, criminals despite themselves.

It is true that personal elements also play their part in Jean's behavior. In my view, private life does not differ basically from public; it is simply another way in which people are totally determined by the social factor. There is also a problem that has always fascinated me, how the private blends with the public in the case of a public political figure. The fact that a man is called upon to play a role in history cannot be merely a matter of chance or a series of coincidences. By combining Marxist and psychoanalytic analyses one ought to be able to show how a particular society and a particular childhood go to form a man who will be capable of taking and exercising power on behalf of his group. But this problem goes beyond *In the Mesh,* in which it is barely touched upon. François's character is very different from Jean's, his private concerns are not the same, and yet he will take over his predecessor's policy.

Adapting to the stage a story written for the film while thinking of what can be done in a film naturally gives rise to serious technical problems. I placed myself unreservedly in the hands of Jean Mercure to solve them, as I had done with Piscator when *In the Mesh* was staged in Germany and with Strehler for the production at the Piccolo Theatro.[4] I know that Jean Mercure wants to make a genuine people's theater, and that is what I like very much about his venture. People's theater should be above all a theater of action, abounding in events and sparing of words, the meaning emerging from the whole of the play silently, as it were, instead of being expounded within it. I must add that at the present time I cannot conceive of a people's theater which does not have a political dimension. That is why I welcome the performance of *In the Mesh* at the Théâtre de la Ville.[5]

NOTES

PART I. **Documents, Lectures, and Conversations on the Theater**

On Dramatic Style

1. Henri Gouhier, *L'Essence du théâtre* (Paris: Plon, 1943) introduced by essays by Georges Pitoëff, Charles Dullin, Louis Jouvet, and Gaston Baty.
2. This was a film to be produced by Henri-Georges Clouzot from a scenario based on *No Exit*; it was to have been entitled *Par les chemins obscurs*.
3. The film *The Lady in the Lake*, directed in 1946 by Robert Montgomery, the American actor, with a script by Steve Fisher based on Raymond Chandler's novel, was shot in its entirety by this "subjective camera" method. Its methodical application proved tiresome in this case, and the experiment is not convincing.
4. *Volpone*, by Ben Jonson, in Jules Romains's adaptation was first staged and acted by Charles Dullin at the Théâtre de l'Atelier in 1928. Jean-Louis Barrault staged and acted *Hamlet* at the Comédie Française in 1942.
5. As illustrated especially by the work of Jacques Copeau and the Pitoëffs.

6. Sartre wrote an essay on Maurice Blanchot's *Aminadab* in 1943 (*"Aminadab* ou du fantastique considéré comme un langage,"* Cahiers du Sud*, April and May 1943). He compares Blanchot with Kafka and shows that the two authors attacked the same problem: "How is one to make [a man] see *from the outside* this obligation to be inside [in the world]?" See *"Aminadab* or the Fantastic Considered as a Language," in Jean-Paul Sartre, *Literary and Philosophical Essays*, trans. Annette Michelson (New York: Criterion Books, 1955), pp. 56–72.

7. The famous production of *The Taming of the Shrew* (*La Mégère apprivoisée*) by Firmin Gémier at the Théâtre Antoine in 1918 marks a historically important break with the naturalistic tradition.

8. Dullin staged Calderón's *La vida es sueño* (adapted by A. Arnoux) for the first time at the Théâtre du Vieux-Colombier in 1921, and again at the Atelier. He produced the play with new settings at the Théâtre de la Cité (formerly Sarah-Bernhardt) in 1944.

9. Camus's *Le Malentendu* had just been produced, or was just about to be produced, at the Théâtre des Mathurins (June 1944) when Sartre gave this lecture.

10. Cf. Armand Salacrou, *La Vie en rose*, impromptu in one act (1931), in *Théâtre II* (Paris: Gallimard, 1944). Henry Bataille's scene is at pp. 250–51; it is footnoted, but no source is given.

11. Eugene O'Neill's play (1928), translated into French by Fanny Pereire and Pierre Minac as *L'Étrange Intermède* in 1938.

12. Play by Henry Montherlant (1942).

13. *Césaire, ou la Présence de l'esprit*, play in two acts by Jean Schlumberger, performed in 1922 by Firmin Gémier and the Chimère Company at the Théâtre des Mathurins; published in *Théâtre* (Paris: Nouvelle Revue française, 1923); revived by Jean Vilar in 1943 at the Théâtre de Poche and later at the Vieux-Colombier, together with Strindberg's *Storm*.

14. Drama in five acts (1898), produced by Jacques Copeau at the Vieux-Colombier in 1922.

15. *Macbeth*, act 5, scene 1, line 56.
16. *L'Échange* (1893) was staged by Jacques Copeau at the Vieux-Colombier in 1914.
17. *La estrella de Sevilla*, comedy by Lope de Vega, prose adaptation by Albert Ollivier, which Sartre saw at the Comédie des Champs-Élysées in 1942, performed by the "Quatre saisons provinciales" Company.
18. The allusion is to Jean-Louis Barrault's production of his adaptation of Knut Hamsun's novel *Hunger* at the Atelier in 1938, in which he mimed mounting an imaginary staircase.
19. In *No Exit*.

Dullin and Spain

1. Lucien Dubech, author of *Historie générale illustrée du théâtre* (Paris: Librairie de France, 1931) and theater critic for *Candide*.

Forgers of Myths (Forger des mythes)

1. Jean Anouilh's *Antigone* was first performed in New York on February 18, 1946, in an English adaptation by Lewis Galantiere.
2. Play in two acts, first performed in November 1945 at the Théâtre des Carrefours.
3. *Caligula* was first performed on September 26, 1945, at the Théâtre Hébertot.
4. Hegel deals with Greek tragedy mainly in the *Aesthetics*.
5. *Bariona, or Son of Thunder* was first published in full in English in Michel Contat and Michel Rybalka, eds., *The Writings of Jean-Paul Sartre*, trans. Richard McLeary (Evanston, Ill.: Northwestern University Press, 1974), vol. 2 (in French, in *Les Écrits de Sartre* in 1970), but the play has never been performed in public.
6. Sartre is no doubt confusing this with another production by Gaston Baty, since Baty never, as far as we know, produced *The Taming of the Shrew*. Unless it is really that play, but as produced by Firmin Gémier with similar effects

in 1918 (see p. 322, note 7, above); Sartre cannot, of course, have seen it.

7. All Sartre's plays, except *The Devil and the Good Lord* (*Le Diable et le Bon Dieu*), *Nekrassov*, and *The Trojan Women* (*Les Troyennes*), have been performed in the United States. The outstanding productions are:

— *No Exit* (*Huis clos*), adapted by Paul Bowles, New York, November 26, 1945; 31 performances. *No Exit* won the prize for the best foreign play produced in New York in 1947 and, like Sartre's other works, was frequently produced on tour and at universities.

— *The Flies* (*Les Mouches*), April 17, 1947, at the Dramatic Workshop, New York, directed by Erwin Piscator.

— *The Respectful Prostitute* (*La Putain respectueuse*), adapted by Eva Wolas, New York, February 9, 1948. Over 350 performances. Banned in several American cities.

— *Dirty Hands* (*Les Mains sales*), as *Red Gloves*, adapted by Daniel Taradash, New York, December 4, 1948; 113 performances.

— *The Victors* (*Morts sans sépulture*), adapted by Thornton Wilder, New York, December 26, 1948.

— *Kean*, musical comedy, based on the play by Dumas and Sartre, book by Peter Stone, music and lyrics by Robert Wright and George Forrest, New York, November 2, 1961.

— *The Condemned of Altona* (*Les Séquestrés d'Altona*), adapted by Justin O'Brien, New York (Lincoln Center), February 3, 1966; 46 performances.

People's Theater and Bourgeois Theater

1. These remarks about the TNP audience stung Jean Vilar to reply in *L'Express* of November 24, 1955: "My theater is called the 'National People's Theater,' not the 'National Workers' Theater.' . . . A people's audience in France nowadays is not solely a working-class audience. Surely that is perfectly obvious? A post office clerk, my stenographer, a small shopkeeper, who also work an eight-hour day, all of them are part of the people. Why does Sartre reject them?

... *Nekrassov* may be a people's play in intention. Is it one so far as the customers are concerned? Sartre should think this over and then give us a good play; I have been asking him for one for four years now. It looks to me as if he would be quite at home in the TNP."

2. CGT: Confédération générale du travail, the leading labor organization in France. TEC: Théâtre et Culture, a playgoing society with backing by the Communist Party.

3. A French sailor sentenced in 1950 to five years hard labor for distributing leaflets protesting against the war in Indochina. The Communist Party organized a campaign for his release, with which Sartre associated himself. Cf. *L'Affaire Henri Martin*, with a commentary by Jean-Paul Sartre (Paris: Gallimard, 1953). For further details see *The Writings of Jean-Paul Sartre*, vol. 1, note 53/233.

4. It must be remembered that there had been very few performances of Brecht's plays in France at the time of this interview (1955). The first of his works to be performed in France was *The Threepenny Opera*, staged by Gaston Baty at the Théâtre Montparnasse in 1930, which Sartre saw at the time (cf. Simone de Beauvoir, *The Prime of Life*, trans. Peter Green [New York: World Publishing Co., 1962], p. 15). Apart from *The Exception and the Rule*, produced by Jean-Marie Serreau at the Noctambules in 1947, and *Mother Courage*, which was included in the TNP repertory in 1951, Brecht's plays were confined to avant-garde experimental theaters. Brecht really began to make his way in France with the performances by the Berliner Ensemble at the Théâtre des Nations (*Mother Courage* in 1954, *The Caucasian Chalk Circle* in 1955). On this see the article by Roland Barthes and Bernard Dort, "Brecht 'traduit'" in *Théâtre populaire*, no. 23, March 1957, pp. 1–8.

5. Sartre himself subsequently adapted *The Crucible* for the screen as *Les Sorcières de Salem*, stressing its social aspect and its denunciation of McCarthyism. The film directed by Raymond Rouleau, with Yves Montand and Simon Signoret, was released in 1957. See *The Writings of Jean-Paul Sartre*, vol. 1, note 56/287 and p. 607.

Theater and Cinema

1. *Kiss Me Deadly*, a film based on Mickey Spillane's novel, was released in 1955.
2. *Greed*, a film on Frank Norris's novel *McTeague*, was released in 1923.
3. Play commissioned by Louis Jouvet, first performed in 1947 at the Théâtre de l'Athénée.
4. Cf. *The Psychology of Imagination* (New York: Citadel Press, 1963) Conclusion: II. "The Work of Art," pp. 273–82.

The Author, the Play, and the Audience

1. *The Roads to Freedom* (*Les Chemins de la liberté*), see p. 329, note 14, below.
2. Play by André Roussin, produced at the Théâtre des Nouveautés in 1947, and thereafter regularly revived with tremendous success. It was produced, in an adapation by Nancy Mitford, at the Coronet Theatre in New York in October 1953.
3. Comedy by James M. Barrie, written in 1903 and produced for the first time in French by Gémier at the Théâtre-Antoine in 1920.
4. See p. 325, note 4, above.
5. First performed in 1879.

Epic Theater and Dramatic Theater

1. The allusion here is to an anecdote mentioned by Horace (*Ad Pisones* 276) and by Boileau (*Art poétique*, chap. 3, line 67), describing Thespis, the most ancient Greek tragic poet, as "smearing his face with wine-lees and taking his dramatic poems around on carts."
2. Sartre visited Cuba from February 22 to March 20, 1960. His visit coincided with the performance of *The Respectful Prostitute* by the Havana National Theater.
3. Serge Lebovici is a specialist on the problems of childhood and adolescence and has written a great deal on psychodrama and psychotherapy.

4. *The Connection,* the play by Jack Gelber, was produced by Judith Malina at the Living Theater in New York on July 15, 1959, and was a great success thereafter. Sartre's summary is very rough; cf. the text of the play published by Grove Press in 1960.

5. This phrase, borrowed by Baudelaire from De Quincey (*Confessions of an English Opium Eater*) and translated by him in *Les Paradis artificiels,* appears in the prose poem "A une heure du matin" (*Le Spleen de Paris,* 10) and in the collection *Pauvre Belgique* (ft. 120). Cf. Baudelaire, *Oeuvres complètes* (Paris: Bibliothèque de la Pléiade, 1932), pp. 240, 416, and 1365.

6. This novel was published in 1921. The incident described occurs in chap. 24, and the sketch is in fact a caricature.

7. See p. 326, note 3, above, under "The Author, the Play, and the Audience."

8. See p. 326, note 2, above, under "The Author, the Play, and the Audience."

9. This is a rough summary of Maurice Donnay's play *Les Éclaireuses* [The pathfinders] (1913), published in his *Théâtre* (Paris: Fasquelle, 1919), vol. 7.

10. Play by Marcel Achard (1957).

11. "New Objectivity" or "New Matter-of-Factness." The "Neue Sachlichkeit" movement emerged from expressionism, and around 1923 its leading adherents included Carl Zuckmeyer, Erich Kästner, Alfred Döblin, Hans Carossa and the early Brecht of *Drums in the Night.*

12. Play by Paul Claudel (1890).

13. Produced by Roger Blin at the Théâtre de Babylone in January 1953.

14. Ionesco's play was first performed by Jean-Louis Barrault at the Odéon-Théâtre de France in 1959.

15. See *The Condemned of Altona,* act 4. Leni gives the *Frankfurter Zeitung* to Franz to demonstrate the revival of Germany objectively to him, and Johanna blames her for it in the next scene. Sartre's summary is rough and does not reproduce the lines accurately.

16. Sartre attended a performance by the Peking Opera in Paris in 1956.

17. Hegel deals with Sophocles' *Antigone* in his *Aesthetics* ("Poetry," Chap. 3: "Dramatic Poetry"). It is also mentioned briefly in his *Lessons on the Philosophy of Religion*.

18. A concept in German psychological aesthetics which made its first appearance around 1910. Literally, the term means the capacity to grasp from within, or empathy. In aesthetics, it connotes the process by which a nonmaterial content is grasped intuitively or emotionally rather than intellectually.

Interview with Kenneth Tynan (1961)

1. First produced in Germany in 1961, *Les Paravents* (*Screens*) was performed in 1966 at the Odéon-Théâtre de France, directed by Roger Blin, and caused a violent uproar provoked by groups of right-wing extremists.

2. Lecture given on March 29, 1960; the full text is reproduced above, pp. 78–120.

3. Cf. Jean-Paul Sartre, *The Words*, trans. Bernard Frechtman (New York: Braziller, 1964), pp. 151–52.

4. Cf. Simone de Beauvoir, *The Prime of Life*, p. 169.

5. Sartre is alluding to the trial of Generals Challe and Zeller, who had just been sentenced (May 1961) to fifteen years imprisonment for their share in the April putsch in Algeria. Jouhaud and Salan, the other two members of the "quartet of generals," were arrested and sentenced the following year, Jouhaud to death and Salan to life imprisonment. All four were pardoned by de Gaulle and released, Zeller in July 1966, Challe in December of that year, Jouhaud at Christmas 1967, and Salan in June 1968 (in return, it is said, for the army's support for de Gaulle during the "events" of May–June 1968).

6. The play has not been published in book form.

7. An allusion to the episode entitled "One-Eye" in the film *Raices* (*Roots*), a series of sketches by the Mexican director Benito Alazraki, released in 1955.

8. Sartre visited the United States for two fairly long periods in 1945 and 1946. He refused to go back again in 1965; cf. *The Writings of Jean-Paul Sartre*, vol. 1, note 65/422.

9. Sartre's script, written in 1959 for John Huston, was some eight hundred pages long. It was condensed and reworked by Charles Kaufman and Wolfgang Reinhardt, the author of a book on Freud. The film was released in 1962 as *Freud, the Secret Passion*. In another interview in *Tribune socialiste* (January–February 1962) Sartre explained: "I withdrew my name from the film not because of the cuts— I knew that cuts would be needed—but because of the way it was cut. It's honest, indeed very honest, work, but there is no point in an intellectual's assuming responsibility for dubious ideas." For further details see *The Writings of Jean-Paul Sartre*, vol. 1, pp. 608–9.

10. This myth is the subject of a play by Euripides.

11. Sartre had very cordial relations with Ilya Ehrenburg (cf. Simone de Beauvoir, *All Said and Done*, trans. Patrick O'Brian [New York: J. P. Putnam's Sons, 1974], pp. 282–3 and *passim*). Ehrenburg wrote a preface to the Russian version of *Nekrassov* (*Tol'ko Pravda*; Moscow: Iskusstvo, 1956) and collaborated on the translation with O. Savich.

12. Sartre did, however, attend the 400th performance of *Lizzie McKay*, the Russian version of *The Respectful Prostitute*, when he visited the U.S.S.R. in June 1962. He said he was very satisfied with the way the play was staged and acted.

    The only two of Sartre's plays that have been performed in the U.S.S.R. are *Nekrassov* and *The Respectful Prostitute*, though both were very successful. A volume was published in 1967 containing *The Flies, The Victors, The Respectful Prostitute, The Devil and the Good Lord, Nekrassov*, and *The Condemned of Altona*.

13. The film, released in France in 1952, was directed by Marcel Pagliano and Charles Brabant, and adapted by Jacques-Laurent Bost and Alexandre Astruc, with dialogue by Sartre and Jacques-Laurent Bost.

14. The allusion is to volume 4 of *The Roads to Freedom*, entitled *La Dernière Chance*, which has remained unfinished and unpublished, except for two chapters published in *Les Temps modernes*, November and December 1949, entitled "Drôle d'amitié." Mathieu, the hero of the novel, was to escape from a prisoner-of-war camp, join the Resistance,

and die under torture (cf. *The Writings of Jean-Paul Sartre*, vol. 1, note 49/192).

Myth and Reality in Theater

1. Cf. Geneviève Serreau, *Histoire du "nouveau théâtre"* (Paris: Gallimard, 1966; "Idées" series, no. 104), which Sartre read when preparing his lecture.
2. The play was first produced in Paris in 1959 at the Théâtre de Lutèce by the African dramatic art company Les Griots, in a production by Roger Blin.
3. Artaud founded the Théâtre Alfred Jarry with Roger Vitrac in Paris in 1926 and directed it till 1928. He produced one act of Claudel's *Partage de Midi*, Vitrac's *Les Mystères de l'amour* and *Victor ou les Enfants au pouvoir*, Gorki's *Mother*, and Strindberg's *Dream* (the first night of which was disrupted by André Breton and his Surrealist cohorts, whereupon Artaud called in the police).
4. Cf. "Théâtre Alfred Jarry (Saison 1928)" in *Oeuvres complètes* (Paris: Gallimard, 1961), vol. 2, p. 27.
5. The quotation in full runs: "A production at the Théâtre Alfred Jarry will be as exciting as a game, as a card party in which the whole audience joins."
6. The play was performed at the Théâtre du Gymnase in Paris in 1960, directed by Peter Brook.
7. Antonin Artaud, *Le Théâtre et son double* (Paris: Gallimard, 1966; "Idées" series), pp. 144–45.
8. Jean-Jacques Lebel was chiefly responsible for introducing the "happening" into France. See his book *Le Happening* (Paris: Denoël, 1966; "Lettres nouvelles" series).
9. Actually, the curtain did not fall on the performances of *US* by the Royal Shakespeare Company (Peter Brook) at the Aldwych Theatre in London in 1966; the actors stood rigid, staring at the audience, who finally got up and left uneasily while the actors remained on stage. Sartre did not attend the performance personally and is basing his description on a report.
10. *Le Dossier Oppenheimer* was produced by Jean Vilar at the Athénée-Théâtre Vivant in 1965.

11. Jean-Jacques Bernard, son of Tristan Bernard, was the inventor and principal representative of the "theater of silence" with *Le Feu qui reprend mal* (1921) and especially *Martine* (1922). He preferred the term "theater of the unexpressed" to "theater of silence." Taking Freud's theories as his basis, he tried to make his characters express their feelings by indirection alone. The result at best was something roughly akin to Chekhov.

12. The allusion is to Knut Hamsun's novel *Hunger*, adapted for the stage and acted by Jean-Louis Barrault at the Atelier in 1938.

13. See Artaud, *Le Théâtre et son double.*

14. Play by Eugene Ionesco, first produced by Marcel Cuvelier at the Théâtre de Poche in 1951.

15. Produced by Nicolas Bataille at the Théâtre des Noctambules in 1950.

16. See p. 327, note 13, above.

The Actor

1. *Fiat*: formula for an act of will, an authoritative legal sanction, an affirmation based on inner evidence (cf. *L'Idiot de la famille*, vol. 1, pp. 159 ff.).

2. In *Psychology of the Imagination*, pp. 22 *et passim.*

The Comic Actor

1. A concept introduced and explained by Sartre in the *Critique de la raison dialectique* (see especially pp. 308 ff.).

   In his Preface to Michèle Marceaux's *Les Maos en France* (Paris: Gallimard, 1971; pp. 10–11), he gives the following definition of "seriality": "An aggregate is called serial when each of its components, although neighbor to all the others, remains alone and is defined by its neighbor's thinking, insofar as this neighbor thinks *like the others*; that is to say, each is other than itself and behaves like another which itself is other than itself."

2. In the passage preceding this extract Sartre discusses a theory of laughter in which he borrows from Bergson

(*Laughter: An Essay on the Meaning of the Comic,* 1899) the well-known example of the man tripping in the street, falling down, and arousing the passers' mirth. The following definition is worth noting: "Laughter is the property of man because man is the only animal that takes itself seriously; mirth denounces false seriousness in the name of true seriousness" (*L'Idiot de la famille,* vol. 1, p. 821).

PART II. Documents and Interviews on the Plays

Bariona, or the Son of Thunder

1. It was Balthasar, the Black King.
2. On *Bariona,* see also p. 39 above.

The Flies (Les Mouches)

1. Pierre Bost, writer and author of film scripts and elder brother of Jacques-Laurent Bost, was one of Sartre's pupils at the Lycée at Le Havre and has remained one of his most intimate friends.
2. On the vicissitudes relating to the publication of *Nausea* (*La Nausée*) by Gallimard, see Simone de Beauvoir, *The Prime of Life,* pp. 227 and 236–39.
3. The backer in question, a con man who "answered to the splendid name of Néron," was a minor civil servant who played the role of an intellectual Maecenas with some aplomb, and Simone de Beauvoir, who tells the story good-humoredly in *The Prime of Life* (pp. 408–10), herself became a victim, though she knew all about him, in 1945 when her play *Les Bouches inutiles* was being staged (*Force of Circumstances,* pp. 49–50). Sartre may have used him to some extent as a model for Georges de Valera in *Nekrassov.*
4. In point of fact, almost all the critics tore both the play and the production to pieces: see the reviews by André Castelot in *La Gerbe,* June 17, 1943 ("Giraudoux's *Électre* re-

thought by a Dadaist or a decrepit Surrealist, and a neurotic one to boot"); Alain Laubreaux in *Le Petit Parisien,* June 5, 1943 ("a ponderous, long-winded play," "a performance which reconstructs for us an avant-garde long passed into the rear guard, in an unlikely mixture of shoddy Cubism and Dadaism"); Armory in *Les Nouveaux Temps,* June 13, 1943 ("Sartre has taken the misfortunes of the House of Atreus simply as a pretext to flog a humanity he detests, wallowing in a negative depreciation, ostentatiously exhibiting everything that is most disgusting in our sad world," "Céline without his gust," "epileptic adoration of death"); Georges Ricou in *France socialiste,* June 12, 1943 ("How well one understands the invasion of the flies into this putrefaction of taste"); Jacques Berland in *Paris-Soir,* June 15, 1943 ("Sartre seems to be more of an essayist than a playwright"); Roland Purnal in *Comoedia,* June 13, 1943 ("His whole rhapsody, in short, gains its effect from a certain state of scatophagical obsession"); etc.

One of the few favorable criticisms was that by Maurice Rostand in *Paris-Midi,* June 7, 1943: "It must be said at once that this is a work of exceptional merit for its breadth of development, cosmic force, and metaphysical resonance." The criticism in the *Pariser Zeitung* was not hostile and stressed mainly the play's defects of form.

Charles Dullin was to write later (cf. *Ce sont les dieux qu'il nous faut,* Paris: Gallimard, 1969): "It was a speedy and total flop, the box office was pitiful." Despite this unpromising start, the play was kept on the program twice a week for nearly the whole season, so that it had about forty performances in 1943 (first night June 3).

5. Cf. Marshal Pétain, *La France nouvelle* (Paris: Fasquelle, 1943), p. 167: "You are suffering and you will go on suffering for a long time yet, for we have not finished paying for all our faults."
6. Cf. the unsigned article (by Michel Leiris) "Oreste et la Cité" in the underground *Les Lettres françaises,* no. 12, reprinted with a few changes in Michel Leiris, *Brisées* (Paris: Mercure de France, 1966), pp. 74–78.

No Exit (Huis clos)

1. ORTF: Office de Radiodiffusion et Télévision Française, the state-owned radio and television network in France.
2. Written in about a fortnight in early fall 1943, *Huis clos*, which was first published as *Les Autres* (in *L'Arbalète*, no. 8, spring 1944), was originally to have been a curtain-raiser in a performance on tour in the unoccupied zone by Marc Barbezat and Marc Beigbeder. The two female parts were to have been played by Olga Barbezat and Wanda Kosakiewicz. Sartre first thought of Sylvain Itkine, but later suggested to Albert Camus that he should direct the play and take the part of Garcin. Camus accepted, and the first rehearsals were held in Simone de Beauvoir's hotel room. The projected tour came to nothing owing to material difficulties and Olga Barbezat's arrest. The play was then accepted by Annet-Badel, the new director of the Vieux-Colombier theater. After Camus withdrew, Annet-Badel commissioned Raymond Rouleau to produce the play and engaged professional actors; of the former team there remained only R. J. Chauffard, one of Sartre's former students, who played the part of the majordomo. For further details see Simone de Beauvoir, *The Prime of Life*, pp. 441 and 461, and *The Writings of Jean-Paul Sartre*, vol. 1, note 44/47.

Dirty Hands (Les Mains sales)

1. In point of fact, Saint-Just's remark has a quite different meaning, since what he actually wrote was "One cannot *reign* innocently," and goes on to say: "only a fool would not see that. Every king is a rebel and a usurper." It is an argument in a demand for the king's death. It appears in the first Discourse on the Judgment of Louis XVI, addressed to the Convention on November 13, 1792.
2. During the fighting for the liberation of Paris in August 1944, a truce was negotiated between the insurgents and the German military command. Serious disagreements about the truce arose within the Resistance: the Gaullists of the

General Delegation were wholeheartedly in favor of it and carried on the negotiations with von Choltitz through the good offices of Nordling, the Swedish consul, whereas the Paris Liberation Committee, in which the Communists predominated, were against it. The truce was negotiated on August 19 and was concluded on the twentieth, but was not fully kept, and was denounced by the PLC on the twenty-first. The political issue at stake in the disagreements within the Resistance was plainly the question whether Paris would or would not be under communist influence after its liberation (see Robert Aron, *Histoire de la libération de la France* [Paris: Fayard, 1959], pt. 4, chap. 3).

Hoederer's attitude in *Dirty Hands* would then be rather like that which might have been adopted at the time of these negotiations by some Communists, who, foreseeing that they would have to come to terms with the bourgeois forces in the government issuing from the Liberation for the sake of economic reconstruction, though this would postpone the seizure of power by the Communist Party, might have declared in favor of the truce.

3. One of them played Olga and the other Jessica at the first performance.

4. Hoederer's actual words in the play are, "In principle, I have no objection to political assassination. All parties do it" (act 4, p. 191). This quotation and those in notes 7 and 8 are from *Dirty Hands*, trans. Lionel Abel, in *No Exit and Three Other Plays* (New York: Vintage Books, 1955).

5. The Rassemblement Démocratique Révolutionnaire was formed in late 1947 and early 1948. The first night of *Dirty Hands* was on April 2, 1948.

6. SFIO: Section Française de L'Internationale Ouvrière, the French social democratic party.

7. In an article wholly favorable to the play published in *Le Figaro* on April 3, 1948. Gabriel Marcel too reverts to this comparison to Hamlet in an article in *Les Nouvelles littéraires* (May 13, 1948), and also points out a similarity to Musset's *Lorenzaccio*.

8. Hugo's actual words are, "As for men, it's not what they are that interests me, but what they can become" (act 5, p. 225).

9. Hoederer's actual words are, "I wasn't the one who invented lying. It grew out of a society divided into classes, and each one of us has inherited it from birth" (act 5, p. 223).

10. Sartre in fact took part in a symposium on "morality and society" held at the Istituto Gramsci, May 22 to 25, 1964. See the extracts from his remarks in *The Writings of Jean-Paul Sartre*, vol. 2, pp. 241–52.

11. This remark, which is quoted by Simone de Beauvoir, who dates it September 14, 1939, actually runs: "Now I am cured of socialism, if I ever needed a cure" (cf. *The Prime of Life*).

The Devil and the Good Lord (Le Diable et le Bon Dieu)

1. This is *El rufián dichoso* (The Blessed Scoundrel).

2. The "Morality" announced by Sartre in the last line of *Being and Nothingness* (*L'Etre et le Néant*) was written in the form of several bulky notebooks in 1947–1949 and has remained wholly unpublished, with the exception of an isolated fragment, an extract from a chapter entitled "Revolutionary Violence," published in *Combat* (June 16, 1949), headlined "Black and White in the United States" (for further details see *The Writings of Jean-Paul Sartre*, note 49/187). The first of these notebooks, entitled "For Morality," alone accounts for 247 manuscript pages, representing 822 pages of typescript. Judging as he does that the concepts he held at that time have become completely out of date, Sartre does not contemplate publishing this work in his lifetime. In point of fact, he went back to treating his whole position on the problems of morality dialectically in 1965, in a work which is still unfinished and unpublished.

3. Speech by Hilda in scene 10, p. 133, of the American edition, trans. Kitty Black (New York: Alfred A. Knopf, 1960).

4. See note 8, below.

5. Vilar took the part of Heinrich.
6. Scene 4, p. 69.
7. Scene 8, pp. 124–25.
8. Cf. Johan Huizinga, *The Waning of the Middle Ages*, translated from the Dutch.

The quotation from Odo of Cluny reads: "The beauty of the body is wholly in the outer skin. For if men saw what lies beneath the skin, were they gifted like the lynx of Boeotia with eyes that penetrate to the entrails, the very sight of woman would turn them sick; the grace of women is but the foulness in the stomach, blood, bile, gall. Consider what is hidden in the nostrils, in the throat, in the belly: all of it muck. . . . And we who shrink from touching mucus or excreta even with our fingertips, how then can we desire to embrace the sack of excrements itself?"

Huizinga notes that this theme and its development are borrowed from Saint John Chrysostom, "De mulieribus atque pulcritudine" in *Opera* (Paris, 1735), vol. 12, p. 523. [The passage is not included in the authorized and revised English translation of Huizinga's book (New York: St. Martin's Press, 1924).—TRANSLATOR'S NOTE]

9. André Malraux, *Man's Fate*, trans. Haakon Chevalier (New York: Random House, 1934), p. 50.

Kean

1. In a Soviet film directed by I. Volkov in 1924. Sartre's adaptation was filmed in Italy in 1957 by Vittorio Gassmann, who took the part of Kean himself.

Sartre's adaptation of *Kean*, translated and directed by Frank Hauser, was acted with great success in England by Alan Badel at the Globe Theatre in London (first performance January 28, 1971).

Nekrassov

1. The play is dated 1928.
2. First performed at the Atelier in 1952.
3. Sartre attended the Peoples' Peace Congress in Vienna

from December 12 to 19, 1952, organized by the World Council for Peace. His participation in this congress may be said to mark the peak of his association with the Communists. An "Appeal by the Writers Meeting in Vienna," signed by 103 writers, including Sartre, stated: "We who believe in the power of the written word, and whose trade it is to bear witness for ourselves and for others like ourselves, have decided to make our works consistent with our will to peace and hereby state that we shall combat war in our writings." For further details on the congress, see *The Writings of Jean-Paul Sartre*, vol. 1, note 52/226–29.

The Condemned of Altona (Les Séquestrés d'Altona)

1. Cf. p. 50, above.
2. Headquarters of the Gestapo in Paris during the Occupation.
3. First performed in 1957, directed by Roger Planchon, at Villeurbanne.
4. The allusion is to *Le Printemps 71*, completed in 1961 and produced by Claude Martin at the Théâtre de Saint-Denis in 1963.
5. See pp. 327–28, note 17, above.
6. *Les Quatre cents coups*, the film by François Truffaut (1959).
7. First produced in 1956 by Jean-Marie Serreau at the Théâtre de l'Alliance française.
8. The title of the play as translated in England was *Loser Wins*.
9. Sartre wrote an article on *Citizen Kane* in 1945, entitled "Quand Hollywood veut faire penser" *L'Écran français*, no. 5, (August 1, 1945).
10. This unexpected reference to Molière's *Les Femmes savantes* is actually an allusion to Malraux, who, during an official visit to Latin America shortly before Sartre had this conversation, had publicly attacked him, asserting that he had indirectly collaborated with the Germans during the war by letting *The Flies* be performed with the censorship's permission. Sartre had replied in an interview: "A private person does not have to defend himself against a minister's

slanders. No dispute between Vadius and Trissotin!" (*Libér-ation*, September 21, 1959).

It is of interest in a fairly recent article (*Le Monde*, January 21–22, 1973) Pierre Viansson-Ponté reported the following remarks by Malraux when he had asked him to meet Sartre: "Can you see me in a dialogue with Sartre: Vadius and Trissotin! What a horrible idea! Two elderly gents all got up in their petty glories merrily pelting each other in a battle of flowers."

11. See the debate on *The Flies*, pp. 192–97, above.

12. Act 1, p. 32. All references to the play are to the Alfred A. Knopf edition (New York, 1961), trans. Sylvia and George Leeson.

13. The father's actual words (act 1, p. 34) are, "You do not love your neighbor, Franz, or you would not dare to despise these prisoners."

14. It is the father who says (act 1, p. 34), "The Gerlachs are victims of Luther. That prophet filled us with insane pride."

15. Cf. act 4, pp. 118–37. Sartre gives the general sense of the scene, but does not quote Johanna's lines exactly.

16. Act 1, pp. 289–30. Here too the lines are roughly sum-marized.

17. Cf. Karl Jaspers, *The Question of German Guilt*, trans. E. B. Ashton (New York: Dial Press, 1947).

18. The father says to Franz (act 5, p. 171): "Both your life and your death are merely *nothing*. You are nothing, you do nothing, you have done nothing . . . Forgive me."

19. Gide's *La Séquestrée de Poitiers* was published in 1930 (Paris: Gallimard; "Ne jugez pas" series). The *Souvenirs de la Cour d'Assises* are earlier (Paris: Gallimard, 1913).

20. Sartre wrote an important article on *La Question* (Paris: Éditions Minuit, 1958), the book in which Henri Alleg tells the story of his abduction by paratroopers and the tor-tures inflicted on him. Sartre's article, entitled "Une Vic-toire," appeared in *L'Express* March 6, 1958; the issue was immediately confiscated. It was reprinted later in book form with *La Question* in Switzerland (Lausanne: La Cité, 1958) and after that in *Situations* V. See *The Writings of Jean-Paul Sartre*, vol. 1, note 58/302.

The Trojan Women (Les Troyennes)

1. Cf. Euripides, *Les Troyennes*, text edited and translated by Léon Parmentier, in *Oeuvres* (Paris: "Les Belles Lettres," 1925), vol. 4.
2. The translated play was performed in 1961 and was published in that year by L'Arche in their "Répertoire pour un théâtre populaire" series, no. 34.

In the Mesh (L'Engrenage)

1. The film was very nearly made by Bernard Borderie in 1949.
2. *Rashomon*, a film by Akira Kurosawa (1952).
3. For the passages in which Sartre expressed his disapproval of the invasion of Czechoslovakia by the armed forces of the Warsaw Pact, see *The Writings of Jean-Paul Sartre*, vol. 1, note 68/496.
4. Giorgio Strehler staged *L'Ingranaggio* at the Piccolo Teatro, Milan, in 1953.
5. Though well received by the audiences at the Théâtre de la Ville, *L'Engrenage* was savaged by almost all the critics.

DOCUMENTS ON THEATER AND CINEMA NOT REPRODUCED IN THIS VOLUME

"L'Art cinématographique" [The art of the cinema], prize-giving address delivered at the *Lycée* in Le Havre, July 12, 1931. Published in *Gazette du cinéma*, no. 2 (June 1950); no 3 (September 1950). Reprinted in *The Writings of Jean-Paul Sartre* (Evanston, Ill.: Northwestern University Press, 1974), vol. 2, pp. 53–59.

"Un Film pour l'après-guerre" [A film for the postwar period], *L'Écran français*, incorporated with *Les Lettres françaises* (underground issue), no. 15 (April 1944). Unsigned article.

"Quand Hollywood veut faire penser . . . *Citizen Kane* d'Orson Welles" [When Hollywood tries to be intelligent . . . Orson Welles, Citizen Kane], *L'Écran français*, no. 5 (August 1, 1945).

"Strindberg var fördringsägare [Strindberg our "creditor"], *Dagens Nyheter* (Stockholm), January 28, 1949. In this article Sartre pays a tribute to Strindberg and shows the influence of *The Dance of Death* and *The Storm* on his own plays.

"*The Maids*" [a study of Jean Genet's play], in *Saint Genet, Actor and Martyr* trans. Bernard Frechtman (New York: Braziller, 1964), appendix 3, pp. 611–25.

"Interview," *Teatr* (Moscow), January 1956, pp. 156–59.

"Quand la police frappe les trois coups" [When the police knock thrice], *France-Observateur*, December 5, 1957. Reprinted in *Situations VII* (Paris: Gallimard, 1965), pp. 308–21.

"Le théâtre peut-il aborder l'actualité politique? Une table ronde avec Sartre, Michel Butor, Roger Vailland, Arthur Adamov, Morvan Lebesque" [Can theater deal with current politics? A round-table discussion by Sartre and others], *France-Observateur*, February 13, 1958. Reprinted in Arthur Adamov, *Ici et maintenant* (Paris: Gallimard, 1964).

"Jean-Paul Sartre vous présente *Soledad*" [Sartre presents Soledad], written for the program of Colette Audry's play, Théâtre de Poche (Comédie Caumartin), April 1960. Reprinted in *The Writings of Jean-Paul Sartre*, vol. 2, pp. 236–38.

"Interview," *Teatr* (Moscow), September 1962, pp. 184–85.

"Le cinéma nous donne sa première tragédie: *Les Abysses*" [The cinema gives us its first tragedy: *Les Abysses*], *Le Monde*, April 19, 1963. An article on Nico Papatakis' film. Reprinted in *The Writings of Jean-Paul Sartre*, vol. 2, pp. 239–40.

"Jean-Paul Sartre présente *La Promenade du dimanche*," in Georges Michel, *La Promenade du dimanche* (Paris: Gallimard, 1967; "Le Manteau d'Arlequin" series).

"Une Structure du langage" [A structure of language], *Le Point* (Brussels), no. 8 (February 1967). An interview on avant-garde theater with J.-P. Berckmans and J.-C. Garot.

"*L'Agression* de Georges Michel," *Bref*, no. 103 (February–March 1967). An interview by Nicole Zand.

"Défendez-vous" [Defend yourselves], address delivered at the TNP on December 28, 1968, to protest against the banning of a play by Armand Gatti. Published in *Complexe* (Antwerp), no. 4 (July 1969).

"Débat sur le film *Le Chagrin et la pitié*" [A debate on the film *The Sorrow and the Pity*], *La Cause du peuple—J'accuse*, no. 2 (May 31, 1971).

Index

352   *Index*

"theater of cruelty," 140, 144–5,
152–3
"theater of silence," 150, 330–1
n.11
"theater of the absurd," vii, 135–6
"Théâtre de la cruauté" (Artaud),
152
Théatre et Culture (TEC), 45,
325 n.2
Théâtre et son double, Le (Artaud),
139, 144
Théâtre National Populaire
(TNP), ix, 44–6, 251–2, 324–5
n.1
Threepenny Opera, The (Brecht),
72
Topaze (Pagnol), 248
torture, 122, 202–3, 254, 287–8,
304, 307–8
Tous contre tous (Adamov), 51–2
tragedy, 3–5, 19, 34, 123. *See also*
French classical drama; Greek
tragedy
translation, problems of, 311
transplantation. *See* cultural context
Trial, The (Kafka), 272
Trojan Women, The (*Les
Troyennes*), 309–15
Trotskyists, 224
truth, in theater, 56, 123, 158–61
Tynan, Kenneth, 121–34

Uncle Tom's Cabin (Stowe), 142
Union of Soviet Socialist Republics,
127, 134, 317; theater in, 46–7,
52–3, 133
United States. *See* America
unities, 41, 56
unrealization, 162–7, 172–7
US (Brook), 146–7, 330 n.9

Vailland, Roger, 107
Vega Carpio, Lope de: *The Lovers
of Galicia,* 30–2; *The Star of
Seville,* 28
Verfremdungseffekt (distancing
effect), 266. *See also* distancing,
in Brecht
Viansson-Ponté, Pierre, 338–9 n.10

Victors, The (*Morts sans sépulture*),
42, 62, 67, 202–3, 271, 324 n.7
Vie en rose, La (Salacrou), 16–17,
322 n.10
Vienna Peace Congress, 249,
337–8 n.3
Vietnam war, 145, 146–7
viewpoints, plurality of, 316–17
Vilar, Jean, 6, 20–3, 44, 147–8,
322 n.13, 324–5 n.1, 330 n.10
Vinaver, Michel: *Les Coréens,* 266
Vitold, Michel, 67, 198, 199, 201
Vitrac, Roger, 330 n.3
Voltaire (François-Marie Arouet),
3, 48, 74

Waiting for Godot (Beckett), 51,
99–100, 128, 156, 311
Waning of the Middle Ages, The
(Huizinga), 236
Weiss, Peter, 135
Welles, Orson, 282
Wiegel, Helene, 75
Wilde, Oscar, 176
Wilder, Thornton, 324 n.6
Williams, Tennessee, 128–9
"Wir alle sind Luthers opfer" ("All
of us are victims of Luther";
conversation), 285–306
Wolas, Eva, 204, 324 n.6
women; in Alcestis legend, 132–3;
in comedy, 258; in *The Con-
demned of Altona,* 272–5; in
The Devil and the Good Lord,
230; in Ibsen, 75; in Kafka, 272
Words, The (*Les Mots*), x
work, as shown in theater, 104–5,
120, 263
Wright, Robert, 324 n.6
writers, obligations of, 249, 337–8
n.3

young people: as audience, 134,
290–1; and communism, 210,
220–1; war experience, 259–60,
288–9

Zeller, General, 328 n.5
Zuckmayer, Carl, 327 n.11

Jean-Paul Sartre was born in Paris in 1905. Educated at the École Normale, he then taught philosophy in provincial *lycées*, and in 1938 published his first novel, *Nausea*. During the war, he participated in the Resistance and completed the major work which eventually established his reputation as an existential philosopher—*Being and Nothingness* (1943). After the Liberation, he founded the socialist journal *Les Temps Modernes*. He has been a prolific playwright, producing among other works, *No Exit* (1947), *The Devil and the Good Lord* (1951), and *The Condemned of Altona* (1959). In 1960, he published his second basic philosophical work, *Critique of Dialectical Reason*. In 1964, his account of his childhood, *The Words,* received world-wide acclaim. That same year he was awarded the Nobel Prize for Literature, which he refused. In 1971–1972, the first three volumes of his ambitious study of Flaubert's life and work appeared.